D0079620

The Essential Guide to Overcoming Avoidant Personality Disorder

The Essential Guide to Overcoming Avoidant Personality Disorder

MARTIN KANTOR, MD

 PRAEGER

AN IMPRINT OF ABC-CLIO, LLC
Santa Barbara, California • Denver, Colorado • Oxford, England

Library of Congress Cataloging-in-Publication Data
Kantor, Martin.
  The essential guide to overcoming avoidant personality disorder / Martin Kantor.
      p. cm.
  Includes bibliographical references and index.
  ISBN 978-0-313-37752-5 (hard copy : alk. paper) — ISBN 978-0-313-37753-2
(ebook)   1. Avoidant personality disorder.   I. Title.
  RC569.5.A93K36   2010
  616.85'82—dc22   2009044857

ISBN: 978-0-313-37752-5
EISBN: 978-0-313-37753-2

14   13   12   11   10   1   2   3   4   5

This book is also available on the World Wide Web as an eBook.
Visit www.abc-clio.com for details.

Praeger
An Imprint of ABC-CLIO, LLC

ABC-CLIO, LLC
130 Cremona Drive, P.O. Box 1911
Santa Barbara, California 93116-1911

This book is printed on acid-free paper ∞
Manufactured in the United States of America

To M.E.C.

Hello Martin. For many years I am spiraling deeper into isolation and only yesterday I read about Avoidant PD and discovered I fit on all counts. I am not sure what to do about it. I am scared to talk to people and my memory is weak.

—letter to the author

Contents

Preface

Sufferers from avoidant personality disorder (AvPD) fear forming and maintaining relationships because of ongoing, engaging, deep, pervasive, multilayered interpersonal anxiety. This anxiety causes them to have difficulty meeting, connecting with, getting close to, and staying involved with other people. According to Oldham and Morris, the disorder occurs in fully "10 percent of patients of outpatient mental health clinics,"[1] whereas Dalrymple and Zimmerman have written that "social anxiety disorder (SAD) [including AvPD] is the fourth most common mental disorder in the United States with a lifetime prevalence rate of 12.1%."[2]

I believe that even these disquieting statistics underestimate the extent of the problem, with this disorder far more widespread than most patients believe and clinicians acknowledge. This is because avoidants themselves overlook AvPD because they don't know it exists, or they downplay AvPD because they believe that having social anxiety is somehow shameful. And their therapists, equally misinformed about, or reluctant to recognize, the disorder, dismiss their suffering as normal shyness, reticence, unfriendliness, cliquishness, or as just part of growing up; or, spotting the disorder, they tell their patients that the problem is insignificant or condone it as acceptable, justified, and even romantic. They then offer reassurances that all is well and say that no therapy is necessary, or if it is necessary, it should be for something else entirely.

On their part, researchers often miss the diagnosis because they fold AvPD into borderline personality disorder (BPD). They fail to distinguish the characteristic chronic distancing patterns of AvPD from those of BPD, which consist of a more acute cyclic, intermittent approach–avoidance shifting. Unlike in AvPD, where the distancing is dynamically, if not clinically, resolute, in BPD, overly close intense relationships characteristic of the object hunger–merging phase of the borderline condition are in turn fitfully undone by an equally intense object satiation–emerging phase. As a result, we see the typical borderline tendency to alternate rapidly between overvaluation of and love for, and undervaluation of and disdain for, other people—the all too familiar "come here, go away, I love you."

More often still, and with even more tragic results, is the widespread proclivity of researchers to subsume the diagnosis of AvPD under the rubric of social phobia and then to report exclusively on social phobia, virtually ignoring AvPD. Thus the PDM, or *Psychodynamic Diagnostic Manual*, refers to AvPD as "phobic (avoidant) personality disorder."[3] In some ways, avoidants do resemble social phobics, and some therapists believe that they can effectively treat AvPD as if it were a compendium of social phobias, expecting the former to "disappear" when the latter are relieved. But to my way of thinking, the two disorders differ significantly diagnostically and therapeutically, in large measure because they differ structurally. For avoidants, unlike social phobics, are not terrified by specific, discreet, easily identifiable, well-delineated *trivial prompts* such as having to speak in public, use a public rest room, eat and swallow while being observed, or enter a crowded room where there is a party going on. Instead, they are troubled by a panoply of mostly negative *personality traits* that have more of an existential than a situational implication. Thus they suffer not from a fear of writing a check in public but from a fear of getting close to others and committing themselves to one someone special. Clearly, to me, while the *dynamics* of the two disorders overlap, each takes a unique *form*, with social phobia being a *symptom disorder* and AvPD being a *personality disorder*, and with the former being a modified, encapsulated, delimited version of the latter. Thus, though sufferers of both disorders are struggling emotionally with a fear of criticism and humiliation, the one, the social phobic, displays the fear as a need to avoid using a public rest room to urinate, whereas the other, the individual with AvPD, displays it as a global need to avoid not only restrooms, but also "all" rooms with people in them, making the avoidant individual reluctant to enter into life and to do all the things that happy people living normally ordinarily do.

This is a crossover text meant for two audiences. The first is for therapists hoping to properly identify and thoroughly fathom AvPD in preparation for developing a dedicated treatment approach to helping their patients cope with, or fully overcome, its ravages. The second is for sufferers from AvPD hoping to free themselves from their painful shyness and self-destructive distancing so that they may emerge from the dark shadows of isolation and loneliness into the bright light of warm, close, satisfying, loving, lasting relationships. Thus this book can be read in two ways: it is a guide for therapists developing a psychotherapeutic technique suitable for effectively treating AvPD and a manual for sufferers hoping to develop a self-help approach to profitably modify their lives and change their lifestyles, as they come to subdue their irrational fears and newly and more successfully cope with their overwhelming, life-sapping, happiness-destroying interpersonal anxiety.

PART ONE

DESCRIPTION AND CAUSATION

CHAPTER 1

Classic or Type I Avoidant Personality Disorder

In this chapter, I focus on classic avoidant personality disorder (AvPD), a disorder whose individuals, as Fenichel noted in 1945, suffer from "social inhibitions consisting of a general shyness [that may lead to withdrawal] from any social contact [because] they anticipate possible criticisms."[1] I start with a summary of the *Diagnostic and Statistical Manual of Mental Disorders*, fourth edition (*DSM-IV*) criteria for AvPD, then add a summary of criteria formulated by Francis and Widiger, Benjamin, Horney, me, and the American Psychological Association Help Center.

DSM-IV CRITERIA

The essential *DSM-IV*[2] criteria for AvPD are as follows:

1. Shyness, timidity, and withdrawal from relationships associated with the willing renunciation of autonomous strivings to avoid the friction and conflict associated with closeness and commitment. (The Quality Assurance Project refers specifically to "fear of commitment"[3] and assigns it a central role in the dynamics of avoidance.)

2. A fear of criticism, humiliation, and rejection.

3. Feelings of inadequacy and low self-esteem.

4. Anxiety in new social situations.

5. Hypervigilance and self-consciousness.

6. Social awkwardness due to an off-putting fearful tense demeanor that, in turn, elicits ridicule and derision from others, which

confirm self-doubts, leading to further awkwardness, causing others to pull back because they see avoidants not as "fearful of rejection *by* me," but as "being rejecting *of* me."

NON-*DSM-IV* CRITERIA

FRANCES AND WIDIGER

Francis and Widiger go beyond the *DSM-IV* view of AvPD as the product of a sensitivity to and fear of interpersonal rejection in the form of criticism and humiliation by others to offer further reasons for social anxiety:

1. A fear of flooding and losing control of various impulses due to overstimulation, for example, the fear that forbidden, even revolting, romantic or hostile impulses are about to erupt— disturbing inner peace or even completely shattering internal equanimity.

2. An associated fear of experiencing "uncomfortable body sensations" such as tremulousness.

3. A fear of failure, accompanied by a paradoxical (masochistic) fear of success.[4]

MILLON/BENJAMIN/HORNEY

These observers emphasize the generally downplayed role free-floating and reactive anger play in the distancing process. Millon describes an "avoidant-passive-aggressive mixed personality"[5]; Benjamin speaks of the avoidant's tendency to become too readily "indignant"[6]; and Horney, according to Portnoy, notes that "the major possibilities of anxiety come to be [not only] rejection or disapproval by others [but also] hostile impulses from within the self."[7]

KANTOR

I propose the following as basic criteria:

1. Self-criticism due to self-condemnation by a harsh, unforgiving, shaming conscience, causing one to become guilty over legitimate desires and ordinary (but to the avoidant extraordinarily shameful), interpersonal foibles.

2. Annoyance with others over the most trivial things, for example, "every time he dries himself he uses a new towel, running up my laundry bill, and that in a recession!"

3. A masochistic desire to be hurt by suffering relationally.

4. A fear that acceptance and closeness will interfere with doing the "me" things avoidants really want to do and thoroughly enjoy doing like a man's watching the TV shows he likes or a woman's becoming fully emancipated both personally and professionally.

5. A fear of acceptance and closeness due to a fear that these will "swallow avoidants up whole," leading to a loss of boundaries and a compromised identity due to becoming overly dependent on, and subject to the full control of, others.

6. Relational idealism consisting of a disdain for relationships that appear to be imperfect, originating in excessive expectations of oneself and others, associated with excessive pridefulness and a hypermorality that too narrowly defines what is and what is not "biblically" correct and so relationally permissible.

7. A fear of depletion due to a fear of letting go with others to the point of significantly dissipating one's life energy.

8. The excessive use of relational defenses. (The *Psychodynamic Diagnostic Manual*, or *PDM*, lists, in addition to the defense of phobic withdrawal/avoidance the defenses of symbolization, displacement, projection, and rationalization.[8])

9. Covalent characterological features, including *histrionic* (oedipal) rivalry that buries the potential for closeness, intimacy, and commitment under competitive struggles with others—as Gabbard notes, "entailing an aggressive demand for complete attention . . . associated with a wish to scare away or kill off all rivals . . . [with the competitiveness] interwoven with a sense of shame"[9]; *obsessive* fretting about the correctness and propriety of one's interpersonal actions—with obsessive overworry about the consequences of making even minor relational mistakes associated with a hypermorality that leads to viewing one's ordinary humanity, including, or especially, one's acceptable sexuality, as shameful and sinful; *paranoid* suspiciousness about the negative things others are, or might be, thinking; *depressive* alarmism and pessimism that nothing will ever work out as hoped and planned for and the worrisome fear that if all is not already lost, it soon

will be; excessive "don't make waves" *passivity*, accompanied by a paradoxical *fear* of passivity and so a need to be on constant alert and continuously active to assure always being in complete control of everything about one's relationships; extreme *dependence* possibly leading to a codependent relationship with one person to avoid having to relate to any and all others; *narcissism* characterized by constant pulse taking, for example, "how you make *me* feel," that implies an unempathic lack of concern about "how I make *you* feel"; *neophilia*—a *need* for newness associated with easy boredom with the old; and *neophobia*—a *fear* of newness, leading to a need for sameness, creating a fear of change and progress.

10. Fear of being different from equally avoidant peers, as if being different from them means defying them, and so becoming a nonavoidant pariah in what is perceived to be, and ultimately too often actually is, one's avoidant society.

THE AMERICAN PSYCHOLOGICAL ASSOCIATION HELP CENTER

1. Canceling social events at the last moment.
2. Avoiding situations that provide positive social interaction.
3. Few or no friends.
4. Avoidance of activities that are otherwise pleasurable.
5. Passivity, pessimism, and low self-esteem.
6. Excessive computer use that is not social in nature and without face-to-face contact with others.[10]

I next offer a more detailed discussion of the some of the previously mentioned criteria.

DSM-IV CRITERIA

1. *DSM-IV: Shyness, timidity, and withdrawal.*[11] Avoidants are shy, timid, introverted, withdrawn, socially inhibited individuals anxiously desirous of relating but conflicted about doing so due to a fear of getting close and committing to others.

Unlike schizoid individuals, who have a severely reduced capacity for relationships, avoidants can relate and are both unable and unwilling to relinquish relationships completely and definitively. As Sullivan suggests, the problem is that their "intimacy need[s] collide with the need for security"[12] so that they feel frustrated and pull back as self-protection becomes more urgent than self-fulfillment.

2. *DSM-IV: Fear of criticism, humiliation, and rejection.* Avoidants are fearful of what other people think partly based on hypersensitivity and a proneness to exaggerate the dangers of a negative evaluation. They avoid taking personal risks because they fear being exposed, ridiculed, and shamed, for example, for crying or blushing publicly. (As the Quality Assurance Project says, "an extreme interpersonal sensitivity to perceived rejection" and a tendency to interpret ordinary slightly negative human interactions as rejection leads avoidants to see "developing involvement with others as hazardous."[13])

A Case Example

An avoidant man, expecting too much from the world, overlooked how some rejection is simply part of life's give and take, and instead, expecting life to always be fair, rewarding, and complete, became highly vulnerable to even minor signs of life's inherent unfairness and imperfections. Regularly expecting relational successes, he would panic when they were not forthcoming, pull back, give up, and cry, "Never again." Too, regularly expecting relational miracles, he would go to mingles events/singles resorts and share singles homes in country resorts, and surf the Internet for dates, thinking, "Tonight, I will connect for sure," then, even though he knew intellectually and from experience that he could not count on connecting every night, he would let one night's failure or one turndown become a commentary on how he was *completely* wasting his time because no one would *ever* love him. His motto soon became, "It's better to have never loved at all than to have innocently loved, then been rejected for having done so."

Sensitivity to rejection frequently results in defensive outbursts meant to destroy what could otherwise easily have been a viable relationship.

Case Examples

A patient stormed out of the house after telling his wife he was leaving her because one day, instead of being there to greet him when he came home from work, she had gone out to do some errands and forgot to leave a note saying where she was, "forcing me to come home to an empty house, causing me to feel 'you left me and so you don't love me,' throwing me into a panic about having to stay home by myself for who knows how long, thinking, 'I did something wrong, this is my comeuppance, and as a result I am always going to be completely alone, and in this, such a hostile, world.'"

A patient kept the same routine for months or years—eating in the same restaurant every night and ordering the same food and drinks night after night, meal after meal. He did that until one "fateful day" he changed restaurants on a slim, slightly paranoid pretext because he felt that his "waiter hustled me for drinks, and served me baked potatoes today that were smaller than the baked potatoes he served me yesterday."

A music critic, preoccupied with "who is being mean to *me*," interpreted any opinion that differed from his own as putting him down in a critical way. When others corrected his mispronunciations, he thought that they were calling him stupid and uneducated for misspeaking. When people expressed any neediness at all to him, he interpreted that as their criticizing him for not giving them what they wanted. A globally anxious protective removal grew out of these negative misinterpretations and led to misunderstandings and arguments that became his reason to permanently rupture even relationships that had, until then, otherwise been going well.

> 3. *DSM-IV: Feelings of inadequacy and low self-esteem.* Avoidants feel inadequate; see themselves as socially inept, unappealing, or inferior; and assume that others view them the same way. Hence they have an undue need for certainty and security and, before they extend themselves to others, require that others pass stringent tests indicating that they will always act in an obviously supportive and nurturing manner. Avoidants also withdraw because they feel unworthy of being liked, making it unlikely that they will expect/ask others to like and accept them. (Avoidants can, however, be intimate when they know that assurance of uncritical acceptance is forthcoming.)

A Case Example

A gay patient withdrawing from a suitable partner as a form of self-apology said, "The new man in my life is a vice president of a large media company here in Chicago. The person that introduced us said he was just looking for an average guy, but I was concerned when he got into his Mercedes and all I have is an old Honda. In other words, he lives a much higher lifestyle than I do, and I am worried that I will not be able to keep up with him. He is also very good looking, and I am just average in looks and make a lot less than he does. But we seem to be hitting it off so far: no sex or anything like that—just enjoying each other's company and I actually like him, to date anyway. I just work as a welder in a large construction company, but I am not after his money or anything. My friends say I am worrying about nothing. Still, I'm going to drop him because I would rather live poor and be happy than force myself on someone I feel I am unworthy of."

> 4. *DSM-IV: Anxiety in new social situations.* Excessive security needs along with doubts about relational certainty in both personal and occupational contexts cause avoidants to become highly anxious in unfamiliar situations, as, for example, when attending large parties.

Although the *DSM-IV* emphasizes that many avoidants are most fearful of strange, unfamiliar surroundings, where they know nobody or are just meeting new people, some avoidants actually function best with strangers like waitresses, for they see them as safe because they are comfortably remote and predictably unavailable.

A Case Example

One timid avoidant, though shy with friends and family, was bold and forceful with waiters and coat check girls—for as strangers, they were unlikely to expect anything from him beyond the superficialities. He was able to feel positively about women he merely passed on the street, but with women he really liked and got to know, to use his own words, when he "got past first base" and was "in a position to score," he "completely froze up."

> 5. *DSM-IV: Hypervigilance and self-consciousness.* Avoidants always have one eye open to what others think. They tensely appraise others' movements and expressions to see if others approve of what they are saying and doing, only to avoid others because they become convinced that others believe the avoidant has done, or is about to do, something wrong.

Their vigilance promotes an excessively rich fantasy life, as they frantically appraise the movements and expressions of others, conjuring up the bad things others might be thinking and doing from slim stuff, thence creating complex, fantasized, fearful scenarios, especially about being alone and its lonely consequences. They routinely have dreams about potential or actual social loss, for example, "I call you on your cell phone but no one answers, you were there in the room with me a minute ago, but now you have simply disappeared; and clearly you don't want me anymore because you find me disgusting, which is why you are telling me to get out."

Often their dreams express avoidant fantasies symbolically, as when they dream of running stuck in place, not being able to move forward, or of waiting for the bus that never comes, then when it does come, it turns out to be the wrong bus or, if the right bus, it goes to the wrong place, or to a dangerous place where one gets mugged or killed. This symbolic expression often takes on a surrealistic cast. For example, a man dreamed of a street at the end of which was a welcoming bar with welcoming neon lights, friendly music, and warm grog. One side of the street was brightly lit, and the other was completely dark. Unable to traverse the lit side, he could only traverse the side that was dark. This side, however, held too many terrors and dangers for him to seriously contemplate making the attempt. So he cowered and held back, effectively freezing in place.

> 6. *DSM-IV: Social awkwardness.* Avoidants can seem off-putting to others who misinterpret their fearful, tense demeanor as rejecting so that others withdraw, often after ridiculing and deriding the avoidant, confirming the avoidant's self-doubts.

A Case Example

A potential lover took a long bus trip to be with a patient of mine. As the bus pulled in, the lover-to-be, from inside the bus, saw my patient waiting for him at the bus station and waved him a gusty hello, only to have my patient respond by going into a panic, thinking, "That big wave turned me off, I am suspicious of people who are just too eager to see me." My patient then adopted a body posture that, virtually oozing remoteness, retreat, and rejection, broadcast his clear regret that an actual meeting was imminent.

SOME NON-*DSM-IV* CRITERIA

FEAR OF FLOODING

According to Millon and Davis, avoidants must "avoid everything which might arouse their emotions [and] seek as far as possible to avoid and deaden all stimulation from the outside."[14] Many come to fear that if they attempt to get close, their positive/romantic impulses will erupt, flooding them and threatening their emotional security and structural integrity and, if men, making them feel and look feminine, and, if women, making them feel and look weak.

A Case Example

One patient gave up playing the piano, though, in fact, he played well and others enjoyed listening. He did this because he couldn't tolerate all the adulation he received when he performed in public. For him, playing in public was shamefully exhibitionistic, a showing off, with "crescendos, moderatos, and other expressions of feeling one step removed from having sex out in the open." He also convinced himself that when he played, others snickered, so that by playing, he made a complete fool of himself. For him, then, avoidance was a way to detach from others to proclaim, "I am in full control of myself and emotionally and physically intact, just like the artist Joseph Cornell, who sensibly died a virgin because he feared that if he had sex, it would destroy his artistic ability."

MASOCHISM

Avoidants withdraw not only because they fear losing when they want to win, but also because they fear winning because they need to lose. Freud, in his 1924 paper "The Economic Problem in Masochism," spoke of individuals who needed to be punished and to suffer due to an unconscious sense of guilt that plays an extensive part in their social lives. These individuals are unable to tolerate the possibility of gratification, so they provoke their own criticisms and abandonments by "do[ing] something inexpedient, act[ing] against [their] own interests, ruin[ing] the prospects which the real world offers [them and risking the] poss[ibility] of destroying [their] own existence in the world of reality."[15] In his 1915 paper "Some Character-Types Met with in Psychoanalytic Work," Freud described individuals "wrecked by success," who fell "ill precisely because a deeply-rooted and long-cherished wish has come to fulfillment [and they can] not endure . . . bliss." "Illness follows close upon wish fulfillment, and [leads to] annihilat[ion of] all enjoyment of it."[16]

Thus these avoidants, anxious not only about the possibility of *rejection*, but also about the possibility of *acceptance*, arrange to be rejected by selecting distant, unavailable people to relate to, or people with a fatal flaw, such as those who dislike them or those who are already taken because they are married. They have rescue fantasies in which they long to bring around situations they know to be inherently nonviable, then focus all their efforts on doing so, even when, or really because, they are convinced that these efforts are virtually certain to come to naught. This way, they see to it that they waste their valuable time, and that way, they provide themselves with yet another reason to be avoidant.

A Case Example

A gay man uninterested in dating people who were available to him wrote to me, "There is not much action in my town and since most of the gays are in the closet meeting people is very difficult. I have taken your advice—I do not frequent bars and of course, I never drank. I am still single. I have had a few flings, but they were just that, flings. I am still very serious about meeting someone and establishing a monogamous relationship. But I can't seem to meet the right person. Maybe I am simply not receptive enough. Or it's because I seem to have a propensity for being attracted to divorced or soon-to-be divorced men with children, who may or may not be homosexual. I suspect that they are, but nothing seems to happen. I really think that I am wasting my time."

I have treated a number of women who form hopeless romantic relationships with married men, consciously expecting them to divorce their wives and spend the rest of their lives with them, all the while un-consciously knowing that a good deal of their attraction is less to the man than to the man's unavailability.

READINESS TO ANGER

Benjamin notes that anger plays a significant role in the psychogen-esis of AvPD, saying, "Usually [avoidants] restrain this aspect [of their avoidance]," but there are times when it breaks through and they tend "to become indignant about alleged humiliations." Benjamin adds, "I believe that the *DSM* should add angry outbursts to the description of AVD [because] occasionally AVDs will identify with their humiliat-ing and rejecting family members, and become quite commanding and judgmental themselves."[17]

Here is an excerpt from a negative "review" on Amazon.com of *Dis-tancing*, my earlier book on AvPD, with the review a missile that I be-lieve hints at the irrational anger (she got the facts wrong, perhaps having read only enough to make her mad) just alluded to:

> The most redundant book I have ever read . . . very superfi-cial . . . some sections . . . are so superficial he should have left them out altogether . . . provides examples (way too many) . . . does not delve into their psychology [for only] 17 pages are devoted to cause (at least 5 of which are examples) . . . you expect some anal-ysis from a psychologist [*sic*], but he doesn't offer any.[18]

Here is the heading of another Amazon.com review written by the same person:

> This flashlight sucks.[19]

Sullivan notes that avoidance is called out by prolonged se-vere hostility, the disjunctive nature of "malevolence," the feeling that "once upon a time everything was lovely, but that was before I had to deal with people."[20] Fenichel suggests that avoidance is an anger equivalent—appearing "on occasions where others would feel rage."[21] Millon describes an avoidant-passive-aggressive mixed per-sonality and notes that a threat equal to personal humiliation or so-cial rejection is the avoidant's own aggressive impulses, for avoidants "bind anger" by withdrawing to protect themselves "against humili-ation and loss."[22] Frances and Widiger note that in some dynamic models, avoidants and passive-aggressives are placed side by side as both "likely to be higher on hostility [than dependents]."[23] Beck notes that "the avoidant personality stays poised to attack."[24]

I believe that avoidance, among other things, is a way to say, "I fear you because I fear your making me mad." I also believe that avoidant hostility is partly defensive: both a way to avoid getting close and a method for maintaining one's (shaky) self-esteem by pulling down the standing of others through disparagement and ridicule.

A Case Example

An avoidant woman pursued a cyberrelationship with a man from Germany, who at first told her that he was royalty, only to later confess, somewhat ashamedly, and to her consternation, that he "picked up waste materials to be moved from here to there on a dispersing truck." "Nevertheless," as she put it, she agreed to welcome him to the United States. But after he promised to cross the Atlantic to visit her, he made one excuse after another for not being able to come, for example, "I can't get time off from my job." Eventually, however, he made the trip and, as she said, "turned out to be a great guy after all." That is precisely when she picked a fight with him, condemning him for his bad grammar and complaining about his using too many towels, always taking a new one instead of reusing the old ones until they absolutely had to be washed. She justified her feelings and subsequent actions on the correct but trivial grounds that any lover of hers should have known without having to be told that doing the laundry took time and effort and ran up the electricity bill. But in actuality, she had become angry with him as her way to get what she wanted: that he pack his bags, stomp out the door, and take the first available flight back to Germany.

Avoidants often get angry when others won't welcome them and let them become as dependent on them as they (secretly) want to be.

Some Case Examples

A housewife saved her money for months to travel to the big city to attend a salon for a complete makeover. Her husband, more dependent on her than he admitted, disliked her leaving him even for the day because he saw that as her rejecting him and even suspected, without reason, that she might be meeting a secret lover. As he put it, "You wouldn't be making yourself over for me, I never cared how you look." Upon her return, instead of telling her, "You look beautiful," he launched into a tirade, displacing his own angry disappointment about how she had left him onto their cat, who, according to him, acted "pissed off because you left her alone all day."

A patient, feeling rejected because her next-door neighbors did not invite her over to join them for a barbecue, got back at them by condemning them for letting their ivy grow onto her fence. Shortly afterward, the next-door neighbors' child was sitting quietly in her own yard, watching the birds over the fence feed at the feeder in the patient's yard. Because the child was part of "that family that had caused me great harm and left me bereft and depleted by not including me in their festivities," the patient yelled at the kid, "Stop watching *my* birds, and stop it right now!"

Angry avoidants often express their rage by getting others to act out for them. It was pets for the patient who kept a half-dog, half-wolf that he didn't discourage from snarling at passers-by, and for the man who let his dog off the leash so that it might wander about upon, soil, and uproot his neighbor's lawns and gardens. It was his spouse for the man who maintained the outward appearance of being the "perfectly delightful one," while he egged his wife on to be the troublemaker of the family. It was her children for the avoidant who publicly played the role of "pillar of the community," while privately encouraging her sons to cut the neighbor's flowers (by wishing aloud for a certain bouquet) and to shout antigay epithets (by criticizing homosexuals within the children's hearing range). It was underlings for the boss who used them to live out his own petty, interpersonal antagonisms, taking A into his confidence, telling A that B had made nasty comments to him about A behind A's back, then saying to B that A had made nasty comments to him about B behind B's back, getting both A and B fighting. It was colleagues for an employee who provoked fights among his coworkers by misquoting them: "repeating" their passing comments out of context and with the qualifiers left out, subtly changing their remarks from positive to negative in the telling. It was patients for a therapist who, unable to get the divorce he longed for, fulfilled his own wishes in fantasy by encouraging his patients to leave their spouses, when instead, he should have been encouraging them to at least try to smooth things over and attempt reconciliation.

EXCESSIVE RELATIONAL IDEALISM

Avoidants, as exacting individuals overly idealistic about relationships, will, before they agree to get involved with someone, demand that the relationship meet certain, usually impossible, conditions. Only they soon discover that their self-imposed irrational, impractical, and overly perfectionistic standards are unachievable, so they pull back in disappointment and withdraw to avoid injury to their pride.

Excessive Defensiveness

Avoidance is not a static, but an active, dynamic condition—what Millon and Davis call an "active detachment,"[25] that is, one with important defensive components. Sullivan describes avoidance as a "somnolent detachment," the protective dynamism "called out by inescapable and prolonged anxiety."[26] In equating avoidance with inhibited function, Fenichel views avoidance as the product of a tendency to neutralize wishes with "countercathexes," that is, with equal but opposite forces. Fenichel also notes that "analysis always shows that the specifically avoided situations or the inhibited functions have unconsciously an instinctual (sexual or aggressive) significance. It is this instinctual significance against which [avoidance, that is, the defense of avoidance] really is directed. What is avoided is an allusion either to a temptation for the warded-off drive or to a feared punishment or both."[27] Therefore some observers, emphasizing how the avoidant inhibits important aspects of living to reduce (social) anxiety, suggest that the term *inhibited personality* could substitute for the term *avoidant personality disorder.*

Avoidant detachment is made up of the following defenses, among others:

Identification with the aggressor. Avoidants create expected losses actively to handle the possibility of experiencing unexpected losses passively, for example, "I fear your rejecting me" becomes "I reject you to avoid being rejected by you."

Masochism. Self-sacrificing, self-abnegating, and self-punitive responses are an avoidant's way to counter forbidden desire. Avoidants commit a kind of social suicide to punish themselves for what they consider to be their unacceptable instinctual urges. They suffer now to avoid suffering even more later.

Repression. Repression is the avoidant's way to detoxify anxious thoughts and feelings by suppressing them, then acting as if they no longer exist.

Displacement. Many avoidants find it advantageous to express their avoidance indirectly by expressing it symbolically. For example, instead of actually staying away from someone, they "merely" avoid shaking hands and so touching the person.

Intellectualization. Avoidants frequently disguise avoidant compulsion as avoidant philosophy, for example, their "philosophy of splendid isolation" is in fact a rationalized fearfulness of connecting.

Regression. Avoidants act like children to avoid having to act like adults. Many deliberately if unconsciously revive old negative childhood fears and actual past traumas to discourage adult interaction, often almost deliberately hanging on to ancient painful parental attachments so that they *can* view anyone available as forbidden because they are "just like my mother and father."

Also regressive is the typical avoidant tendency to too readily form *conditioned* responses so that they *can* reflexively shrink from a new situation because it elicits an old displeasure. Regression also accounts for avoidants' too readily forming *transference* responses that facilitate their viewing present relationships in the light of troublesome relationships from the past and present so that they *can* respond to people as if they are old problematic parents, rival siblings, difficult childhood friends or enemies, or one or more other of their current bête noires.

Associated Characterological Problems

Obsessionalism. Avoidants are worrisome individuals, *brooders* with one eye always wide open to the potentially negative consequences of everything they say and do to others, and others to them. They are often *rigid, inflexible* people who, stuck in routine, have difficulty adapting to unexpected life changes. Also, *ambivalent* about relationships, instead of settling in to a given relationship, they *do and undo* it: attempting to relate, becoming anxious, pulling back, then trying again either with the same person or with someone different, ad infinitum. Thus an obsessional avoidant went to New York City, had a successful career and lived a sophisticated lifestyle, gave it up to get married and move to the suburbs, got a dog, and had children, when, unhappy about and bored with being a housewife, she hired nannies to help care for her children so that she could resume working at something "more gratifying than just being a homemaker." Her outside work then gave her the money she needed to become independent of her husband, and her independence gave her the emotional foundation she needed to get a divorce, whereupon she returned home to her birthplace and family, which, as she now believed, she should never have left in the first place.

Paranoia. Avoidants are hypervigilant individuals who fear something bad can or will happen to them unawares, "when they are not looking." They take impersonal matters far too personally and see rejections that are not there as a clear and present danger, or actual attack. A difficulty with basic trust leads them to become highly skeptical of everyone, convinced that no one will show them any goodwill whatsoever, and certain that either they will trust everyone and get burned, or trust no one and get dumped.

Passivity/dependency (fear of being assertive). Avoidants fear self-assertion because they believe that being assertive means being aggressive. Peers, teachers, entertainers, religious leaders, and media all seem to be warning them that assertion, like dissent, means not being "healthily individualistic and productively rivalrous," but "aggressively killing off the competition."

Narcissism. Avoidants tend to be pulse takers who think more about how they feel than of how they make others feel, for example, "I fear what you do to me," not "I worry about what my pulling back from you might do to you."

Depression. Avoidants tend to be depressed individuals with intense negative moods that often commence when someone does not compliment them adequately or rejects them openly. In the absence of daily praise, they experience full and permanent stroke deprivation, associated with a sense of hopelessness about ever winning in the relationship game. They hold the pessimistic view that when it comes to relationships, there is no sense even trying since there is little chance of ever succeeding. Depressive cognitions prevail, particularly the tendency to think catastrophically in the "for want of a nail the ship was lost" mode, so that they readily come to believe that any sign of disinterest in them constitutes a turndown, a turndown a rejection, and a rejection an epochal tragedy.

Neophilia and neophobia. Avoidants paradoxically display both neophiliac and neophobic traits. As neophiles, they are always seeking new people because they are easily bored with the old. Some become serial daters who, as Freud notes, show "a lack of stability in object-choice [evidenced by a] 'craving for stimulus'" that is the product of a need to have an "endless series of substitute objects, none of which can ever give full satisfaction."[28] As *neophobes*, avoidants seek not newness, but familiarity. They fear being unprepared and taken by surprise with their defenses down. So instead of trying new situations, they strive for sameness, as Frances and Widiger note, avoiding rejection by retreating into routines with the same few old friends, "going to the same restaurant, the same table, and eating the same entrée."[29]

IDENTIFICATION WITH ONE'S PEERS/SOCIETY

Avoidants are often most attracted to friends, family, and society who are avoidogenics, that is, avoidance makers encouraging avoidance in others and having an especially devastating impact on avoidants as individuals already prone to shyness. Avoidogenics typically embrace and advance in-vogue avoidant philosophies such as religious (biblical) damnation for positive/sexual feelings; the Beatles' exhortation to not trust anyone over 30; Zen philosophies of withdrawal aimed at reducing personal anxiety by the expedient of removing oneself from others and the world; and "do-your-own-thing" philosophies that overstress the importance of freedom, independence, and individuality, while fretfully condemning even the relatively modest submission and deindividuation that are in fact necessary to form close, loving relationships. Avoidants who do obeisance to this avoidant crowd come to view committed long-term relationships as the essence of boorish and uncool, and antithetical to their only true and meaningful goals in life—to be free of encumbrances ("a man thing") and to be fully emancipated ("a woman thing").

For one avoidant, embracing the belief that all intimacy is troublesome dependency was her way to be politically correct and so to gain approval from her equally avoidant peers. Hoping to belong if she accepted her group's avoidant ideals, she went along when the group proclaimed, "Never cling too hard, it makes you into an invasive vine that only grows well with support from the very people it will ultimately strangle." She, like so many other people today, clung to this avoidant philosophy because she valued her reputation with others over her satisfaction with herself.

Case Examples

A patient, after having gone to a great deal of trouble and expense to move from the "crowded large city in which I live to a small town with fewer inhabitants where I can have less contact with people," could do no better than complain about the daytime noise in his new home—the leaf blowers, the gas company repairing the mains, and the like, really because they were the accoutrements of life and living. To "get away from all the oppressive activity," he moved again, this time to a farmhouse surrounded by acres of land and enclosed by a high fence to keep intruders out—only to move still again to an even more remote place in the desert because "on the farm, I'm frightened by the shadows in the woods at night."

After years of being unemployed, he took a job working in the mail room of the post office. He took that particular job, even though it was "beneath him," because it allowed him to have as little contact as possible with coworkers whose minor slights and rejections he took so personally that after arriving home after a day's work, he began to brood about who said, meant, and did what to him. Unable to sleep at night, he was too tired to function effectively the next day and so unable to fully concentrate on his work. As a result, he became so distraught that he called out sick the day after, only to become so guilty for calling out sick that, once again, he was unable to sleep at night and had to call out sick the day after that, as well. Eventually, he became a secretive, isolated, sullen, and uncooperative worker who was diagnosed as having "burnout" and put on temporary disability leave. In response, he quit his job so that he could once again be able to live the lonely, completely isolated life he really had always dreamed of for himself.

A patient manifested a fear of commitment in his occupational life as a dreamy restlessness and desire for change whenever things were going well professionally so that he quit one perfectly good job after another and moved on, rationalizing his behavior as "for more money" or "for better working conditions"—ultimately illusory. A doctor, he kept many licenses in different states in case he wanted to relocate, and for a long time wouldn't buy the house or apartment he wanted, and instead rented one so that he wouldn't be tied down to one spot. Whenever he did move, he found that the old job he had left behind was as or more worthy than the new one. Though he recognized this after the fact, the recognition had no effect on his future behavior so that he continued to look at ads and apply for new positions. Of course, with each new job, the same difficulties arose, for his avoidant tendencies reasserted themselves, and he felt a new urgency to move on.

In his personal life, he suffered from a severe fear of commitment that took the form of intense object love alternating with a consuming desire to "get away from them all." One night, he had the following dream. After waiting in a restaurant for his take-out order, and noting with mixed pleasure and envy the many generations all working under the same roof in splendid cooperation, he heard himself begging his wife to "throw him out" so that he could be alone. In his waking life, he had mixed feelings about his wife and their marriage (he was later actually to get a divorce). These took the form of an obsessive fear that his (consciously) beloved wife would get into a fatal car crash. Associated were a series of escapist distancing fantasies and behaviors involving shopping alone; going alone on vacations to exotic places or to a remote shack in the woods with a warm fire and steamy kettle; reading escapist books on exploring the Antarctic; traveling *Through the Looking Glass* and going "Over the Rainbow"; wandering alone through the seaside mists listening to the fog horn; taking trains by himself north, to isolated places, or to distant stations at the end of the line, not because of the pretty, interesting, or welcoming things he might find there, but because there, in his private, remote Oz, he would be as far away from home base as possible; taking fantasized trips in time to an imagined better past or future; and taking fantasized trips in person assuming another identity such as that of a troubadour in the Middle Ages playing ancient music alone in the woods, or that of an archaeologist who uncovered the past, not so that he could study, but so that he could live in it.

He once decided to actually buy a shack in the woods. He couldn't wait to go there every weekend, and even went in winter, using as his excuse, "I have to water my plants." However, when he got there, he promptly panicked because now he was all alone with nothing to do. So he called all his friends in the city just to make contact with other human beings and drank in local bars just to be where other people were, although he hated drinking and disliked the people in the bars as well as the contact he had with them, for as he saw it, they were "all predictably superficial and limited." So he sold the lonely country shack and bought an apartment in the city, only to find that he constantly dreamed of the splendid times he had when alone in his house in the wilds—of the pleasures of getting into his car in the middle of winter, the cold snow everywhere; driving to the bars with their warm, welcoming lights, sounds, and people and wonderful, body-strengthening food and soul-building drink; and of the times when he was isolated, in his "beautiful digs," with its beautiful furnishings, "living in sin" (as an acquaintance once put it) "with the wall board."

A woman lived at home with her parents, being the good, dutiful, but resentfully compliant daughter who drew a magic circle around herself, letting the family in, keeping a few friends whom she saw occasionally, and having an occasional blind date, but accepting no close intimates into her life. She mainly filled her days with impersonal interests such as collecting things and attending craft shows. While sometimes she complained about being lonely and isolated, at other times, she insisted that she was enjoying her life fully because she was living it exactly the way she believed she wanted to. When she tried "to fight the good fight attempting to relate," she was only able to do so with difficulty and deficit. Thus she occasionally went to singles bars, mixers, and parties, only, once she got there, to function below par, standing off completely by herself or speaking only to the person she came in with. She might complain that she was dissatisfied with the narrowness of her life, but would then regularly add that however hard she tried to change her luck, she could never seem to do any better and truly "get lucky."

She feared starting and maintaining intimate relationships because she was highly fearful of rejection. Partly this was because she was a perfectionist, who, when it came to relationships, failed to accept that any rejection was part of life's give-and-take, and otherwise expected too much positivity in a world full of negativity. Partly it was because her self-esteem was extremely low so that she would anticipate rejections that might never arise and take those that actually occurred much too seriously—because for her, a rejection meant that her greatest fear had come true: that no one could ever love her because she was completely unlovable. Often even a mild rejection led to a catastrophic reaction, where she panicked, pulled back, gave up, and cried, "Never again." A doctor once diagnosed her as having a depersonalization disorder. Fearing acceptance because it could only lead to rejection, when faced with the "danger," as she saw it, of being embraced by other people and getting close to them, she would go into a trancelike state that reminded her of a rabbit freezing in the headlights of a car, so that her trance, meant to be protective, instead turned out to be self-destructive. For in her trance, she shrugged men off with a "yeah, sure," put them off by acting silly and giggly, or drove them away by becoming preoccupied and remote—her mind wandering to other things, even (perversely) going from a present satisfactory contact with a real person to a future affair with a mysterious stranger. Particularly when introduced to someone she really liked, she became defensively hazy, actually fainted, or even called on one of her multiple personalities to save her—one of the alter egos she reverted to temporarily at times of danger—created by suppressing parts of her old personality, by borrowing new personality parts through identification with someone she admired, or by becoming once again like her old self: the rebel she had once been but was no longer. Only later, after she had eliminated any possibility of a serious involvement, did she come to her senses, wonder what she was thinking about at the time, and "kick herself" for allowing the one that got away to escape. Then she pressured herself to "go out and meet someone new," only to start the entire pathological cycle once again.

An avoidant woman consulted me because of her inability to "meet the man of my dreams." She sought treatment for being so shy with men that it had become difficult for her to get close to the men in her family, to make male friends at and outside of work, and to get beyond accepting a first date with a man to be able to go out with him a second time. As a result, she feared, and with reason, that she would never fulfill her wish to get married, have children, and live a "normal life with a husband and kids in the suburbs."

Just having wishful thoughts about marriage frightened her. She first thought, "I better get serious and start looking for a husband, for after all, I'm not getting any younger." Then she took that back with, "Marriage isn't right for everyone, and it may not be right for me. I think I would be much better off single, being able to come and go as I please, and beholden to nothing and no one. As far as I am concerned, the single life is not only just as good and valid as the married life, in many ways it is even better. I really enjoy being single, and just having a few good friends. I actually prefer that to having a husband, because with friends you can beat a path out of the relationship whenever you want to—and without a lot of stupid paper work."

Often the normal travails of dating left her feeling severely depressed. For example, when a man was just a few minutes late for a date, she convinced herself that that was the end of the relationship, for he had died in a car accident, and "there goes my last chance to get married." Because the nice things men said to and did for her eluded her completely, she saw even a highly positive relationship with a man as entirely negative and would break off the relationship precipitously and without explanation. Part of the problem was that feeling she deserved no better, she picked men who were unavailable, either because they played hard to get or because they were already married. Then she complained that relationships with men could never amount to much or go anywhere, so that her fate was only to be hurt, abused, and alone, her sole source of love coming from tearful, caring, concerned friends and family rushing to her side and rescue, pitying her, and taking her under their wing, to nurture her and salve her wounds.

Soon she became paranoid as well as depressed. She began imagining that even a man's compliments were criticisms, so that when a man told her that she looked great one day, she thought that he was actually telling her that she looked terrible the day before. She convinced herself that all men were just out to seduce and abandon her: planning to take advantage of her sexually and financially before dumping her precipitously. Serious feelings of jealousy also began to plague her. When a date was just a few minutes late, she convinced herself that he was not going to come at all because he was out with someone he liked better. So his being late was his way to send her a message that he would soon leave her for another woman, and she would be all alone in life now and forever. She even became jealous when a date looked at another woman on the street just to make sure he would not run into her, spoke to another woman at a party, said more than hello, looked as if he were enjoying himself, got excited not bored like she thought he ought, did not look uncomfortable as if he couldn't wait to get away, and said more to the woman than (she was almost actually counting his words) he said to her all day. Once she became jealous of a boyfriend's having close friends at work, even though he was only going out to lunch with his buddies. She panicked if she called him at work and he didn't answer the phone, for then she started worrying about "what he might be up to." She even started writing down where his odometer was set to make certain that he wasn't making extra trips on the side to see another woman. She began to demand that he be available/accountable to her at all times so that she could keep tabs on him 24 hours a day because "since all men are secretive, you never know." Ultimately, she even came to believe that she could read his mind and pick up the negative signals he was sending her. She then confronted him with her imaginations. There would be a fight, and should he try to defend himself, that meant that he was defiantly challenging her. So she pulled back permanently, believing that he was not only being unfaithful to her, but that he was also lying about it.

Men were sometimes able to get beyond these relational impediments by handling her "therapeutically," only to come up against an even more distressing problem: boredom that tempted her to break off what had finally become a working relationship so that she could move on and look for someone else. A little into what had, in spite of all, become a positive encounter, a pervasive sense of aching dullness impelled her to give up, move on, and meet a new man, for "every day with the same man was just going to be the same old, same old, tired experience for the rest of my long, troubled life." Her need to move on became so pressing that she completely forgot how painful it was to have to look for someone new: having to reexperience all those terrible letdowns and disappointments where all she could salvage were a pleasurable self-pitying feeling and (a progressively dimming) hope for better luck next time. There were times when she gave up on all men completely, feeling that she would willingly undergo the lesser pain of permanent isolation to avoid suffering what was for her the greater pain of the vast emptiness predictably associated with being connected.

In therapy, we focused on how a measure of her "boredom" with the old was a defense against her fear of being controlled. Thus she was reluctant to make plans with any man in advance, even a dinner date, because she feared she would not be able to "wriggle out from under." When a man called her and invited her over for "dinner this Saturday," she accepted, only to feel trapped and cornered, so she added, "I will call if anything comes up," leaving the man wondering, with reason, if she would actually make it over at the appointed time, and thinking, "Maybe I better back out first so that I don't save the date only to have her cancel out on me at the last minute, leaving me with no plans for the big night." Feeling trapped, she longed for her space and started thinking about how wonderful it would be to sit at home by herself "surrounded by the things I love, like my valuable collection of lovely appliquéd teacups that fill the shelves in what used to be my basement bar (no longer working because all the china on the shelves left no room for liquor)." She might contemplate having a man over to sip from her cups, but afterward, she would ask herself, "How am I going to get out of this?" and cancel the engagement with only a few minute's notice using a flimsy excuse, such as claiming she had caught a cold or had a last-minute family emergency.

We next uncovered how part of her distancing from men was attributable to her anger with them. She rarely expressed this anger with men directly. Mostly she expressed it indirectly and subtly: by becoming remote as her way to quietly say, "You make me mad."

A great deal of this anger toward men was defensive: her way to seek out negative things about them to give herself the excuse she required to remove herself from their presence. She actively looked for reasons to complain that a man did not love her; didn't accept her for herself; criticized her for anything she said or did; only saw her weaknesses and ignored her strengths; and subjected her to ridicule. She made certain that she interpreted anything that a man said that wasn't a compliment as a criticism and that she saw his disagreeing with her as exactly the same thing as his savaging her completely. Humorlessly, she would deliberately take the mildest joke at her expense far too seriously. Once, for example, she confessed to a friend at a dinner party, "I have brittle bones." She then asked a man seated next to her, "What about your bones, are they bad?" Others at the table, overhearing the exchange, jokingly remarked, "Don't tell her! Your bones are *your* business!" So the man she asked, also as a joke, said, "I'll never tell." Whereupon she began to sulk aloud: "I told you about my bones, now why won't you tell me about yours?" And she meant it, and refused ever to speak to that man again.

Her anger was especially fierce when she believed that men were trying to control her—to "get me to do their bidding by roping me into a relationship I am reluctant to pursue"—and when she believed that men thought they were better than she was simply because they were men. Even fiercer still was her anger over the possibility that a close relationship with a man might be compromising her identity—by keeping her from being herself, stifling her right to be free and emancipated, and thwarting her creative urge to do what she wanted without interference by any man. As she put it, "I hate having to change myself around just for men I don't respect or care about that much anyway. I am an independent woman. For me closeness and intimacy with a man overwhelms, strangles, and pulverizes me into dust. Doesn't it do that to any woman alive?"

We also discussed how she was too much the relational perfectionist for her own good: a woman who sought the ideal man, while refusing to consider and accept any man who was less than perfect. Thus, before contemplating getting serious with a man, she demanded full compatibility. A man had to be not a calm, stoic type, who thought that all fretting was a waste of time, but as much in touch with his worries as she was. He wasn't for her unless he was "the sort who gets hysterical over nothing." Shared interests became much too important for her. Thus she left one viable relationship because "he loves boorish baseball and I love the much more sublime chamber music." She would also demand full exclusivity right from the start and break off a promising relationship at the first sign that she was just one of several in a man's affections. Otherwise, she was just "lowering her standards by hanging around with someone beneath me; someone who doesn't deserve me, or merit my faithful love."

We profitably identified and worked on two of her counterproductive security maneuvers. The first involved identifying with the aggressor. She would actively abandon men to deal with her fear that they might abandon her. She would also deal with her fear of being devalued by men by actively devaluing them so that it wouldn't matter if they devalued her. As she put it, "I actually like weak men because they lack power over me: the power to put me down."

We also worked on her paradoxical fears: that giving herself any breathing room in a relationship would mean that she was going to be abandoned; that retaining her identity in a relationship would result in her being left out in the cold, punished and sacrificed for being an individual by being thrown over for another more cooperative, compliant, conciliatory, and passive woman; and that involvement with a man necessarily meant compromising her career only to find herself not only alone, but also unemployed. Too, we worked on her destructive competitiveness, marked by her need to turn a cooperative relationship into a struggle for power and supremacy. For she saw friendly, cooperative men as rivals, turning a relationship into a contest either over small things, like who would be the one the dog came to first or whose lap the cat always sat on, or over big things, like who was or would be more successful than her professionally. This competitiveness led her to actively rejoice when something bad happened even to a man she liked. For that way, she could win, without feeling guilty about having caused him to lose.

Throughout, and not surprisingly, she complained that she was "dead in bed." She postponed having her first sexual experience indefinitely because she believed that abstinence alone was conducive or even essential to moral superiority. As she once put it, not entirely humorously, "The only way I can even think of having sex would be in the missionary position, with a Bible in one hand, and a washcloth in the other."

She saw sex not as lofty or spiritual, but as dirty and animalistic: to the point that she often provoked an argument to avoid having relations. On those few occasions when she actually tried sex, she would stop prematurely because she couldn't relax, lost sensation, and felt cold. To avoid self-blame, she convinced herself that "I really don't like how the man looks, or the way he behaves in bed, so it's best that I see to it that it is over immediately."

We discovered that much of her sexual difficulty developed out of the early fear that men would hurt her now, as her parents had hurt her when she was a child. She saw all men as father clones, who terrified her the way her father had done when he threatened to whip her if she didn't "behave" and "cooperate." All men had also symbolically become her hurtful mother, who never supported and always criticized her, even for a thing and its opposite, such as being messy (for not keeping her room clean) *and* for being excessively neat (for being a compulsively finicky dresser). Too, she believed that all men would infantilize her the way both her parents did—treating her like a helpless child with no rights or acceptable ideas of her own, yet demanding that she grow up fast so that she wouldn't be a burden to them forever. Worst of all, as she put it with tears in her eyes, "when, after a good deal of effort, once I managed to tell my parents that in spite of it all, I loved them, they nevertheless remained unmoved. So I never uttered those words to them again. Or to anyone else."

Unfortunately, she resisted therapy throughout. Rather than admit to being avoidant, she developed a number of rationalizations to normalize her behavior. She transformed fear into disinterest, and disinterest into preference, so that a fear of rejection became a fond desire for personal isolation, and that was "not something we ever need to discuss."

Ultimately, after a few months, she left treatment, saying that her life wasn't so bad after all and she didn't need to waste her money and time working on something that didn't really amount to much. For, as she put it, almost incredibly, "I am not hurting at all. If I am an avoidant in the first place, it gives me very little grief personally, and no trouble whatsoever professionally."

Just recently, I heard from her once again. Therapy had worked after it ended, for she could accept treatment from me now that she was no longer struggling with me about "how to think and what to do." She had gotten married, had a large family, and made a peace with her parents that was, however, imperfect, for "I still resent them for making me an avoidant, causing me to lose so many years out of my life to all the fearful isolation I had to endure all that time, and strictly on their behalf, and account."

CHAPTER 2

Counterphobic Avoidants

I divide avoidants into two broad classes of individuals: Type I, typical, classical avoidants; and Type II, atypical, counterphobic avoidants.

TYPE 1: TYPICAL, CLASSICAL AVOIDANTS

These avoidants, discussed in detail in the last chapter, display the classical *Diagnostic and Statistical Manual of Mental Disorders*, fourth edition (*DSM-IV*) profile of pervasive shyness and fearful isolation. Within this class, variations of severity exist on a continuum. Some of these individuals live by themselves or with their family, either staying at home and not socializing at all, or socializing only with a few selected individuals, attempting to meet people but having difficulty connecting as they try, but fail, to form sustained and sustaining relationships. Others form relationships that are only partially avoidant: limited in degree or of reduced intensity such as bicoastal marriages; serial monogamous relationships; or relationships that are stably unstable, dysfunctional because being with unattainable partners makes the relationships unlikely to come to fruition, or if they do, sooner or later, they are destined to dissolve.

TYPE II: ATYPICAL OR COUNTERPHOBIC AVOIDANTS

Type II avoidants do relate, but their relationships take the form of isolating social rituals. The *Psychodynamic Diagnostic Manual* describes such individuals collectively under the heading "Converse Manifestation: Counterphobic Personality Disorders": individuals who are "psychologically organized around defenses against their fears." These avoidants handle relational anxiety through "denial [and] reaction formation," that is, by using the characteristic pathological defense of "I can face anything without fear."[1] There are three subtypes, IIa, IIb, and IIc, which I now describe in some detail.

Type IIa

Type IIa avoidants characteristically display avoidance Sullivan describes as consisting of isolative social rituals. He calls these "pseudosocial ritual[s]," where individuals are "busily engaged with people, but nothing particularly personal transpires."[2]

Coleman seems to be referring to individuals with isolating social rituals when he describes a kind of relationship discord consisting of numerous love relationships that are often short-lived, and generally intense and unfulfilling, in one of the following ways: compulsive cruising and multiple partners, where cruising is ritualistic and trance inducing; compulsive fixation on an unattainable (or deficient) partner; compulsive multiple love relationships; and compulsive sexual behavior in a relationship (sometimes associated with compulsive autoerotism).[3]

In the realm of selecting unattainable people to relate to, these avoidants pick distant, remote people who are already taken to convince themselves that they are attempting to relate but failing to do so for reasons not fully under their control. Their cry "it won't work" is consciously or unconsciously part of their original plan to make certain that when it comes to their relationships, much goes on, but little actually happens.

A Case Example

A woman picked a married man to be her lover, then, when he "threatened" to become available, discouraged him from divorcing his wife—first by dissociating (not hearing his thoughts about marriage or, hearing them, passing them off as an aberration of the moment, not to be taken seriously) and second by becoming personally just remote enough to create sufficient doubt in the man's mind to make him hesitate to take the final step. All along, she suspected that this man being a proven cheat on account of his record with her made him unlikely to be a suitable candidate for marriage.

On his part, the man, to ease his guilt about having an affair, selected this woman in the first place, suspecting that her need to have an affair with a married man meant that it was likely that she would lose interest in him should he actually "threaten" to get a divorce and propose marriage. He sensed that she would be intolerant of real intimacy because of her need to be "the interloper," in her case, part of what he saw as her pattern of an all-too-apparent fear of success.

The man's wife knew that her husband was cheating on her from evidence that would have convinced even the most trusting and innocent of people that he was being unfaithful. But because she, being an avoidant herself, unconsciously needed to permit and encourage the affair, she failed to spot the obvious, and even (when she could no longer fool herself) refrained from confronting him and having a showdown, thus giving the affair her imprimatur: by being complicit in its neglect.

Many Type IIa avoidants are what I call "mingles" avoidants: individuals whose fear of closeness and commitment is either sufficiently mild or under adequate control to permit significant forays into relationships that are, however, tenuous because they are easily fractured, often by minor insignificant stress. Clara Thompson, describing such individuals, states, "Problems of intimacy are among the most disturbing interpersonal difficulties. . . . There are detached people who are not particularly hostile, who live as onlookers to life. They have an impersonal warmth so long as no closeness is involved, but they fear any entanglement of their emotions. . . . Many of these people get along very well in more superficial relationships. In fact, they may be the 'life of the party' or 'the hail fellow well met' so long as no permanent warmth or friendliness is demanded."[4]

Some typical Type IIa "mingles" avoidants look hypomanic due to their tendency to quell relational fears by making numerous but superficial "devil-may-care" contacts. They become serial daters or serial monogamists who meet new people/partners easily but have difficulty sustaining and developing the ensuing relationships so that quality becomes a casualty of quantity as they keep others, often many at one time, at bay through a gun-notching hyperrelatedness that covers an underlying remoteness and isolative tendency, which together create the self-fulfilling prophecy that "I can't meet anyone substantial and so am doomed to remain alone for the rest of my life." Typically, never seeming to be able to settle down, they become overly active in the singles scene. They frantically socialize looking for a mate, only to jump from one situation that does not work to another that works just as badly, continuing that pattern in spite of its obvious frivolity and ultimate futility. They juggle many ongoing but resolutely superficial relationships within a chic and sophisticated lifestyle that fills their days with insignificant others who function for them as self-esteem enhancers: mere hood ornaments, pretty girls or handsome men on the arm, worn like a badge that says, "View me favorably because if I can get something this stunning, I must be someone special myself."

When rejected, hypomanic Type IIa avoidants make an especially frantic attempt to feel loved once again. They rush about looking for new lovers, grabbing the first accepting person who comes along, not for any winning quality that person might have, but to get unrejected, to undo a sense of despair and a feeling of emptiness, as they become too much the life of the party in order to deny the feeling that they have been disinvited from the ball.

A Case Example

A man put ads on the Internet just to see how many hits he would get, only he then did not reply to the people who wrote to him, or, what was worse, replied, in essence, "I'm a young, virile guy longing to meet you, rich and famous, and I'm sure we can get along because you sound just right for me, but I'm so busy now that I just can't take the time to meet someone as wonderful as you seem to be, but I will get back to you as soon as I can, but meanwhile feel free to meet other men, though I hope you will wait, because I will call, if only you will be patient." Although he consciously feared he would never have a partner, he nevertheless once abruptly arose in the middle of a date with a new, rather exciting, adoring woman to leave for home because he couldn't wait to download a new love song from the Internet. Another time, under similar circumstances, he abandoned a woman to go home to check to see if he had left his sound equipment on—thinking he was afraid it would overheat and he wouldn't be able to play soft, soothing music during subsequent sexual encounters. Still another time, under similar circumstances and for the same reasons, he left to check to see if he had scratched and ruined a CD by playing it on a damaged machine.

In the singles bars he attended he played Berne's game of "Kiss Off" or "Buzz off, Buster."[5] He dressed to look sexy, stood in alluring poses, and gave others come-hither looks, only at the first sign that others were interested in him he removed himself, becoming aloof and disdainful even though he was the one who had first extended an invitation. In ongoing relationships he said, "We must get together again sometime," but he never made the next date, or, making one, broke it, reassuring the victim that this was the very last time it would happen, just so that he could make it happen again. In his sexual behavior premature withdrawal was the order of the day—not to prevent conception, but to first tempt and excite then to frustrate by starting just so that he could stop short and avoid fulfilling the woman completely.

Many such men and women form these pseudorelationships based on a fascination with other peoples' superficial qualities so that they pick others according to such surface attributes as their looks or possessions, substituting impersonal for personal relationships by relating to attributes rather than to people. Still others relate, but to an anonymous, collective "them," as did the avoidant who was active with his fan club to avoid having relationships with any one personal fan. Notable for many are a lack of affectional reciprocity: they give affection when it is unlikely to be returned, but withhold it should it appear to be forthcoming.

Unlike Type I, shy avoidants, who are *neophobes*—that is, individuals who cannot initiate relationships because they fear the new as something unknown—Type IIa "mingles" avoidants are *neophiles* who want to, can, and like to attend social functions and initiate relationships once there. Only they have to move on because they long for the challenges involved in meeting someone new. Becoming restless and impulsive in familiar situations and feeling contemptuous of present company, they grab at the latest, newest thing. Underneath, many fear success due to a masochistic need to suffer that makes it difficult for them to accept being happy and fulfilled. When these avoidants say, "This relationship is wrong for me," they really mean that it is wrong: because it is too right.

Many of these avoidants join groups of other avoidants with the same or similar problems. Now they all head together for, but never seem to find, a conquest. All concerned roam in "packs," hoping to "snare a man" or "get a woman into bed." Instead, all they relate to is the collective, with each group member making certain that the other members don't bolt, while simultaneously maintaining group cohesion by ostracizing outsiders from their magic inner circle. Often heavy drinking and drug usage are part of the picture and can even become the main purpose of the group, the group's real, or even only, "social" activity.

Not all type IIa avoidants with isolating social rituals actually get to the point of burning through relationship after relationship. Some, instead, compulsively plan for, but never actually proceed with, a seduction, as did the individual who decorated and redecorated his apartment so that "women will yield when they see my beautiful place," only to never actually invite women up to visit, and developed an all-consuming and all-surpassing desire to be "where it's at, with the in crowd," at "in" resorts, rubbing elbows with "celebrities, not lowlifes" in the trendy bar or restaurant that only special people know about, a place "where you can really meet women," although during all the years I treated him, he rarely went to such places, and when he did, he never once even attempted to say hello back to the many women who, clearly interested, came over to say hello to him.

TYPE IIB

Type IIb, or seven-year itch, avoidants seem able to form more or less full and satisfactory relationships, but only for a time. Unlike Type IIa avoidants, who have difficulty relating/committing fully right from the start, they at least seem to relate well/commit fully in the beginning. But all the while, they are planning their escape. Not atypical is the patient who, after a three-year engagement, seemingly without warning announced that he was taking a hiatus from the relationship and would call again after the few months' time he said he needed to work things out in his mind. A year later, he had become a bitter, lonely man, who still hadn't made the promised contact.

Many of these avoidants are typical "dumpers," who opt out by precipitously rejecting an innocent and unprepared victim, spurting out something like, "I want some down time to think," "I need a break," "I want to be free," "I met someone new and fell in love, so I want a divorce," or saying nothing, just disappearing forever out of a formerly significant other's life—even when, or just because, the relationship seems to be working. They leave their innocent victims feeling mystified and hurt, thinking "I didn't do anything to deserve this," especially because when they go, they typically cite their partners' defects exclusively, while whitewashing their own limitations entirely.

A Case Example

A personal friend, a dental school student, called me up once or twice a day to unload his serious emotional problems on me. After several months of this, he suddenly stopped calling. Concerned, I called him up to ask him what was wrong. To my question, he replied, "I can no longer speak to you. I just got an important sensitive academic position and I cannot even let on that I know you. You know much too much about me for that."

Type IIb avoidants are often narcissistic individuals who typically leave after using people up, dumping others precisely when they seem to want something from them in return. Often they actively provoke their partners to get annoyed with them so that they can have the excuse they need to abandon them. This way, they can look more like the victim than the victimizer. A husband wants to go out drinking with the boys, but his wife disapproves. He has no trouble antagonizing her by picking on her for small things like vacuuming when he is trying to watch television. She gets defensive, saying, "Who else is going to clean around here?" and now he has the reason he needs to stomp out: he is a poor, henpecked husband, undeservedly married to a harpy.

Type IIb avoidant adolescents characteristically have a history of having dumped their parents without warning. Many elope, saying they did it to break free from long-resented parental domination—but the domination is more fantasized than real because they are acting on fearful fantasies of being controlled that are, in reality, the product of their own avoidant transference toward their parents.

A Case Example

My daughter Carley was a girl all set to go to nursing school. The hospital where she worked was going to pay 80 percent of her tuition if she promised to work for them for three years afterward, and she had so wanted to be in the medical field for years that she even used to go to the medical school cafeteria dressed in surgical scrubs to pretend she was a doctor (weird, but no weirder than the crush she developed on her dermatologist, whom she used to follow around with a girlfriend, who was also in love with him). So what does she do to avoid the responsibility of developing herself and a career, as I had hoped? She runs off with a schizophrenic stalker who believes the president of the United States is going to send him to Iceland to develop an energy formula, cuts off everyone in her family who can give her a reality check, drops all of her former friends, and immerses herself in his crazy family where she can live in the land of the blind as the one-eyed queen. She has basically reinvented her life from scratch, embracing everything she used to hate about her former life (she used to hate it when I had relatives over, referring to them as "hellatives," but she is now entrenched in a numerous-clan family); and then she would never go to church, even when her religious school required it, but now she goes every Sunday because her husband's parents are religious fanatics. She marries after only knowing her husband-to-be for a short period of time—and this after she told me she is part of an age where it is considered wiser to live with someone first. She then rushes to have a baby to lock herself into her predicament so that she can avoid having to go back to who and what she used to be. Cutting off her entire old personal history and roots was her way to avoid taking responsibility for her life by escaping into a totally new fantasy world, where nothing is expected of you in terms of developing yourself and working at a career, and all that is now demanded of you is to be physically present for your husband.

TYPE IIc

Type IIc avoidants remove themselves from others via a process of reaction formation, where they distance from all by becoming overly involved with, or actually immersed in, a regressive relationship with one. This type is exemplified by the codependent individuals described by Melody Beattie,[6] some of whom are avoidants who move away from home and in with a steady partner or spouse to become immersion junkies, who seem nonavoidant because they are in a close, all-encompassing, loving permanent relationship with one person, but are, however, not relating to one out of love, but hiding out from all out of fear as well as out of anger that leads them to show their dislike of, and try to defeat, all the other people in their lives.

Sometimes these bosom relationships work, and last, but if the number of books written on how to overcome codependency is any indication, all is not well in the codependent life. For codependent relationships are often not as loving as they seem to be; rather, they can be unhealthy hostile-dependent relationships that, though they often last, less often really work.

Other Type IIc avoidants stay too close to their parents, living at home with no partner or spouse, as did the man who worked at home from his computer as a stock trader and had few or no friends, didn't go out on dates, and watched pornography all day long on the Internet. Then, after years of refusing to marry a woman because he didn't want to hurt his mother, he finally acquiesced—but he never told his mother, or the rest of the family, that he had done so, and instead, to the full detriment of his marriage, hid his wife from all concerned and continued to live at home and otherwise act as if he were single, hoping to avoid disappointing his mother, just so that he could keep from causing her to get sick over him.

CHAPTER 3

Healthy and Normal versus Pathological Avoidance

HEALTHY AVOIDANCE

Avoidance can be healthy when it is, as Sullivan suggests, a conjunctive force used to "enhance security."[1] Healthy avoidance can also consist of a rational philosophical desire to be alone. As such, it is *preferential*, that is, something individuals have reasonably decided is both good and good for them and so have comfortably built into their lives—a splendid self-sufficient self-containment that allows them to achieve their desire to remain independent of others, be their own masters, and enjoy the peace that comes from removal and detachment. For such avoidants, the song that refers to jangling spurs that say that you should roll merrily along, being glad that you are single, is apropos. For these are independent souls who aver that relationships, and particularly marriage, are not right for them because they want to come and go as they please, because for them, being "me" does actually require "being free."

Some Case Examples

One such avoidant would regularly and comfortably eat dinner in a restaurant all by herself reading the Sunday newspaper on Saturday night and go walking alone by the seashore day in and day out. Most of all, she liked closing her eyes and putting hot compresses over them; having a few drinks at home alone; rocking by herself on her porch in her favorite rocking chair; self-hypnotizing by submitting to the drowsy nirvana- and sleep-inducing drone of the lulling train or car ride; being soothed by monotonous ragas; and performing repetitive activities like crocheting or knitting. She also relished reading escape

literature that took her away to the cold North or out West to the lone
prairie, where she fantasized riding a horse by herself under the stars.
If she suffered at all, it was not from her isolation, but from the social
pressures that made her feel guilty about being as isolated as she really wanted to be. She wanted to eat, live, and play alone, but a critical world, and an uncomprehending therapist, made her ashamed of
feeling that way, although that was what she wanted and exactly what
seemed right for her as an individual.

A married writer felt, "I would like to retreat from the world, line
my room with cork like Proust, and write, write, write, alone, all
day long." Then he did essentially just that: he purchased a house
trailer, which he parked in the driveway of his home, and worked
there "to avoid having my family disturb my concentration." Eventually, he moved from California to New York, leaving his wife and
children behind, commuting but only on occasional weekends. He
acted not out of a pathological fear of closeness, but out of a desire
for separateness—in the belief, later proved correct, that distance
would lend enchantment both to his work and to his relationship
with his wife, who, "fortunately" being an avoidant herself, was even
more comfortable than he was with the arrangement.

A middle-aged patient had a job working as a blackjack dealer in Las
Vegas gaming halls. One day, she had an epiphany. Tired of "stealing
money from drunks," she instead decided to buy and go live by herself
on five acres of land in northern Arizona. Her land was a piece of desert without water or electricity, two miles from her nearest neighbor,
a place whose extreme remoteness she called "the main advantage of
living in the wild." With her own hands, she built a log cabin out of
limbs she cut from the trees in her backyard. She now hauls her water
from 30 miles away in her Chevy truck, uses solar panels to make electricity, and heats her home with other logs cut from the trees around
her house. She never gets bored because "she has to work too hard for
that," and she loves her existence because daily she reminds herself
that life is all about not what she has, but what she has left over to give
to others.

Avoidance is also healthy when it is a limited, small-scale, creative,
distancing maneuver appropriate to specific circumstances or for the
ultimately greater nonavoidant good of providing a welcome escape
from a tumultuous world too much with one: a world full of uncomfortable, unimportant, but upsetting relationships likely to spread to
contaminate, undermine, or destroy what potentially more meaningful social and personal contacts remain. Such avoidance as a useful
method for dealing with stressful external situations is a justifiable

self-protective reactive response that wards off properly anticipated or actual humiliation or rejection at the hands of the inconsiderate or hurtful others that come into everyone's life, such as the intrusive, backbiting professional colleague or the undesirable, overly aggressive personal suitor. Potential lovers *should* at least consider avoiding partners who do not reciprocate and offer love back, and we all should at least consider avoiding people who torture us by nagging us, hurt us by being prejudiced against us, or threaten to harm us, if not physically, then emotionally, by reviving old, unmanageable traumatic interpersonal agony or by suddenly rejecting (dumping) us. Nor is there any sense in being a hero with wild, potentially dangerous paranoids, having a fight that wins points but costs lives. In short, there are many self-help books out there on how to get along *with* difficult people. What many avoidants need is a self-help book on how to get along out there *without* them.

Avoidance is also healthy when it is a defense that provides a welcome resolution of or escape from reactive *inner* turmoil. It is healthy to want to escape from one's own sadistic impulses by avoiding wild kingdom animal shows that rub one's nose in the laws of the jungle, and even to want to avoid facing sexual desires that provoke guilt— staying away from X-rated movies less for the moral reasons generally cited and more because the close-up anatomical view revives unintegrated/unmanageable primal-scene experiences or activates quiescent prior traumatic sexual molestations. A particularly bright side of the defense of *obsessive-compulsive* avoidant procrastination is pause thus allowing time to think. That permits internal conflicts and difficult real life situations to be resolved implicitly, and in the longer run by simply waiting for the tincture of time to kick in.

NORMAL AVOIDANCE

Avoidance that is not entirely *healthy* can still, under certain circumstances, be *within normal limits*. For example, avoidance is within normal limits when, as part of grief, it permits the individual to be alone with his or her nostalgia, with his or her faded clippings and reminiscences, dwelling on a pleasurable past to deny an intolerable present, indulging in a better-days, if-only fantasy. One patient, after the death of his wife, retreated into arranging and rearranging his old photos and the sympathy cards he got when his wife died, doing so in order to keep alive her memory to avoid suffering the pain associated with having to live his life without her. He also stayed alone in the large house they once occupied together just so that he could continue to be surrounded by the pleasant memories there, even though the house was too large for his needs, too difficult for him to keep up, and in the suburbs, although all his activities were in the city. And at a shore house they once shared, he kept and nurtured all his wife's plantings, even though, or in a sense just because, the yard, although it was becoming overgrown and wild, still remained in its "original" state.

However, a continuum exists between normal and pathological grief, with pathological grief becoming avoidance when it is excessive, overly intense, continuous, and prolonged, as in the following case.

A Case Example

A patient informed me, "One of my friends made his first million right out of college writing some kind of innovative software, so he retired and followed his dream to sing folk songs with his guitar. He got a gig at a famous restaurant and bar. Later on he married, then divorced, but apparently he still loved his ex-wife. Then she died a few years after the divorce. Now he had to stop singing because he would unpredictably start crying at the thought of her death. When he wrote to me to express his condolences about my own wife's death, he told me all of this and how he now lives out in the woods somewhere, like a hermit, telecommutes for an advertising company, and has for his only 'friends' the business cable channel, which he leaves on all day. He never leaves his home, and never will, according to him. And the tears still come, unexpectedly."

Avoidance can also be within normal limits when it is *part of the normal developmental process*, for example, part of "adolescent turmoil," where adolescent rebellion has the beneficial purpose of paving the way for the child to grow up and become an adult who, having turned into a more independent man or woman, can now leave home without second thoughts and free of guilty regrets.

Avoidance is also normal when it is a rational reflexive response to a difficult partner. Is this the case here? (And who in the following exchange is avoiding whom?)

A Case Example

I recently got the following letter:

Can you please direct me (well, my husband) to someone in or near Fargo, ND who might be able to help him. He has avoidant personality disorder and has "ended our relationship" countless times. I am not only heartbroken each time, but am at my wit's end, and his doctor has recently referred him to a social worker who specializes in women's addictions of all things. I just don't know where to turn, as I love this man dearly and don't know how to get him the help he needs, and I don't know how I can cope with this, short of ending the relationship which I really don't want to do.

I replied that I wished I could help but I didn't know of anyone in her area. She shot back in what I thought might be a somewhat passive-aggressive fashion, as follows:

Dear Dr. Kantor. Thank you for answering my email. I am not very hopeful for my husband finding the help that he needs in this town.

Was she expressing anger toward me—for being less than help-ful—in the form of disappointment? At any rate, I felt bad, and wished I were somewhere else. Was I being highly attuned to her unspoken anger, or was I just being hypersensitive out of my sense of guilt?

Avoidance is also normal when it is an *interim, transitional, planned part of psychotherapy.* In fact, therapy well done works partly by tempo-rarily enhancing avoidance—by offering the avoidant not only a sanc-tuary from everyday cares, but also a time out where he or she can temporarily stop, take stock, retreat, and reconsider life options and goals: becoming more avoidant for now, in preparation for becoming less avoidant in the future.

AVOIDANT PERSONALITY DISORDER

The following section attempts to clear up what appears to be wide-spread confusion about the differences between avoidant *personality traits* and the full avoidant personality disorder (AvPD) syndrome as well as about *comorbidity*, where AvPD coexists with one or more di-agnosable Axis II disorders, resulting in a mixed personality disorder. (Comorbidity is discussed at length in chapter 7.)

PERSONALITY TRAITS

In this book, although I do not always spell it out, many of my dis-cussions of AvPD are in fact discussions of avoidance; that is, they are not about AvPD, but about the individual *traits* that together go into making up the AvPD. *These traits by themselves do not constitute the personality disorder, which consists of a cluster of personality traits.*

Personality traits are primary behaviors, the product of rigid, armored attitudes that are in turn set ways of viewing things, coming from within, weakly and only with effort influenced from without: overly rigid, fixed, repetitive, predictable, and often inappropriate responses barely subject to the dictates of reality and common sense. Traits resemble overvalued ideas—preoccupying beliefs, close to convictions, that lie somewhere on the continuum between rational beliefs and irrational delusions. An example of an overvalued idea is emotionally based, rigid, inflexible, unvarying, and off-the-mark ideology from the politically far Left or far Right. Some traits, like excessive worry, are ego-dystonic, that is, they feel like unwanted foreign bodies in the mind, while others, like withdrawal, can be ego-syntonic, that is, they feel acceptable, desirable, and enjoyable.

Dynamically, traits originate in developmental fixation or regression; are products of learning and experience; can be the result of identification with others with similar or the same traits; constitute the behavioral manifestations of active defenses; can be the product of an unpredictable (sometimes overly lax and sometimes overly harsh) superego or conscience structure; and can represent the lingering legacy of early, unintegrated trauma.

Generally speaking, traits may be either adaptive, as the trait of ambitious competitiveness can be, or maladaptive, as are the traits of lack of self-assurance and masochistic self-destructiveness. Personality traits are not inherently either normal or pathological. This is so because legitimate individual personality differences exist, with some people normally more introverted than others, and such different personalities as uncomplicated Type A and Type B personalities both within the normal range. Also, in determining the presence of normalcy versus psychopathology, external circumstances have to be taken into account. Thus a trait that is pathological under some cultural and environmental circumstances is nonpathological under others, for example, on vacation or at a special time of the year, with such terms as winter doldrums reminding us that we as individuals, and society as a whole, often make cultural allowances for some deviation from year-round norms.

Personality Disorder

In exceptional cases, a personality disorder can consist of the use of one favored trait employed either only under certain circumstances or

continuously. The former is exemplified by dissociation that only occurs in the face of "acceptance emergencies," or "projection" that only
occurs under extreme stress and is meant to create a resolutely "not-me"
excuse to avoid feeling guilty about one's unacceptable thoughts and
actions. Generally, however, a personality disorder is made up of multiple traits. These tend to be selected on the basis of affinity with each
other, for example, shyness and submission or withholding and withdrawing. Also, unless the traits selected are inherently distinctive,
and, if multiple, combined in a unique way, personality style, not personality disorder, will result. In the realm of "inherently distinctive,"
the traits that constitute a personality disorder are generally abrasive
and pungent, with negative traits favored over positive traits, so that
Mr. Lowdown predominates over Mr. Loveable and maladaptive traits
are favored over adaptive traits. In the realm of "combined in a unique
way," unless there is a critical mass of traits that additionally synergistically distort the personality, we will not have a personality disorder, but a pattern less dramatic in presentation, startling in nature,
and devastating in effect than a true syndrome needs to be. Put another way, unless the resulting psychological construct makes waves,
ruffles feathers (one's own and others), and attracts psychiatric attention because the individual, for any one of a number of reasons, develops difficulties that are sufficiently overt to be obvious, and sufficiently
intense to become noticeable, that is, unless there are discrete, obvious, and generally troublesome interpersonal/social behavioral consequences, the diagnosis of a personality "style" or "type," rather than a
"personality disorder," should be considered.

In the realm of comorbidity, many, if not most, avoidants do not
exhibit avoidant personality traits or disorder alone. AvPD is commonly not diagnosed by itself; rather, AvPD is often part of a complex
syndrome characterized by more than one personality disorder, the
elusive "pure singular syndrome" rarely ruling in a given individual.
In great measure, this is because the individual component traits of
AvPD are not distinctive enough to suggest only one diagnosis so that,
for example, the trait of withdrawal can also be schizoid or phobic,
leading the diagnostician to call the withdrawn individual a "mixed
avoidant/schizoid" or to say that he or she is suffering from a personality disorder "best described as avoidance due to a social phobia
generalizing." Like many personality disorders, AvPD is a somewhat
elusive entity due to being made up of traits that are in themselves
undistinguished and assembled into a tentative and shifting psychological edifice, rough in outline and construction, that is less a firm
unvarying entity than a proclivity to move in a certain direction, in

this case, anxious withdrawal, as distinct, for example, from suspicious remoteness.

Conversely, only a few personality disorders have a relatively hard-edged identity: the obsessive-compulsive and the paranoid representing two exceptions.

A caveat is that a personality disordered label cannot be attached to an individual unless an experienced clinician has seen the patient in person, carefully studied him or her over a significant period of time, and determined if overall behavior, not just one or two examples of it taken out of, or even in, context, warrants that such a determination be made.

CHAPTER 4
Sexual Avoidance

There are two broad categories of sexual avoidance: innate or essential (asexuality) and acquired (anxious).

DESCRIPTION

Innate or Essential Sexual Avoidance (Asexuality)

Innate or essential sexual avoidants suffer from a sexual hypoactivity disorder, a kind of "sexual alexithymia" where the individual experiences diminished or absent sexual urges and believes that that state of affairs is normal, welcome, desirable, and acceptable. The cry is, "I don't feel sexual, I don't want to feel sexual, I just can't have sex, I won't have sex, who needs sex, sex is not for me." Some asexual men and women complain only of a lack of desire, while others also complain of a lack of genital sensation. Some once felt sexual but lost that feeling later in life. Others claim that they had nothing to lose because they never had strong sexual feelings in the first place. Some retain the capacity for romance. Others are as personally unromantic as they are sexually unarousable.

A Case Example

One of my asexual patients half-jokingly said that he was "perfectly happy being in love with his truck." He cracked that he was so in love with her that he had fallen in love with her "head over wheels." He spoke of how sad he was to have to let his truck go now that he bought a newer, younger girl, for his truck was a faithful companion, but getting on in years. She had 315,000 miles on her and had been with him for a decade. If he sold her, he couldn't get much money for her because of all her mileage. But the person who bought her would be getting a great little woman because she was still in very good shape and in a position to serve. True, not all of her anatomy was still intact, but anything anyone needed was still there, and she could still do everything important she needed to do, and do it as well as any girl half her age.

This man had had sex with his wife a few times in the beginning of their marriage. After they produced a child, he started thinking that sex was evil, so to get away from his wife's sexual advances, he built her a separate house attached to the main dwelling so that they could live together, yet apart, and go their separate ways: she to France to have a series of affairs, and he to his job, driving his beloved truck by day and even sleeping in her at night.

On those rare occasions when his wife still approached him for sex, he would tell her in essence, "We did it already—we had a kid; why do we have to do it again?" He would then make the following excuses as he went off to sleep by himself:

- I can't sleep with you in the same bed; you snore and toss and turn.
- You don't keep yourself up.
- You are too old.
- I am too old.
- It's the same thing over and over again.
- The kid will overhear us.
- Every time I do it, I get irritated down there.

In passing, he also noted that not only his sexuality, but also all his biological functions were slow—so slow, indeed, that he only had a bowel movement once a week. Then he added that anyway, for companionship, he was content with his 20 cats, each of which had a special personality, which he would then go on to describe in detail as if he were talking about 20 parts of a wife, split among 20 different souls. This one purred when he stroked her, that one slept with him, this one kissed him good night, that one woke him up in the morning, this one gave him the feeling that he was wanted, and so on.

Both he and his wife agreed to keep their one son at home as much and as long as possible. They even homeschooled him as part of their plan to groom him to be as interpersonally avoidant as his father was sexually avoidant: a day trader in the market, working from his home computer, able to support himself adequately without ever having to leave the house—and Daddy.

My patient loved his life, and he loved his wife, but he never missed nor complained about not having sex with her. Nor did he have relations with other women. He was not homosexual either. As he put it, "I am simply content to go about my business from the waist up, without having to attend to each and every one of my body parts from the waist down."

He never sought nor felt he needed treatment. Originally, he had come to see me because his wife had asked him to go for a consultation "just to see if something is wrong and if so what could be done about it." But, uninterested in continuing therapy beyond our initial meeting, he made another appointment, then cancelled it and never returned.

His wife dealt with her own strong sexual needs by having a series of affairs. Though he knew about them, he didn't really seem to mind. He did not deny that she was being unfaithful to him. What bothered him most was the possibility that she would meet someone new and leave him, then not be around to help him bring up their son and take care of the cats. He even agreed to pay for her trips to France, though he knew that she went there to actually meet and have sex with men she had initially contacted through the Internet. He figured "that a man should pay his wife's transportation, and since she didn't have her own car it is only fair that I pay for a plane trip to France now and then." He would do anything for her—but one—as the price of her staying with him. Her reassurances that she sought only affairs, not divorce, were enough to keep him calm and happy.

This man claimed that he no longer felt any sexual feelings. He denied that he was suppressing them out of a sense of guilt originating in psychological conflict, social teachings, or religious tenets. His asexuality only bothered him when someone he perceived to be knowledgeable and in authority told him that something was wrong and that he was missing something, or when he started worrying that his wife would leave him for sex and that he would grow old and alone. For him, asexuality was not pathology, but philosophy. And because his wife accepted him as he was, the pairing worked, the marriage lasted, and both he and his wife claimed to be happy and well adjusted just the way things were.

ACQUIRED SEXUAL AVOIDANCE

While true asexuality is innate or essential, acquired sexual avoid-ance, what Fenichel calls "psychogenic sexual impotence,"[1] is the product of inhibition arising out of conflict. This psychogenic sexual impotence is often the product of an erotophobia, or "love phobia." This becomes manifest in various ways, including guilty hesitancy about doing anything at all sexual, resulting in transient or prolonged fearful celibacy; limiting oneself to substitute gratifications such as hobbies used to partially or fully divert oneself from getting sexually involved; sexual coldness and frostiness; a paradoxical, counterphobic hypersexuality; or physical sexual symptoms such as diminished geni-tal sensation, erectile dysfunction/impotence (inability to get or main-tain an erection), premature or retarded ejaculation in the man, and dyspareunia or vaginismus in the woman.

Erotophobia is itself the product of a constellation of underly-ing fearful components. Some erotophobes fear touching and being touched because they view anything sexual as dirty and disgusting—as did the patient who feared shaking my hand because of the possibil-ity that I would contaminate him with a sexually transmitted disease. Others fear that their sexual feelings will flood them so that for them, it becomes as difficult to tolerate sexual as any other form of intense pleasure. Still others, obsessively scrupulous individuals, fear that sex is forbidden because it is immoral and therefore to be avoided without simultaneously putting some form of countervailing cleansing prohi-bition into place.

In one such cleansing prohibition, the individual can only enjoy in-tercourse with a lover, but not with a husband or wife, for now, as Freud noted in his 1912 paper, "The Most Prevalent Form of Degra-dation in Erotic Life," "the condition of [necessary] prohibition is re-stored by [the] secret intrigue [of being] untrue."[2] Another cleansing prohibition involves having sex, then taking it back, by condemning what one just did immediately afterward, say, with postcoital revul-sion manifest as a desire to get away from one's partner quickly, what one avoidant called my "take a shower and get dressed right now syn-drome." Still another involves keeping tenderness out of sexuality to the point that, as Freud states, a man might actually perceive a "check within him"[3] so that, as Jones suggests, he is "only capable of intense physical pleasure with a woman socially, morally or aesthetically of a lower order."[4] Frequently, the condition of prohibition is restored by developing strong attractions to many and often only to unavailable people, as does the straight man who pursues serial affairs with prostitutes or the gay man who only likes stevedore types, or by demeaning one's partners or sexuality itself by picking someone already devalued, say, "rough trade," or by picking someone valued then demeaning him or her by refuting the value of sexual exclusivity by becoming openly or secretly promiscuous.

A Case Example

Recently, I received the following letter (lightly edited) asking for my advice:

About six months ago, I had a breakup. I was really hurt, and I decided that I was tired of being the monogamous, romantic one who was the only one that seemed to really care and the only one that ever seemed to get hurt. I have since been a slut, in all honesty, going from guy to guy not even caring to learn the person's name. I honestly have guys in my phone that are labeled "A guy" and "Guy 1," "Guy 2," etc. But I am getting tired of not having a someone. Not being loved by a unique partner. Still I feel that all gay guys are stuck up, selfish whores that can't give a damn about anyone but themselves.

I'm in the military, navy to be exact, and we aren't exactly allowed to be gay, but everyone knows I am. I met a guy on post about two weeks ago that I slept with and eventually became fond of. I don't know why really. I have only been with one guy since I met him. I actually care about him. Nowhere near "Love," but I do care about him. I cry when he's sad, I smile when he's happy—a crush if you would. Still I posted an ad the other day on Craigslist looking for sex. I got about 40 responses, 30 of which I accepted and agreed to hook up with within the week. Well, the next day I started thinking. I e-mailed all the guys and told them I was no longer looking for sex. I feel like my life is so fake right now. I would use the commonplace term "empty," but I don't like that word. I don't exactly feel empty, rather full of superficial things that are not really me. Henceforth, I will say I feel "fake"—just compiled of things I don't really want (but pretend I do).

So, I canceled all these offers. And after about four to five lonely hours of feeling sorry for myself (because I found out that the guy that I like is married and is trying to avoid getting close to me emotionally), I decided to get up and feel good about myself even with the nothing I have and the nothing I've done lately.

I often have low self-esteem. I feel inferior or inadequate. I'm definitely too femme and emotional. I've never had a decent relationship that wasn't online (sadly enough). And I know I have so many great qualities and so many people would be lucky to have me. But why am I attracted to people I cannot have? And why do I attract people that I would not get with? Hopes and dreams are big to me. I am definitely a lover boy and I like to be proper. Exquisite dates. You know, the whole charade. But I often feel like I am being lied to and used by the only guys I meet. I often feel like guys tell me they like me but in the same breath try to push me off. "Oh, sorry, I'm busy. Can we do it tomorrow?" Then I let my emotions take over, and I give them about eight pieces of my mind.

If you have any advice, motivational words, or words of wisdom, such would be highly appreciated. Because I could use all the advice I can get.

Perhaps the commonest cleansing prohibition involves having only virtual sex—displaying an excessive fondness for pornography—which becomes acceptable because it doesn't involve actual people.

Surprisingly, erotophobic individuals are not necessarily personally cold-blooded types. Outside of the sexual arena, they tend to be normally related people who, though their capacity for sex is diminished, often retain their capacity for personal warmth and affection. Surprising, too, is that unlike individuals suffering from innate sexual avoidance, who claim that "that's just the way I am," patients with acquired sexual avoidance tend to be insightful about why they are sexually removed. In contrast to the asexual avoidant who says, "Who knows and even cares why I don't feel anything," they often know that they desire sex and have performance difficulties because they have buried their passions, and it is this that leaves them with reduced sexual feelings and ones that they are unable to translate into decisive erotic action.

DEVELOPMENT

More is understood about the development of acquired than of innate sexual avoidance, the latter seeming to "come from out of the blue." Acquired sexual avoidance in the adult often results when a

child's healthy sexual development is thwarted by unhealthy contain-
ment at the hands of rigidly suppressive parents, who encourage the
child to carry on his or her parental sexually suppressive tradition, one
supported by repressive elements in the society the parents happen
to, and often choose to, live in. To illustrate, when he was a child, one
avoidant's mother whipped him whenever she sensed he "felt sexual."
She meted out one particularly intense whipping when she caught him
"playing doctor" with a neighbor's little girl, saying "nice little boys
don't play such naughty games." After the beating, he "ran away from
home" to a neighbor's apartment, only to be beaten again, this time
for disappearing without telling his mother where he was going. After
that, his mother tried to make certain that he stayed away from all the
girls in the neighborhood so that he didn't "ruin their lives the way he
ruined hers."

Many parents like this mother are themselves erotophobes, who
make it clear that they harbor negative feelings about most or all sexuality. They do this either directly, say, by criticizing the child for masturbation, or indirectly, say, by issuing warnings to "not get married
and leave home because your mother needs you." Children who in-
ternalize the parental erotophobia implode sexually and come to view
their own sexuality through the eyes of a rigid punitive conscience
composed of the adopted harsh, shrill, intrapsychic, hateful, self-
destructive messages antithetical to desire, love, and sex, with no forgiving nuances anywhere to be found to soften the inner blows the
conscience rains down on the sexual self.

Sons whose parents humiliated them for normative sexual feelings
often go on to develop a fear of masculine sexual activity.

Some Case Examples

A father beat his son and threatened to cut off his funds for school
if he did not see a psychiatrist to be cured of being promiscuous,
which, according to the father, consisted of his "having more than
one girlfriend at a time." The father's overall message, "I am ashamed
of you for being so sexually preoccupied," soon became the son's
"I am ashamed of myself and my sexuality." Next, the son developed
a defensive retreat, first into sexual passivity, and then into studied
femininity.

As a child, a boy preferred playing with girls. His father, becoming
concerned that he would "grow up to be a sissy," abused him personally by calling him a faggot in order to frighten him straight. Later in

life, the son demeaned himself both for his sexuality and for enjoying almost anything he did, sexual or not. Eventually, the son attempted suicide because "I hate myself so and deserve to die."

Daughters who grow up with an overly possessive, excessively controlling father may become women with dyspareunia.

A Case Example

A woman's father repeatedly made the point that he did not want any teenage daughter of his talking to those creeps on the Internet. Then he forbade her to go online at all. Then he declared that she should not date men until she was 30 years old. Then he stopped her from having overnights at houses where there were any men in the household because "who knows what you might do in the way of diddling each other should I leave you alone with them."

Both parents punished her for "premarital petting" by selling her their house, knowing, but not telling her in advance, that a building project across the way was going to block the ocean view. To rub salt in her wounds, they built a new and better house and gave it to her brother. They also gave him a thriving business they had built up over the years. Almost predictably, their daughter morphed into a self-destructive, self-hating, remote woman distanced not only from her own family, but also from all potential and actual friends and lovers. She felt too undeserving to enjoy the company of good people and too personally worthless to allow herself to have a great life, especially one that included fulfilling sexual experiences within the context of a happy marriage and big family.

Not surprisingly, early discrete sexual traumata tend to have great lingering inhibitory effects on adult sexuality. In a common scenario, childhood rape or incest experience(s) lead women to view all men as predators, then to detach themselves from adult sexuality because they have come to view all sex, even when consensual, as being forced upon them.

This said, a degree of erotophobia is so common as to be virtually normal. While some is personal due to having introjected negative parental and social messages, some is also innate, part of sexuality's inherent tendency to elicit guilt in everyone, straight or gay. For reasons not entirely known or explainable, guilt is a universal negative, attitudinal mind-set toward having a body and using it sexually, one that makes all sex into something wicked and sinful, unless the sex is between a man and a woman, in the missionary position, in the dark, and strictly for the purpose of procreating—and sometimes even then.

PSYCHODYNAMICS

In contrast to asexuality, which is endogenous, primary, or innate, involving not the presence of conflict, but the absence of discernable desire (and so no determinable conflict), a sexual avoidant's sexual feelings are there, but suppressed—generally at the behest of a guilty conscience full of shame and embarrassment over having a body and wanting to use it. A belief that sex is sinful develops out of irrational self-criticism for one's sexual feelings (where rational self-congratulations for being only and fully human are, in fact, indicated). Typically, this guilty conscience is associated with a need for retaliatory masochistic self-torture, which is often additionally externalized to become the sadistic torturing of others, also for their sexuality. Thus a man who hates his own sexuality develops a Madonna complex, where he puts women on a pedestal, while making them feel guilty for being whores, as he makes clear: "You are a woman, and women don't want sex, or like my mother, may want it but shouldn't have, and have not actually had it." (Women put in this nonsensical position often themselves embrace sexual avoidance, hoping that the man will stop debasing and instead start respecting and idolizing them.)

A Case Example

An avoidant man with a Madonna complex felt uncomfortable when he saw his wife's head turning to look at the display as they passed a pornography shop. He didn't mind it if he did the looking because he felt that it's OK to do if you are a man, but he hated to see his wife's devaluing herself and all women by getting down into what he considered to be the mud and muck of sexuality. He also determined which movies they were allowed to watch at home and in the theater because he worried that his wife would laugh at the double entendres and dirty jokes, revealing that she was just a slut. Ultimately, they couldn't even attend social events because the men and women there would always talk about sex, and he wanted his wife to neither see nor hear such evil. Central to his guilt-laden relationship with sexuality was the belief that sex was lowly, dirty, and disgusting, a belief that partly originated in his almost daily "appalling rediscovery" that the genitals were too close for comfort to the excretory organs so that touching his wife sexually could lead to his being contaminated by her and getting an infection.

Of course, also contributing to sexual avoidance are the interpersonal, fearful mind-sets characteristic of avoidance in general, especially as shown in table 4.1.

Table 4.1
Fearful Mindsets

Fear of exposure.

Fear of intimacy as confinement.

Fear of yielding, with yielding = dissolution of the self and ego.

Fear of dependency and with it helpless passivity; paradoxically associated with a fear of independence and that with isolative remoteness.

Fear of becoming too emotional and being flooded by overly strong feelings, associated with a fear of letting loose, as if the slightest stirring of emotion might cause all emotions to spin out of control and overwhelm the individual, leaving him or her no longer in charge of the self.

Fear that a demarcating moral line might be crossed.

Fear of failing and being humiliated, often based on a negatively distorted body image that leads avoidants to sell themselves short, expect little, then withdraw defensively to avoid being humiliated and, in a case of misplaced altruism, to keep from disappointing others.

Fear of succeeding then being defeated: in men, castrated, or in women, deemancipated.

Fear of rejection that in turn originates in sensitivity to and readiness to experience even the most positive feedback as shatteringly negative, based in part on excessively high and often perfectionistic expectations of the self and others.

Fear of pleasure on the part of ascetic masochistic individuals who so eschew having fun in any form that they make certain not to take any pleasure and enjoy themselves at all, or at least to do so as little as possible.

Fears that self-assertion = aggressivity, making sex = rape.

Fear of admitting one's own problems so that others are to be avoided unless *they* agree to change and be the ones to make all the sacrifices.

SPECIFIC SEXUAL SYMPTOMS

Pathognomonic (characteristic pathological) psychodynamics can sometimes be linked to specific sexual symptoms. Broadly speaking, sexual symptoms tend to be mostly associated with the following:

- an inability to merge intimate and sexual feelings due to an overly scrupulous morality and fear of closeness
- a histrionic fear of genital vulnerability and mutilation

- a generalized regressive mind-set that promotes a throwback to infantilism and with it immature and so infantile sexuality

More specifically, using men as examples, many men with *premature ejaculation* tend to be excessively impulsive and show a narcissistic lack of concern for a partner's fulfillment along the lines of "I come when I'm ready to, and who cares about you." Such men are often also easily bored and want to get it over with so that they can go on to have sex with someone new and presumably more enticing.

Some men with *erectile dysfunction* may fear that penetrating equates to hurting because the penis equates to a weapon, so they spare the woman in order to avoid brutalizing her. Some are paranoid individuals who see in any mutual attraction the possibility that a woman is forcing them to perform. Still others are sadists, who, devaluing women emotionally and physically, come to feel that no woman deserves anything much from them, so "why give them what they want?"

Men with *ejaculatio tarda* are often insecure individuals who are spectatoring: observing themselves having sex and making each performance a test of their adequacy, while predictably disparaging themselves for not measuring up—brooding right throughout their performance about what might go wrong (e.g., they won't be able to come to orgasm) as they constantly judge their sexual prowess as if they are on public display and about to embarrass themselves through failure. Ejaculatio tarda can also arise in the context of an intense fear of closeness due to the belief that closeness equates to merging, or in the context of the histrionic fear that being tender necessarily means being feminine and, as such, becoming emasculated. Further problematic, and perhaps most common of all, is a negative mind-set that won't allow the man to deny the seamier aspects of sex, leading to frustrated excitement due to the intrusion of negative fantasies originating in disgust.

CHAPTER 5

Course

Sometimes avoidant personality disorder (AvPD) can improve spontaneously as the individual grows older. This improvement often results when psychological maturity associated with increasing insight based on ongoing introspection and continuous learning are coupled with new fortuitous, corrective social experiences. As a result, the AvPD fades, leaving in its wake self-awareness in the form of the commonplace youth-to-age wisdom expressed as the retrospective amazement of "what was I thinking then, and why did I act as I did?"

At other times, AvPD may not have so favorable an outcome, as the avoidant, succumbing to his or her avoidance, fails to emerge from, or sinks further into, the beckoning quagmire. This often happens because adolescent hormonal fires that stoke relational neediness die down at about the same time that adult relational fears strengthen, societal prohibitions begin to wield greater influence, and new negative interpersonal experiences traumatize the individual, all leading to feelings of resignation and a pervasive sense of doom, accompanied by existential murmurings of hopelessness, creating a generalized inability to experience relational joy. As a result, paraphrasing Berne's reference to the lonely consequences of playing off-putting games, because avoidants are "not stroked [their] spinal cord[s] . . . shrivel up."[1]

Also, as the years go by, depression can become superimposed on the avoidance, leading to increasing awareness of how much one is missing in life. This depression can also be intensified by escalating isolation due to withdrawal and panicky agoraphobia. Consequences of the depression, such as neglecting one's appearance and allowing antagonistic behavior toward others to proceed unchecked, may occur along with vicious cycling between withdrawal from, and rejection by, others, ultimately resulting in family members and potential friends and lovers leaving, really being driven away. Millon describes a typical vicious cycle where avoidants' timidity and shyness antagonize people who withdraw from the avoidant, thinking not, "he is afraid of me," but "she doesn't like me": "the patient's discontent, outbursts, and moodiness frequently evoke humiliating reactions from others, and these rebuffs only serve to reinforce his self-protective withdrawal. . . . He often precipitates disillusionment through obstructive and negative behaviors [then] reports feeling misunderstood, unappreciated, and demeaned by others."[2]

As time goes by, anergia and anhedonia can also appear, as defensive avoidance continues to consume energy that would otherwise be available for relating and diverts it into denying and binding one's natural/healthy inclinations. Anergia and anhedonia can also appear because second-line defenses develop, bolstering, fixing, and protecting the remoteness. These defenses include hypomanic denial, consisting of resolutely not caring about being loved; inertia in the form of a protective striving for familiarity and sameness; rationalization; identification with the aggressor; and acting out.

RATIONALIZATION

Avoidants who say they want to be alone are often really expressing a fear of connecting. Protesting too much about the splendid nature of isolation, they come to insist (not quite convincingly because of the modest gratification to be obtained from the advantages they list) that "I like being alone because at least my apartment stays straight, I can sleep through without a lover's snoring, no one stains my upholstery and wall-to-wall rug, and for companionship I have all that anyone needs—my two delightful, loving cats."

Other rationalizations include the following:

I don't have time to meet people. One man placed a personal ad on the Internet and then, making it look as if his work left him no time for fun, arranged to always be too busy to respond to any takers.

I'm not ready; young men like me should play the field a while longer. Some field players are profitably studying the terrain, but many are commitment phobics excusing their inability to play, while others are neophiliacs abandoning old lamps for new because being thrill seekers, and easily tiring of what they already have, they pursue the unfamiliar, seeking variety as the only spice in their life.

The world is a terrible place, full of terrible people. Examples follow: "Out there I have nothing but bad luck," "I never met anyone any good in my whole life," or in extremely unfavorable cases, "There aren't any people where I live worthy of me." A sample uninsightful/cruel statement made by a woman in a singles bar as to why she would never try meeting people over the Internet follows: "The creeps in here are bad enough; imagine what I'd find if I actually entered the chat rooms."

I can't help myself; it's not my fault. It is true that some avoidants are in fact so anxious and fearful that they cannot help but retreat when faced with the possibility of forming a relationship. But others, whose anxiety and fear are relative, not absolute, could, if they would, struggle against their anxiety, try to relate, and do so successfully. However, they choose not to use willpower to fight their anxiety. Then, out of shame or guilt about being derelict, they say, not "I choose not to," but "I can't."

The grapes are sour. One patient, afraid of women, thought instead, "Who wants one?" and gave as his reason, "After all, insides beneath that lovely exterior make a woman nothing but a well-packaged bag of dirt," then added, "and anyway, all wives cheat on their husbands."

A Case Example

A patient had several ways to rationalize his unrelatedness. He announced, "Relationships are really not that important or essential." He dwelled on what he believed to be the philosophical meaninglessness of everything interpersonal until, as he later suggested, he became so "preoccupied with the sound of one hand clapping that I can't erupt into spontaneous applause." He constantly told himself, "What's the use of trying to meet someone, we are all going to die anyway?" and convinced himself that the world was a terrible place because of life's little sardonic twists such as, "You can't get a partner unless you have relationship experience, and you can't get relationship experience unless you have a partner."

Too often, other people buy into such rationalizations, thus perpetuating them. An avoidant friend of mine threw her husband, a PhD psychologist, out of the house after three months of marriage. I mentioned to the psychologist that though his ex-wife later said to me that she couldn't meet anybody new because there were no eligible men where she lived, I thought that what was keeping her back was not her geographical location, but her personal problems (and he should know all about those!). Yet in spite of his recent firsthand negative experience with her, he shot back that her difficulties weren't created by, but for, her, due to her being stuck living in the boonies—a place where all the men were already married so that the only men you could meet there were either cheating on their wives or complete losers who stay single not because they want to, but because they have no other choice.

A caveat is that it is necessary to distinguish rationalization from its opposite: guilt about being oneself. In rationalization, things that are feared are turned into matters of natural preference. In guilt about being oneself, matters of natural preference are turned into things that are feared. Thus one woman who wanted to remain single but was embarrassed to say so said, instead, "I am an avoidant, and as such too fearful to even try to connect."

IDENTIFICATION WITH THE AGGRESSOR

In the realm of *identification with the aggressor*, relying on how the best defense is a good offense, avoidants reject others as a way to defend themselves against being rejected by them. The idea is to put others down before they can do the same thing to you. Theirs is, however, an unfortunate quest for immediate gratification, without concern for collateral damage and long-term consequences, for they overlook how, in the long run, putting others down changes the avoidant in others' eyes: from a person to be pitied and succored into one to be feared and ignored.

Finally, avoidance can also worsen with the failure of helpful defenses already in place so that avoidants can no longer handle their anxiety adequately. Now we see panic, increased self-monitoring due to spreading fear, and breakthrough depression accompanied by behavioral regression, appearing because avoidants can no longer deny, and finally have to face, their sad predicament—which, for them, becomes one that they feel entirely helpless to change.

CHAPTER 6

Differential Diagnosis

In this chapter, I discuss differentiating avoidant personality disorder (AvPD) from panic disorder, specific phobia, and social phobia, all Axis I disorders, and from borderline personality disorder, an Axis II disorder.

DIFFERENTIATING AVPD FROM PANIC DISORDER/SPECIFIC PHOBIA/SOCIAL PHOBIA

According to the *Diagnostic and Statistical Manual of Mental Disorders*, fourth edition (*DSM-IV*), patients with *panic disorder* have discrete anxiety attacks in "places or situations from which escape might be difficult (or embarrassing)."[1] According to Ballenger, these panic attacks commonly lead to avoidance of certain situations "because [the patient] fear[s] that if a panic attack occurred in these settings, it would be embarrassing, frightening, or both."[2]

According to the *DSM-IV*, patients with *specific phobia* tend to experience "fear[s] that are excessive or unreasonable, cued by the presence or anticipation of a specific object or situation."[3]

According to a vast body of literature devoted to "differentiating" AvPD from *social phobia*, there is no real difference between the two disorders, and AvPD should be subsumed diagnostically under the rubric of social phobia. Thus the *Psychodynamic Diagnostic Manual* (*PDM*) calls AvPD "phobic (avoidant) personality disorder"[4]; Anthony and Swinson state that "avoidant personality disorder is just a more intense form of Social Phobia"[5]; and Rettew, wondering if it is possible to diagnose one without the other, notes that APD may represent a more severe form of generalized social phobia with respect to levels of symptoms, fear of negative evaluation, anxiety, avoidance, and depression.[6]

While clearly both disorders overlap psychodynamically, that is, they share many of the same dynamics as feelings of inadequacy and hypersensitivity to negative evaluation, I view the two disorders both as *somewhat* distinct *psychodynamically* and as *significantly* different *structurally*. For example, many individuals who are, dynamically speaking, shy and withdrawn do not complain of being afraid of speaking in public or of anything like that. Indeed, as many actors point out, as shy people, they actively come alive when on stage, undergoing a kind of temporary antiphobia—what the *PDM* calls a "converse manifestation: Counterphobic Personality Disorder,"[7] only to revert to type when the "play" is over.

Millon and Davis also strongly suggest that AvPD and social phobia are two separate entities, for, as they note, social phobia is a *symptom* (Axis I), while AvPD is a *personality problem* (Axis 2). Thus, as Millon and Davis say, in AvPD, "there is a pervasiveness and diffuseness to the personality's socially aversive behaviors, in contrast to the [social phobic's] specificity of the phobic object and the intensity of the phobic response."[8] For characteristically avoidants express their anxiety in the form of what Reich calls "character armoring,"[9] that is, in pervasive and diffuse interpersonal withdrawal behaviors that run the gamut of severity from modest problems with meeting, mingling with, moving close to, and remaining intimate and involved with other people to full shyness. Conversely, as Millon and Davis suggest, in social phobia, the "phobic symptom is not associated with the broad range of traits that characterize the [avoidant] personality, such as 'low self-esteem' [or] the 'desire for acceptance.'"[10] As Benjamin notes, social phobics do not possess the AVD's sense of being "socially inept [and] personally unappealing, or inferior to others,"[11] which lead the patient with AVD and not the social phobic to be "less likely to be married [and more likely to be] content (even relieved) to stay home by himself or herself."[12]

In short, individuals with AvPD, unlike individuals with social phobia, are not primarily bothered, or bothered at all, by reactive situational anxiety attached to discrete "trivial prompts" such as signing a check in public or urinating in a public restroom—that is, they are not bothered by situations not particularly meaningful in themselves that they make significant by investing them with catastrophic implications. Rather, the life of the typical individual with AvPD is primarily consumed by diffuse, ongoing, *dysfunctional relationships* characterized by remoteness, shyness, and a tendency to recoil from closeness and intimacy. Patients with AvPD fear closeness, intimacy, and commitment itself, not a symbolic substitute, stand-in, or replacement for those things. In contrast, social phobics withdraw not from interpersonal *relationships*, but from interpersonal *activities* that are *discrete trivial prompts* that *symbolize* fears associated with interpersonal relationships—neatly packaged, tangible cues that act as stand-ins for interpersonal upheavals condensed and externalized to become outwardly expressed hieroglyphic representations of inner conflict. Because social phobics keep their personality as a whole out of their phobias, they generally remain outgoing and retain the ability to form close and lasting relationships. They might well be happily married and professionally successful. Their problems tend to consist "merely" of troublesome islets of panicky withdrawal—an insular expression of social anxiety that in turn spares the rest of their lives, island(s) of seemingly impersonal difficulty in the mainstream, with a mainland full of satisfactory personal relationships.

Examples of how social phobias refer to specific relational anxieties in a condensed form include a phobia of blushing signifying being criticized for turning red hot sexually; a phobia of speaking in public signifying being exposed as deficient and hence humiliated; a phobia of eating in public signifying being criticized for using the mouth in situations where observed (with homosexual issues implied); a phobia of urinating in a public men's room signifying exposing one's genitals to the man standing in the next urinal, in turn implying both homosexual vulnerability and fear of emasculation; and a phobia of signing one's name to a check while others watch signifying a fear of yielding and hence of being submissive.

Some Case Examples

A patient expressed his generalized social anxiety indirectly and symbolically by pouring it into specific terror about urinating in public and signing his name to a check while others watched. He also condensed his fear of relating into a fear of driving to his partner's home through *green* lights and over bridges. He was ultimately able to reach his partner, be romantic, and have sex, only during sex he would suffer from pangs of fear of commitment, which he expressed as a severe ejaculatio tarda (delayed ejaculation) that made it difficult for him to complete the sex act. Dynamically speaking, he was expressing deep interpersonal fears, but *structurally* speaking, he was expressing them in a condensed and displaced fashion, walling off and containing the fears in short-lived, discrete, pseudointerpersonal encounters that simultaneously referred to, obscured, and to an extent spared the real thing.

This state of affairs contrasts to that which existed with an avoidant, whose interpersonal life was globally tense and unfulfilling. People afraid of public speaking can take a job where they don't have to do that, but this avoidant could not exist comfortably because he was unable to shake proffered hands, was so fearful of relating that he could not go outside without hiding to some extent, and not only developed an isolating telephonophobia, but also installed an answering machine not to receive, but to screen, messages, then neither answered the phone at all nor returned the messages that people left for him.

I believe that patients with AvPD have effectively made an *unconscious choice* to deal with their anxieties by developing mild to severe *generalized* relationship difficulties. In contrast, social phobics have made a different *unconscious choice*. They have chosen to remain interpersonally outgoing and related. They desire and hope to keep their whole personality out of things, and to do that, they limit their illness to part of their personality only—precisely so that they *can* remain generally outgoing, although with specific exceptions in the form of delimited deficits.

Importantly, social phobia differs from AvPD in its *effect on others.* Speaking figuratively, I divide psychological disorders into hot red pepper, garlic, and onion styles. *Hot red pepper* disorders trouble only the self, "upsetting the stomach," while others escape distress. *Garlic* disorders trouble others through "bad breath," but the self escapes "emotional dyspepsia." *Onion* disorders trouble both others and the self as "interpersonal bad breath" accompanies "personal dyspepsia." While social phobia is a hot red pepper disorder, mainly interfering with one's own functioning, AvPD is an onion disorder, for it both affects the avoidants' personal well-being and happiness *and* is troubling to and detrimental to others in the avoidants' world.

This said, Benjamin notes that especially troublesome problems of differential diagnosis arise when social phobia generalizes.[13] This was the case for a socially phobic adolescent afraid of going to school because of a painful startle reaction to the loud school bell. This child soon also became so fearful of all street noise that she was unable to leave the house at all without her mother. Eventually, as an adult, she stayed home with her mother all day, every day, her phobia having spread so that the only meaningful relationships she could have, besides the one with her mother, were the close relationships she developed with her cats.

A careful developmental history can help distinguish patients with generalized social phobia from patients with AvPD. As children, people who go on to develop AvPD are more likely to pull back from others than are people who go on to develop social phobia. The latter as children tend to have normal relationships both at home and outside of the home, for example, they play well with others and their peers aren't focused on picking on them. But they are more likely to suffer from childhood phobias such as agoraphobia—limiting their movement more than they limit their potential ability to relate.

Therapeutically speaking, social phobics respond to treatment that emphasizes developing cognitive insight into the symptom ("you fear public speaking because you feel that if you make a minor mistake then all will be lost"); informal or formal behavior therapy that offers the patient tasks of graded difficulty geared to overcoming the specific behavioral inhibition(s) involved; and possible pharmacotherapy to reduce anxiety. In contrast, patients with AvPD tend to do best developing insight into the full nature and meaning of the interactive problems that keep them from becoming, and remaining, intimate with significant others. Conversely, it is just common sense that cognitive-behavioral techniques, particularly techniques of graded exposure, will not likely be as helpful for treating an ongoing and generalized fear of closeness, intimacy, and commitment as they might be for treating an encapsulated fear of public speaking. While a patient afraid of public speaking can ask himself or herself, in a reassuring manner, "What is the worst that can happen?" then expose and habituate himself or herself to the anxiety associated with the feared situation until he or she can perform comfortably and safely, shy avoidants afraid of intimacy and commitment have difficulty using exposure methods therapeutically because getting over their "dating anxiety" would require trial intimacies and commitments, which, if at all possible, would be selfish and cruel to others in the extreme.

Invoking an ad hominem argument I base on my own personal observation, I feel that behavioral therapists' vested interests (in doing behavioral therapy) tend to tempt them to obscure the diagnostic difference between AvPD and social phobia so that they can treat all concerned the same way, that is, behaviorally. In contrast, psychodynamically oriented therapists' vested interests (in doing insight-oriented, psychodynamically oriented psychotherapy) tempt them to emphasize the differences between a phobic symptom and a personality problem such as AvPD so that they can reserve cognitive-behavioral interventions for the social phobic and use strictly psychodynamically oriented psychotherapy for the patient with AvPD.

DIFFERENTIATING AVPD FROM BORDERLINE PERSONALITY DISORDER

The full, fundamental and frequent alternate merging and emerging of borderline personality disorder has to be differentiated from Types IIa and IIb avoidant partial, infrequent, and mostly defensive shifting between closeness and distancing. As the *DSM-IV* says, the borderline process is notable for a "pattern of unstable and intense interpersonal relationships characterized by alternating between extremes of idealization and devaluation."[14] This ambivalence about forming and maintaining interpersonal relationships leads borderlines to alternately love too well and hate too intensely: to develop close ties then drop people impulsively, seducing then abandoning them suddenly and without provocation or warning. We see a pattern where the borderline closes in and distances (merges and emerges) along the lines of Freud's quaint simile of porcupines, who, seeking warmth, approach each other because they are cold but who then, pricking each other with their quills, move farther apart to relieve the discomfort, only to feel cold again and move closer together once more. One day, borderline individuals feel lonely, hunger for contact, and call and come over constantly, and the next day, they remain aloof, refusing invitations to visit or be visited, not even returning phone calls. Now they are relentless seekers of love and affection, and now, however much they unconsciously fear loneliness and abandonment, they disrupt potentially workable relationships offered or already in progress. When they are involved in relationships, they dream of how wonderful it was to be alone and grouse vocally that relationships invade their space and feel too close for comfort. Then, when they arrange to be alone, they dream of how wonderful it was to be involved in relationships and complain that others do not get close enough quickly enough. But when they are once again involved in relationships, they provoke others to provide the match that lights the fuse that explodes the tumescent bomb of their long-simmering avoidant fantasy—so that they can blow up over things that people concerned with relationship maintenance would at least try to forgive and forget: not replacing ice cubes after using them; not covering the unused portion of the cat food thus allowing the food to dry out; or putting feet up on the sofa, even when the sofa is old and the feet are clean.

Too, unlike the avoidant, who distances as a way to handle *fear* associated with being close, the borderline merges and emerges as a way to gratify *need*. Borderlines first merge after overestimating others as all good, assigning individuals the qualities of savior wise and true, and actively courting them out of a need to relieve intense loneliness and achieve a sense of comfort and satiation. Only then, brought up short in disappointment, they come to underestimate others as all bad and actively dump them out of a need for vengeance, seeing only others' real, perceived, or delusionally perceived minor flaws so that they can award them the qualities of villain, fool, and cheat, in turn so that they can now avoid embracing them and instead consign them to complete oblivion.

Some Case Examples

My team and I saw a patient without an appointment as an emergency for a two-hour visit, then offered follow-up care the next day with both me and a psychologist. At first, the patient felt, "You people are wonderful—look how much time you spend with me." Then, in short order, she changed her mind to say, "You people are dreadful—you are trying to overwhelm me, get too close, and press me to open up and tell you my problems before I am ready. Besides, you are only doing this for the money."

This patient had, in the emerging phase, confined herself to activities that had little inherent interpersonal context—dull, lonely things like watching television supine on the couch, or self-destructive lonely things like excessive drinking and/or taking drugs. In contrast, in the merging phase, she had met and married a man after knowing him for only a few days, then, shifting once again after another few days, claimed that she and he were incompatible and filed for divorce.

A patient, after breaking up a relationship with a lover over his wearing a designer belt (as part of an attack skillfully geared to put the blame on him for his pseudosophistication instead of on her for her unrelatedness), thought twice and called the lover constantly, begged him to give her one more chance, and added, as often as she could, "I really like designer belts and, most of all, the people who wear them." Her life ultimately deteriorated into shifting from the two-bedroom apartment with unloving roommates to the lonely studio apartment with the loving cat, then back again; placing personals ads on the Internet but constructing them in a way that assured they were geared to get few to no responses because they were too noncommittal to be consonant with their stated purpose; and frantically cruising singles bars, functions, and resorts, but drinking heavily to the point that she got too drunk to function effectively, then, after sobering up and staying home alone for months on end, starting to think, "I miss my social life," and returning to her old ways of heavy drinking and frantically seeking "Mr. Right, right now."

A patient told me of how a borderline man alternately seduced and abandoned her, keeping her involved in his charade by taking advantage of how her loving neediness rendered her too helpless emotionally to deal effectively and definitively with his alternate merging and emerging:

Here is a cross section of my conversations with Oscar:

Oscar avoided me through his not matching his action to his words and lofty promises. Our conversations went something like this:

O: I can't live without you. This life here in Paris holds nothing for me. It is a life where [*sobbing*] no one even caresses me.

F: If you can't live without me, how come you ditched me when I went to Paris to see you?

O: Because I don't mean I need you for a week or two weeks, *I need you for all of my life and forever.*

F: A person that loves that much would have at least helped me when I telephoned, confused and panicked about what train to take to make my appointment with you—but you, working in your office at the train station, said you didn't know, and had to hang up.

O: Well, if that is how you feel, I respect your feelings. I never try to force anyone to think differently than they do, that would be disrespectful and everyone is a sacred creature of God.

F: I don't know which part of you to believe, the one who cries because he loves and wants to be with me, or the one who is never there and seems to have no urgency at all to see me.

O: Oscar is not a liar [*he often referred to himself in the third person*]. He is not a liar because when he was five years old his grandmother gave him a lesson he never forgot. When he tried to steal a candy when they were out shopping she slapped his hand, humiliating him, and made him bring it back. He has never lied again since.

Also, his emotions were phony. When he would cry, it would be with intense drama, but only for about five seconds, and then he would laugh or start a different conversation. It was more an obligatory wailing with a time limit.

Also, I am still not over the fact that he would never return my grandmother's tablecloth. My grandmother had made it by hand (she used to do cut work when she came to this country). He inherited an apartment from his mother and said it was to be for us. I had brought the tablecloth and 12 napkins over for what was to be our place together, but we never got there because he told me the workmen were fixing it up and he was allergic to dust so we shouldn't go. The next time I went to France, he told me he had rented the apartment out because I wasn't clear enough about when I would move in with him. So I asked him for the tablecloth back. He said he still had it and treasured it because he treasured everything I gave him, but he would give it back to me, but he never did, although it meant a lot to me and nothing to him. Once I got really upset and he told me he had sent it and it was on its way. When I opened the envelope he sent me (yes he actually sent me an envelope!) there was one thin, worn cloth napkin (not my grandmother's) with a hole in the middle. I asked if this was supposed to be a joke, and he started crying, saying he couldn't do anything right, and please forgive him, God made him imperfectly.

Also, every time we got together, after passionate e-mail exchanges in the year in between, saying how when we met we were going to plan our future together—he would find a way to hedge. Here were some of his excuses about not making plans:

- I wasn't prepared to talk about this. You take me off guard. You jumped in too strongly and didn't wait for me to bring up the subject.
- My son Sacha is still under 18. I need to protect him from my wife, Josette, who is crazy, and I'm afraid of what she might do to him.
- My brother-in-law is gay so if I leave my son now, he may have too much of an influence on him.
- Your being upset with me made me too upset to talk with you about a plan.

Sometimes when I was with him I felt only hope that we would be together forever. Sometimes instead I felt only despair that we would always be apart. Just as I couldn't live without him, I couldn't live with him. As far as he was concerned, it seems as if he could, and did, live very well either way: one minute with, and the next minute without, me.

CHAPTER 7

Comorbidity

Comorbidity with other personality disorders distorts the "pure" clinical picture of avoidant personality disorder (AvPD). For example, Millon describes an "avoidant-passive-aggressive mixed personality,"[1] which adds a dimension of annoyance with, to the anxious withdrawal from, others.

Comorbidity alters the treatment approach to AvPD, and it does so in at least two ways. First, the therapist must treat all the disorders that constitute the final picture. Thus, while nonparanoid avoidants need to focus on, expose themselves to, and immerse themselves in relationships so that they can connect with others without becoming unduly anxious, paranoid avoidants need to start not with exposing themselves to relationships in the real world, but with rethinking their suspicious ideas about the real world to which they will hopefully soon be exposing themselves. Second, comorbidity determines the nature of and increases the number of resistances that crop up to impede therapeutic progress. Thus avoidants who also, in paranoid fashion, wonder, "What did he mean by that?" tend to be reluctant to think and act less avoidant just on the therapist's say-so. Avoidants who are also depressed tend to resist therapy because they view the therapist's exhortations to do something as a criticism that they didn't already do it. Avoidants who are also masochistic tend to resist therapy because they respond to getting better by feeling worse. Avoidants who are also obsessive-compulsive tend to resist therapy because as stubborn individuals, they respond to therapeutic exhortations by taking one step backward—to "rethink," really undo, every step they just took forward.

COMORBID AVPD AND PARANOIA

Here the classic AvPD fire of sensitivity to the possibility of criticism, humiliation, and rejection is fueled by suspicion of what others might be thinking and up to. Such suspicion originates in large measure in a lack of basic trust resulting from projection, where "I dislike myself" becomes "you feel antagonistic toward me and so must be out to get me." These avoidants primarily withdraw because they become wrongly convinced that others dislike or even hate them, as they view a cancellation of a date due to sudden illness as a personal rejection; an ogling look from a stranger not as a come-on, but as a hostile stare; an offer of friendship or love as sexual harassment; an attempt to matchmake as trying to humiliate them for being so desperate that they need to be fixed up; and the best-intentioned advice, including that from a concerned therapist, as criticism for prior wrongdoing and/or as an attempt to control them for the personal gain of the advisor.

Projection also leads avoidants to unfairly blame others for their own need to withdraw. They weave the threads of their pathological fantasy, cognitive error, and the prophetic but unrecognized self-fulfilling consequences of their own provocative behavior into the cloth of external "stress," then, coming to view their inner anxiety as external fear, attribute their isolation and loneliness entirely to the machinations of the world around them. Illustrative is the familiar example of singles blaming their loneliness entirely on the absence of suitable partners where they live, when such a conclusion is in fact an illusion, created mainly out of their own problematic concept of "suitability" and a false distortive environmental assessment based on externalization of self-hatred to become "others hate and avoid me." Beck's method of cognitive treatment, as revealed in taped interviews of sessions with a patient he calls Audrey, devotes itself in some measure to correcting paranoid blaming of others for having it "in for me," as Beck shows Audrey how her withdrawal from others is in large measure a response to her belief that others are distancing themselves from her.[2]

Ultimately, paranoid avoidants even come to welcome their perceived "stress," "bad luck," or the nebulous "incompatibility" of everyone they meet, for it provides them with the excuse they are looking for to keep to themselves—the rationale they are seeking to distance themselves from others so that they can break free of them, exactly as they wanted to do all along.

COMORBID AVPD AND DEPRESSION

While nondepressed avoidants fear not being loved, depressed avoidants become convinced that they can never be lovable. Their cry is, "What's the use of trying to relate to anyone, no one will want me." Now they become apathetic, give up, accept the hopelessness of things exactly as they imagine them to be, inure themselves to the rejections they feel are inevitable, and steel themselves to the predictable loneliness they are convinced is bound to be their fate and as such will plague them throughout their lives.

As self-demeaning individuals, depressed avoidants become like the depressed hardware store salesman who told self-deprecating jokes on his first date: how when handing out a flier for his sale merchandise, he said, "Read this only if you are having difficulty sleeping at night." As guilty individuals, they feel that to err is inhuman, to forgive themselves unallowable. They view themselves as sinners unworthy of loving themselves or being loved by others—partly based on a hypersensitivity to criticism that leads them to misinterpret a neutral question or positive remark as a personal devaluation, take a little joke as being seriously at their expense, and even interpret noncritical idiomatic expressions in a concrete, defamatory manner. To illustrate, I stopped using the expression "in case you haven't heard" to convey something positive ("everybody has heard it, so I am sure you have, too") because several of my avoidant friends thought that I was being critical of them, as if I were saying that the reason they didn't hear of something was that they were completely, hopelessly, and stupidly deaf to the world.

Some Case Examples

A shy, depressed avoidant customer struggled to ask a salesperson in an upscale food store a question regarding the merchandise. The salesperson patiently explained his wares to her and then said, meaning it as a compliment, for he actually liked and took to this person, "I have never spent so much time with a customer before." The customer, being depressed as well as avoidant, thought he was criticizing her for taking up his whole afternoon. As a result, she complained to management that he had sassed her, then refused to return to the store ever again.

A depressed avoidant emergency ward patient severely castigated members of the Department of Psychiatry for referring to her as a "walk-in," a status she had convinced herself was somehow inferior to that possessed by "those who have an appointment." In our interview, in the course of trying to assess the quality of her social life, I merely asked her, "Do you have many friends?" To this she replied that I was putting her down by criticizing her for being a loner and was even implying that "you are the sort of person that nobody could ever want."

While nondepressed avoidants tend to confine their somatic complaints to those related to their anxiety, such as hyperventilation or tremor of the hands, depressed avoidants tend to develop a variety of off-putting messenger somatic complaints like the familiar "not tonight, dear" headache, Epstein-Barr "leave me be" chronic fatigue, or the physical weakness and need to "retreat in order to rest" of hypoglycemia, all of which are their way to proclaim, "I am withholding and withdrawing for physical reasons." A hypochondriacal fear of catching an illness often leads depressed avoidants to become remote due to worrying about contamination, especially from sexually transmitted diseases, another isolating curtain they draw around themselves, having come to feel that "closeness is beyond emotionally precarious; it's physically dangerous."

For nondepressed avoidants, every new potential relationship promising a rosy future is a fresh sign of hope. For depressed avoidants, every new potential relationship recalling a dismal past is a new reason for despair.

COMORBID AVPD AND GRIEF

Grievers pull back into themselves and avoid others because they feel pain so unbearable that it fully preoccupies them and saps their life energy. They also pull back out of a need to uninterruptedly chastise themselves about the bad things they guiltily believe they did to the lost loved one. Additionally, they pull back for more positive reasons: so that they may think of the person they lost full time and recreate the lost relationship inside of themselves, in their fantasies. Then they stay remote because coming to overvalue the lost object, they feel that no one new can ever match up to that person and take his or her place.

COMORBID AVPD AND OBSESSIVE-COMPULSIVE PERSONALITY DISORDER

These avoidants tend to withdraw less out of fear than out of a need to maintain relational correctness, honor, and propriety. As perfectionists, they discard relationships because of others' minor flaws, doing so just because the other person has merely made a single, insignificant social blunder such as "you passed me on the crowded beach without even saying hello." They also remain remote because they fear making relational mistakes. As one individual describing her excessive perfectionism put it, "My record stands for itself: in my whole life I never made a slip of the tongue, because I rarely speak so that I can avoid saying the wrong thing. For me slips of the tongue are like wrong numbers. If you dial one you didn't get a wrong number; you dialed the number wrong."

As worriers over nothing, they hurt relationships by subjecting them to constant evaluative questioning, always asking, "Can he or she be the only right one for me?" then answering the question as "maybe, or maybe not," then remaining aloof due to "not knowing the correct answer." Uncertain as to whether they do or do not want to relate to others and to a given person, they tease, then disappoint, blowing hot and cold as they alternate between interest and detachment, playing Berne's game of "Kiss Off,"[3] as they beckon others to come, only to change their minds at the last moment and push them away should they actually arrive.

A Case Example

One such man entered multiple chat rooms then did not reply to the people who replied to him or told them that he was busy now and couldn't take the time to get back—"but I will contact you, if only you will be patient." In singles bars, he dressed to look alluring, stood in sexy poses, and gave others seductive looks. Then, at the first sign of interest on the part of others, he became aloof and disdainful and removed himself, even though he was the one who had first extended the invitation. In his relationships, he said, "We must get together sometime," but never made a date, or, making one, broke it, reassuring the other person that this was the very last time that it would happen, just so that he could make it happen again. When having sex, premature withdrawal was the order of his day—not to prevent conception, but to first tempt and excite, then to frustrate by stopping short of fulfillment. Ultimately, he married to get away from home, but, feeling unfaithful to his mother, divorced his wife so that he could go home again, only to complain about the singles life, about his inability to tolerate living with his mother, and about the difficulty older men have in meeting someone suitable and getting remarried. Eventually, he met someone he felt strongly attracted to, only to then take a job that required him to work every weekend and on holidays so that the few days he could take off were on nonholiday weekdays—which, not surprisingly, was the very time his new partner couldn't be at home with him.

Nonobsessive avoidants are detached, distanced, and disinvolved partly because they have difficulty expressing their positive feelings. Obsessive avoidants can and do express their positive feelings, but only in situations where they can take them back; when they can express them paradoxically, that is, when others, having given up, no longer anticipate or are open to anything positive from them; or when they can express them indirectly, for example, to a person other than to the one who is the actual recipient of those feelings.

Some Case Examples

One obsessive avoidant man gave negative responses to acquaintances' positive gestures, reserving his positive responses for when the gestures had been withdrawn—because the other person no longer cared and had chosen to move on. For many years, he had saved money by only having one date, never to repeat the experience because he became intensely angry when she ordered the most expensive item on the dinner menu. Then, later in life, after he saved a nice nest egg, he thought, "It's time," and permitted himself to fall in love. Only now he found himself making bad investments in the stock market, thinking, "Better to lose it honestly than to have it taken away from you by some gold digger."

Speaking of a new, suitable man she had been seeing regularly for weeks, a patient said, "He's handsome, funny, very presentable, and I love how he deals with me, especially how he listens and remembers what I have to say. But it's really confusing. I see him one time I like him, I see him the next time I don't like him. He really wants me. I gave him my card and he called me right back. But I just cannot commit to him. I hear my mother's voice going around in my head, saying, 'What are you holding out for, someone who will treat you like a piece of crap?' It's the old story: you want the ones who don't want you, you don't want the ones who do. Anyway, my intense feelings for him completely disappeared when I discovered that his body type was all wrong for me. He doesn't have any body hair, and his legs are too short, a shock when you see him naked for the first time. So I started telling him negative things about myself: how after all I am not perfect and that right now I'm not going to object if he pushes for a relationship, but I'm not going to encourage one either." The final choice for this woman: a man who regularly criticized her for being a cheapskate for saving money by using in-store coupons, "something we just don't do in my family, and where I come from."

Additionally, obsessive avoidants are stubborn, controlling individuals. They may express this stubbornness in minor ways, for example, by sending "belated birthday cards" (with the additional element of a narcissistic shift in focus from "your birthday" to "my having forgotten your birthday"), or in major ways, as when they make an appointment then cancel at the last minute. Caught up in control issues, they don't so much turn away out of fear as they run away out of need. They look for what others want in a relationship just so that they can refuse to give it to them so that now they can gratify their need to be the one to call all the shots.

Obsessive avoidants characteristically struggle with harsh matters of morality. They resolve their good versus evil struggles interpersonally by deeming others immoral so that they may now avoid them. While nonobsessive avoidants stay away out of a need to maintain safety, obsessive avoidants stay away out of a need to more closely approximate sainthood.

COMORBID AVPD AND HYSTERICAL (HISTRIONIC) PERSONALITY DISORDER

Histrionic avoidants exaggerate the dangers associated with closeness, intimacy, and commitment. In the milder cases, a cancelled dinner date becomes a signal that a given relationship, and every relationship to come, is troubled and doomed. In the more severe cases, closeness becomes commitment, commitment becomes entrapment, and entrapment becomes fatal smothering to the extent that we hear, "Freedom is completely out of the question within the bounds of a close, loving relationship; and complete freedom is what I want out of life, for I want to be me, and I need to be free." Because of such fears, histrionic avoidants love unwisely so that they do not have to love too well. They typically display that characteristic fear of closeness by avoiding suitable men in favor of attaching themselves to men about whom they have mixed feelings. Typically, they ignore a potentially workable relationship in favor of relationships that are likely to sputter or fail. Not only do they react negatively in positive situations, but they also react positively in negative situations, forming strong attractions where the possibility of fulfillment is weak, and vice versa, as they get turned off by those who are warm, yielding, permissive, and available, and turned on by those who are distant, unfeeling, forbidden, and unavailable. In their pursuit of negative situations and unavailable people, they sometimes become enamored of movie stars to the point of stalking them. Basically, they favor oedipal triangular situations, pursuing people who are already involved with and committed to someone else, particularly "almost divorced" lovers who promise to leave their wives and marry them, but never actually do. All told, they suffer from what amounts to a fear of success, where they do attempt to relate—but only in those situations where they are virtually guaranteed to fail to do so.

COMORBID AVPD AND DISSOCIATIVE PERSONALITY DISORDER

Avoidants who dissociate undergo flight—not only from the possibility or actuality of rejection, but also from the possibility or actuality of acceptance. When acceptance looms, they flee to the distant, remote, unfamiliar, foreign, strange terra incognito where what they perceive to be the discomforts, harassments, and fears of the old world of relationships, or of a specific relationship, no longer pertain. If others approach them, they, in essence, tell them, "Corner me and I will retreat," then pull the curtains around "me," exclude "you," and disappear out of what they perceive to be danger. They laugh off a serious approach or seduction that comes their way so that any work they have done until now to promote a relationship evaporates and the relationship comes to naught. Some, speaking of needing to take a break from an actual relationship, call for a hiatus early on. Others make it as far as the marriage ceremony, then, at the last minute, get cold feet, leaving their groom or bride at the altar. Some even have minifugues consisting of detached, trancelike, and confused states in which they might view a potentially satisfactory relationship virtually as a terrorist attack. At times, they develop a chronic and persistent aloofness to others that is the product of their constant detaching themselves from feelings they perceive to be dangerous or forbidden by the expedient of removing themselves from other people who elicit those feelings. They also become aloof to themselves—not allowing themselves to feel through creating a protective remoteness inside that, in essence, says not, "I am afraid you find me uninteresting and will reject me," but "I find you uninteresting and reject you."

Ultimately, they calm down and once again become rational, as they become painfully aware of opportunity missed. Now we hear recriminations about how they utterly ruined their lives and the lives of those who loved them. Unfortunately, however, their past regrets usually do not readily translate into improved future performance.

Developmentally speaking, these avoidants often describe a past marred by constant parental warnings of the dangers of relating overall and of those associated with forming certain relationships specifically. For one little girl, the danger consisted of the loss of family, and for one little boy, the danger consisted of a symbolic castration as the father told his son that "all marriage is a ball and chain around your ankle, just like the one with which your mother ties me down and ruins my life."

Some Case Examples

A gay man who routinely dissociated when the big moment arrived—not registering it or, registering it, denying it—still remembers an incident 40 years ago, when a handsome sailor made it clear that he wanted him, but instead of replying in kind, he ignored him, sloughed him off, to use his words, "laughed off the approach like a silly girl." He doesn't know why he did it, but he suspects it was because he became anxious. Forty years later, he was still bothered by his tactical error, still had fantasies of making it with the sailor, and still brooded, "Was the pleasure dangerous—the pain desirable? Did I perceive danger though there was none, see risk in the absence of a reason for concern?" His only consolation, which he ceaselessly repeated to himself for reassurance, was that had he gone with this sailor, he wouldn't have gone with the other man he met that night, and that was the man through whom he ultimately met his lifetime lover.

A wistful patient announced his future plans to live his life by himself, camped alone under the stars in an adobe in the Arizona desert, on a farm with only the animals for companions, or on an island off the coast of Maine. The following two dreams regularly recurred during his childhood:

He was running down a long corridor in order to escape an unknown danger. At the end of the corridor, an object variously described as the tassels of a riding crop, the straws of the head of a broom, and the feathered tail of a rooster appeared through the wall and shook at him, tracing an up and down trajectory. The sight of this terrified him, although he did not know why. He remained terrified until he progressed further along the corridor, when he saw a sign that read, "Safe to the left, danger to the right," whereupon he ran to the left and into the "arms of safety." In the dream's aftermath, he wet his bed and awoke. In association to his dream, he recalled how one day, after his grandmother caught him playing doctor with a childhood sweetheart, she whipped him, then took him aside and showed him a picture from a Bible: a harp whose pillar was carved in the shape of a nude body of a man, genitals absent. The grandmother suggested that he would become that man if he continued to play such dirty little games.

The shaking tassels/straws/rooster tail both represented his being whipped and the whip itself, and so both his threatened emasculation and the symbolic reassurance that his phallus was still there and intact. His running in the dream was both a running away from being whipped and emasculated and a running to a place of safety.

In a second dream, there was a park "over there" with skyscrapers arising intact from an excavation pit. His childhood sweetheart in reality lived on a street bordering the park. In the dream, he wanted to go there but was afraid and couldn't find his way. And at any rate, he felt he didn't deserve to be there because he hadn't the right clothes. Ultimately he arrived, only to discover her home had been bulldozed and in its place another, taller structure, a skyscraper, had been erected.

In his associations to this dream, he described himself as a distant and lonely avoidant preoccupied with futile searching for new people whom he would like better and for new places where he would be happier. In later life, he actually fled from city to city looking for a relationship in a new place, even when many satisfactory relationships were available to him in the old one. On one occasion, he moved for no better reason than that in the new city, the skyscrapers were taller than in the old. The old city without tall skyscrapers referred to being devalued, punished, and emasculated for his sexuality now, just as he felt his grandmother had threatened to do to him when he was a kid. Fleeing to the new city, the "park with big skyscrapers, and one big one in particular" represented a restitutive attempt to avoid/undo emasculation and become physically intact once again. Fleeing also represented heading to a place characterized by safety in numbers because a bigger city was "more anonymous, a place where no one would know who I am, and hurt and abuse me for what I do."

For successophobic avoidants, dissociation is particularly "suitable" for "acceptance emergencies," when by chance, bad luck, or in a moment of weakness, they find themselves in a potentially happy relationship they were unable to foresee and so avoid.

In an unfortunate turn of events, the avoidant "vanishing act" often comes across to others as rejecting, even though it is not, for the dissociating avoidant is not being rejecting of, only protecting the self from rejection by, others.

Too often, these avoidants' protective aloofness filters down from personal to impersonal pursuits with distortive results that affect choice of profession or choice of job within that profession. As a general principle, with plenty of individual exceptions, serious avoidants tend to become physicists even when they really want to become doctors, and within the medical profession, anesthesiologists even when they really want to become psychiatrists.

COMORBID AVPD AND POSTTRAUMATIC STRESS DISORDER

Some avoidants pull back in the here and now to steel themselves from a potential or actual current relationship that reminds them of a traumatic relationship from the past. They confound new people they might love or who might love them with old people whom they loved once, only to discover that in reply, they hurt them badly and irrevocably. Unable to discriminate between bad past and good present relationships, they instead continue to generalize from old bad experiences to new, unrelated, good, and potentially satisfying involvements.

A Case Example

As a child, an avoidant was raised in the same bedroom as a delusional grandmother who regularly and, because of her age and status, with some authority, announced that through the window, she could see "kidnappers, and I worry that they will whisk you away." Later in life, he stayed away from all involvements with people who were overly intense like her. Instead, he preferred people who were bland, unemotional, and uninvolved, which unfortunately, and predictably, meant that they were also remote.

He also had a hypochondriacal father who worried constantly that he might get polio and even kept him at home for months in quarantine so that he would not come into contact with the polio virus. "To ice the cake," as the patient said, "he dressed me up in high shoes, like the ones actual polio victims wore, and forced me to wear knickers that had gone out of style and were made out of wool that, because of my allergy to lanolin, itched me so intensely that I could hardly function in social situations unless I wore shortie pajamas underneath to act as a lining—only to be regularly humiliated when, as predictably happened, my pajamas spontaneously fell down and stuck out from below." Not surprisingly, later in life, the boy developed a pervasive shyness that in effect said, "I am too ashamed of myself to get close to anyone, for if I stay away from people, I won't be dangerously on display and mocked as a result."

COMORBID AVPD AND PARAPHILIA

Paraphiliac avoidants are disabled in loving because they limit their attraction to the (paraphiliac) object or situation—one that, by definition, represents only part of normative patterns of arousal and activity. An example is an overfondness for a particular body part such as a foot. For paraphiliac avoidants, the attraction to the part is an aspect of the process of distancing themselves from the whole. Part of the process is that paraphiliac avoidants find themselves compulsively attracted to relationships that are dysfunctional because they are nonreciprocal. Thus a subway marauder experienced a decrease in sexual arousal when a partner promised (threatened) to get close. So he rubbed women in the subway because with such strangers, a full personal and sexual relationship was completely out of the question.

COMORBID AVPD AND NARCISSISM

Narcissistic avoidants tend to avoid less out of fear and more out of a preoccupation with their own needs, one that can be selfish in the extreme. Thus a single man at the beginning of the evening complained to his blind date, "I had to interview 90 women just to get you," and at the end of the evening, "I've dated women with small breasts, and I've dated women with large breasts, but no matter how hard I try, I can't seem to find a woman whose breasts are exactly the right size."

Narcissistic avoidants don't get close to, and maintain a solid relationship with, others because they jealously guard an identity of which they are inordinately fond. They have difficulty giving up "being me" in order to become "us." They feel that "who I am" (my masculinity, my identity as an independent man, my emancipated status as a woman) is more important than "who I am with." They are entirely too willing to stand on principle, even though that means standing alone.

COMORBID AVPD AND PASSIVE-AGGRESSION

Passive-aggressive avoidants antagonize others in *subtle* ways. Their goal is to provoke others to withdraw from them in a way that allows them to deny that they are the ones orchestrating the withdrawal from others.

COMORBID AVPD AND AGGRESSIVE PERSONALITY DISORDER

The same avoidant individual can be, and often is, both afraid of criticism and highly judgmental and critical of others.

A Case Example

One aggressive avoidant had few friends/lovers because, as she herself complained, she couldn't keep from criticizing everyone she knew both for things beyond their control, like their looks, financial status, and emotional problems, and for things within their control, but essentially unimportant, like wearing yesterday's clothes or recommending and taking her to all the "wrong" places. For example, she was very close to a colleague for many years, until that colleague got slightly depressed and needed someone to talk to, at which time she told her, "I am not interested in doing therapy with my friends" and refused ever to see her again. She also often criticized people for things that were her own fault. For example, "utterly shattered" over having missed a bus stop (though the next stop was only a few blocks away), she found herself severely castigating the bus driver for not reminding her to get off—even though, assuming (incorrectly) he knew her from earlier trips, she had not bothered to tell him the location of her stop. She often attacked innocent people just because they were around and available to be savaged. Sometimes it was the messenger, sometimes it was the next person to come along after the last person who troubled her, and sometimes it was the repairman who was trying to fix the problem. For example, she excoriated the bus driver of the bus that came (for there being so few busses) because she was angry at the driver of the bus that did not come. She excoriated an airline ticket agent when her luggage was lost, although it was the person who handled the luggage, not the ticket agent, who, if any abuse were deserved, was the one who merited it. Finally, she often went back in time to tease out one thread from the skein of life's normal give-and-take, stretch the simple unremarkable strand, and weave it into a tapestry horrific enough to give her the reason she needed to act out negative feelings about potentially positive relationships. Thus, after 43 years of not seeing a childhood companion, she was reintroduced to him at a large party she gave, whereupon she spontaneously announced, loudly and unforgivingly, and to all present, "Here's the boy who, when we were both two years old, threw dirt in my carriage."

COMORBID AVPD AND PASSIVE-DEPENDENT PERSONALITY DISORDER

Some Type IIc passive-dependent avoidants "actively" surround themselves with a protective shell to effectively hide out from a world they perceive to be threatening and rejecting They do this by forming a (possibly unhealthy) dependent relationship with one to avoid having healthy relationships with many. They might become overly close to a parent to avoid having a lover (or to avoid having to go to work) or form an overly close codependent relationship with a single partner to avoid other outside relationships. Some seek safety by becoming dependent on groups of like-minded avoidants. On the positive side, these groups enhance self-esteem through imparting a sense of belonging that makes all concerned feel wanted and involved. On the negative side, by becoming overly possessive, they enhance pathological intragroup attachments that isolate the group members from the outside world.

Other passive-dependent avoidants are simply too inactive to actively relate to others, for that means doing the work required to meet someone like Mr. or Ms. Right. I advised one patient from northern New Jersey desperate for, but unable to meet, a partner to go to New York and try hanging around a special place where bachelors go to meet women. In response, he could do no better than complain, "Too far. Too hard to get there."

In still other cases, the passivity is not the cause but, rather, the result of the primary avoidant problem. One avoidant, afraid that being active could lead to being rejected, refused to follow her friends' advice to be more forward with men. For example, when a man she liked said good-bye to her, ignoring her friends' advice to say, "I won't let you get away until I get your phone number," she merely said good-bye back and let it go at that. In her case, it was guilt and shame about her humanity that led her to hold back, for she believed that simply acting interested in a man meant that she was proposing to have an illicit liaison with him.

When passive avoidants like her find themselves in a troubled relationship, they tend to both welcome the troubles and make little or no active attempt to fix them. Typically, they ask or allow others to take full responsibility for the outcome of their lives—deputizing virtual strangers into telling them what to do. Rather than looking for problems and coming up with solutions on their own, they write letters to newspaper columnists, or to me, asking, "What do you think I should do?" or they find therapists who tell them whether to stay or go. Predictably, they select that columnist or therapist they know, intuitively, by reputation, or from past experience, will encourage them to leave. Then they lead them on by only giving them information that would seem to suggest they should go and censoring information that might suggest they should stay.

On a more favorable note, passive-dependents are *nonavoidant* when they suppress their hostility in order to maintain their dependency. They act kind when we would expect them to be unkind, say "it doesn't matter" when they should be setting limits, say yes when they should be saying no, suppress their sexuality should they deem it somehow troublesome to others, and generally behave in a self-sacrificial fashion—all in order to avoid offending others in a way that might lead others to retaliate by rejecting and dismissing them.

COMORBID AVPD AND MASOCHISM

Nonmasochistic avoidants want to relate well in order to avoid personal distress. In contrast, masochistic avoidants want to relate poorly in order to induce personal suffering. Some, looking to relate to people who cannot or will not relate to them, deliberately extend themselves only to those who are unlikely to accept them. Disinterested in people who overlook their flaws or see them as virtues, and wanting most of all to get approval from someone who already disapproves of them, they become unaccountably attracted to and actively seek out critical, humiliating, and rejecting persons, or at the very least choose those who are too different from them to be sufficiently compatible to make suitable companions and partners.

When these relationships fail to hurt and punish them as hoped and expected, they arrange to hurt and punish themselves through these relationships. After seeking them out, they stick with unfulfilling people and make a concerted effort to convert their harshest and most disdainful critics, the harsher and more critical the better, from negative to positive. They willingly (though resentfully) become submissive and do almost anything, even things that are not in their best interests, just to make these relationships work. They even gladly excuse the most outrageous behavior in their partners just so that the relationship can continue, as did the masochistic woman who excused her husband for cursing and reviling her in the foulest of terms on the basis of "anyone who hurts another person like that must be in pain himself." And should their relationships "threaten" to work, they imagine negativity in a neutral or positive situation. A man might call and leave a message for someone on Friday and, "forgetting" about the weekend, think he was being rejected because the call was not returned until Monday. They look for, and find, flaws in others because now they can make a cause célèbre out of the deficits, deliberately marring a relationship that works so that they can give themselves the excuse they are already seeking not to make repairs, but instead, to give up and leave.

Some Case Examples

A masochistic bisexual avoidant avoided people who treated him with respect in favor of relating to people who were unpleasant, hurtful, or abusive to him. He shrank from people he sensed would accept and love him by placing ads on the Internet and then not replying to responders who seemed interested in him. He also turned down promising introductions from friends and family who wanted to fix him up when he sensed that the fix might work out. Instead, he felt most strongly attracted to remote women, prostitutes, in particular. In an attraction to heterosexual prostitutes, the money transfer was avoidant because it convinced him, "I don't love, I buy." In a sideline attraction to transgender prostitutes, he knowingly involved himself in a situation where "confusion precluded closeness." (For the prostitutes, the avoidant attraction often was, "I do it with many people, not one, and not for love, but for money," which both precluded closeness and provided them with an opportunity for expression of hostility toward people who can't "get it" but have to "buy it.")

A masochistic single woman came to me complaining of a burgeoning successophobia typified in a recurrent dream "that my driving phobia"—a symptom of which she long complained in reality—had "lifted enough for me to be able to drive, but when I tried to park the car, I would swing it widely, and into traffic, bumping, hitting, and destroying other cars in the process."

When speaking of her relationships, she complained, "I have searched the world and there is no one in it for me." I suggested she ask her relatives, who knew many eligible bachelors, to fix her up with blind dates. They did, and the dates were not bad. But to defeat herself, her relatives, and me, she announced, "Blind dates never work out," and refused to accept ever being fixed up again. For her, blind dates got an undeservedly bad reputation because as a masochistic avoidant, she needed to be certain that no relationship would ever develop. To that end, she saw to it that her self-destructive behavior continued into the blind date itself.

Drawing additional inspiration from a successophobic belief that what was bad for her was good for her, and the reverse, she made a masochistic choice in her final selection of the man who was to be her husband. As she put it, looking back, "I avoided all the attractive men I met. Instead, I married the man who was unattractive, impotent, thin, reserved, self-preoccupied, and mother-fixated." Later, after meeting her goal of getting married to a man she found unattractive, she was actually surprised, as if she were learning it for the first time, that they had nothing in common, or that, as she put it in more specific, sexual terms, "His penis doesn't fit my vagina." After some years of couple treatment, she decided to try to get along with him. "He is really not a bad guy," she finally admitted. But then a new symptom arose— her "seven-year itch." Unlike nonmasochistic avoidants, in whom the seven-year itch is a longing for variety originating partly in a sense of boredom that can be reality based, her seven-year itch appeared precisely in order to disrupt a relationship that was finally going well: her husband had begun to respond to her positively, surprising her by becoming loving, just the way she once thought she had always wanted him to be, but which now "turned her off completely."

Many avoidants act out as masochistically with place as they do with person. In a self-destructive geographical maneuver, they choose to live in a place where they sense they are not wanted and can never be happy. They have a civil right to be there, but more important, because they do not fit in, they get stuck in what is for them a hopelessly deaffirming culture, where they aren't nearly as happy as they might be in another location, one where they had both a right and a reason to be.

In therapy, masochistic avoidants tend to be especially resistant to improvement. They find ways to keep their avoidance in order to continue their suffering. They call their loneliness preferential and attempt to convince their therapists of the same thing. They claim to value their privacy and independence over all else. They say that "marriage isn't right for everyone and it's not right for me." They note that having regular sex is not all it is cracked up to be. In the words of one such avoidant, "The best things in life are only for the isolate." Should therapy appear to be working, they find a way to defeat it by having a masochistic triumph that consists of cutting off their noses to spite their therapist's face. This was the motivation of an unmarried woman who allowed her goal of meeting people to become secondary to her goal of proving to everyone trying to help her—family, friends, and me—that "No matter what I do, I still can't find Mr. Right, and no matter what you do, you still can't help me catch him."

Not surprisingly, in couple therapy, masochistic avoidants respond negatively when a partner improves. In their headlong rush to a painful divorce, they deliberately, if unconsciously, continue to view a mate who has newly become interesting as still boring, who has learned to be nice as still insufficiently positive for their taste, and who has changed from remote to close as a newly developing threat to their valued freedom, independence, and identity.

COMORBID AVPD AND ADDICTION

Avoidants who are also addicts gamble or take drugs as a substitute for having relationships. For example, they gamble not to be involved with, but to retreat from, the world and the people in it via entering the substitutive fantasy arena of the casino, their figurative opium den. A man gambled in Las Vegas to get away from his wife. He thought of himself as a "guest of the owner" of his favorite casino, as if the owner wanted not his money, but him personally. He viewed the casino as the perfect home with the perfect people in it, in contrast to "my own shabby surroundings and impossible home life." As anyone who has tried to make eye contact with a serious gambler in a casino can attest, he, like many gamblers, hardly noticed anyone around him. He was blocking out the possibility that someone might be interested in him personally or sexually—as if the gambling (as intended) made human relationships, at least for the moment, entirely beside the point.

COMORBID AVPD AND BISEXUALITY

Bisexual avoidants indulge in Types IIa and IIb avoidant behavior when they behave homosexually to avoid heterosexuality, and the other way around.

A Case Example

A patient was at first a heterosexually oriented child. But, as he recalled, because he threw a baseball underhanded, his peers humiliated him to the point that his self-esteem fell precipitously. So as an adult, he "became bisexual to protect myself from rejection and the consequent loss of self-esteem by surrounding myself with two different kinds of people and fleeing protectively from one to another whenever I felt criticized and humiliated."

He also traced the origin of his bisexual shifting to problems in his early relationship with his parents. According to him, an overattachment to and identification with his mother fostered homosexual fantasies as he acted toward male companions in a way that reproduced his mother's seductive behavior toward him. But heterosexual fantasies came to the fore as he fled from homosexual relationships because they made him feel too much like a woman and so much too much like his mother. Also, every time a woman was unpleasant to him, she "sent me to men" because she reminded him of his mother's hostility toward him, while every time a woman was warm/seductive toward him, she "sent me to men" because she aroused oedipal/incestuous anxiety related to "my mother fixation."

He also traced his bisexual shifting back to his relationship with his father. He believed that his complete disrespect for his father put a damper on his heterosexuality because he had no male figure to identify with. And a restitutive need for a good father accounted for his never-ending search for an imperfect man he could make over into an ideal male parent.

As he concluded, overall, "I use my bisexuality to reduce anxiety about getting close to any one individual, for my being bisexual means that I will never be stuck in one place, and with one person only."

COMORBID AVPD AND MIXED PERSONALITY DISORDER

I diagnosed the following individual as a man with avoidant, including sexually avoidant, passive-aggressive, and narcissistic, personality features:

I recently was given your book as a gift and I must say that I find some parts of it very helpful to my situation. I have spent hundreds on counselors in the past few months and have not received any direction from them on understanding why I do the things

I do and what I can do to change. Your book has helped me get a better understanding of who I am and I must say I do not like myself for it.

My story goes like this: I was with my wife for seven years and for the first part everything was fine. We moved in together after six months. Three months afterward, my sister moved in with us (arriving on a student visa from Greece). She interfered all the time with my relationship with my wife, and it became too tiring to deal with her as she had issues of her own (she was 30 when she arrived, she is now 36). This took a toll on my relationship with my wife. Yet I was unwilling to tell my sister she had to go home then kick her out. She would sign up for college courses in English as a second language and just not go (she needed to be enrolled in a class to keep her visa). She would go once a week to make an appearance then spend the rest of the time sleeping during the day and staying up all night watching TV or cooking. When my wife learned I was the one paying for all my sister's expenses and she had sucked up all my savings, she asked me why I needed to support my sister like this and said she was using me. I explained it was a cultural thing and she would not understand.

Around the same time I got money from my parents to buy a new home. My wife and I found a nice loft in Center City but I insisted we get a two-bedroom to accommodate my sister. We all moved in and things got worse. The two-bedroom was an open concept with wall partitions going up 8 feet while the ceiling height was 14 feet, so you could hear every sound.

Our sex life went from very little to even more so. We were never really that sexually compatible to begin with since my wife was more the romantic type that needed the candles flickering and soft music playing in the background, while I was more spontaneous and aggressive and liked to be adventurous. As our sex life became worse I got to the point that I was more into porn than into her. I would rather just lie beside her and relieve myself than do anything, and if she tried to touch me, I would push her away, and this even when my sister was not home. I would not let her have me unless I was drunk or high and she was not into that as she said she would feel she was taking advantage of me and making me do something I did not enjoy.

My wife got sick of the situation and started to hook up with other guys on the side. She learned that with others, she could have the sex she wanted and enjoyed, the sex that she could never get from me.

Spring last year, we decided to move to a new place with more privacy. My wife begged me to get rid of my sister, and I kept telling her that since my parents gave me the money for the place I did not want to do that, even though our parents also wanted my sister to go back home and live her life there, and my sister owns her own place back in Greece. My wife got to a point where she felt alone because she was in a ménage à trois relationship with me and my sister. My wife also complained that she put all the money she made into our home, yet every day she would come home to find the house a complete mess as my sister would do nothing around the house but cook a meal she saw on a cooking show that day.

My wife begged me to do something but I refused as I said that it is not her house as my parents gave me the money for it. I told her that this was not her home even though everything she made went toward it. She began to feel like she was working toward nothing in her future. She even started contemplating suicide.

She had enough. She had to get away, so she flew to London for a week to clear her mind and distance herself from the relationship to evaluate what she should do. She came back with as few answers as she had when she left. When she returned she connected with a guy (John) that she thought was very nice even though he was 11 years older. They started talking and got to know each other well; they hooked up and she said that the sex was the best she ever had.

Next she decided she had had enough of being the third person in her marriage and moved out and in with John. She knew this was not the brightest of ideas but she felt like she finally met someone that she could connect with on all levels of a relationship and she was not willing to pass up the opportunity to be happy for once.

So four months ago she filed for a divorce. It was only then that I finally sent my sister packing for home and begged my wife to come back home and work out our problems. During that time, though, she fell hard for John, and they seem to have a great relationship. The exception is that John gets mad that my wife and I still have a business and work together.

My wife feels torn. While now I would like to have an exclusive relationship with her, she is unsure of what to do. I feel like after all those years of my being stuck with my sister from hell, she should give me a second chance and try to work out things with me. I know she is cheating on me, and while I am willing to forgive, I would be unwilling to open up the relationship since I go for exclusivity. On the other hand, she says her relationship with John is great, sexually things are fantastic, and it all just feels right for her without her having to try.

So reading your book made me feel like I'm behaving inadequately. I have tried to get professional help for this to get her back. The situation is driving me to the point where I do not know what to do. If you could tell me what to do, I would forever be in your debt.

CHAPTER 8

Cognitive-Behavioral Aspects

According to Burns and Epstein, emotional disorder is the product of "negative cognitions or [negative] automatic thoughts" and "stable underlying [incorrect or partially correct] assumption[s]"[1] that distort and disrupt interpersonal relationships through the creation of irrational disjunctive beliefs about oneself, others, and the world. These irrational beliefs, developed and maintained in the face of evidence to the contrary, lead to decreased interpersonal objectivity due to flawed interpretations of interpersonal events. These flawed interpretations feed back to firm up the original distortive beliefs to the point that the latter become unwritten laws—"activat[ed] stable underlying assumption[s]"[2] such as "if someone doesn't like me, then that means that I am unlikable." These unwritten laws lead to catastrophic thinking such as "since I am unlikable, all is lost" so that the avoidant becomes unable to differentiate between real and imagined dangers, having lost realistic internal reference points by which to judge his or her own behavior and its consequences, further escalating the antagonistic interpersonal schemas.

PROJECTIVE (PARANOID) THINKING

Avoidants who think in the paranoid mode create outer stress from inner turmoil by attributing their personal negative biases and guilt feelings to others, turning their own worries, fears, and self-condemnations into objective convictions of assault and attack. Projections largely account for suspiciousness and suspiciousness for the avoidants' classic fear of criticism, humiliation, and rejection, reflecting an impoverishment of basic trust.

Here are three common projective assumptions avoidants make about others:

I feel unworthy and devalue myself. Projection of unworthiness and self-devaluation becomes "you devalue me." Therefore a cancellation of a date due to sudden illness becomes a personal rejection, an offer to matchmake becomes humiliation for being so desperate that one needs to be fixed up, and the best-intentioned advice, including that from a truly concerned therapist, becomes a criticism for prior wrongdoing.

I am guilty about my sexuality. Projection of sexual guilt turns a friendly look from a stranger from a come-on or a "cruise" into a hostile stare or "sexual harassment."

I fear being controlled. Projection of fear of being controlled becomes "you are controlling me," turning a potential partner's request to have a close or exclusive relationship into an assault on one's independence. Good advice becomes the advisor's attempt to manipulate for personal gain, and a personals ad on the Internet becomes not an offer to meet meant to attract, but a pack of lies designed to attack.

THE MAKING OF FALSE EQUIVALENCIES (SIMILAR = THE SAME THING)

Avoidants think negatively due to emphasizing the similarities, while overlooking the significant mitigating differences, between A and B. They perceive a little questioning of them to be a shattering critical assault upon them, see mere disinterest on the part of others as full negativity or hatred, and misinterpret advice from others ("this is what you can profitably do") as a demand made upon them ("this is what you should do"). They see kidding as humiliation; turn constructive criticism into a put-down or a personal attack; and interpret friendliness as inappropriate sexual interest, or even sexual harassment. They believe any assertiveness on their part to be the exact equivalent of aggressiveness to others so that acceptable forwardness equates to unacceptable pushiness. They believe merely thinking about something bad equates to doing bad things; view the passivity associated with being in love as dangerous neediness, helplessness, and vulnerability; and see their minor flaws as completely disqualifying lesions. Commitment becomes entrapment; ordinary desire comes to equal desperation; co-operation with a friend or intimate comes to equal submissiveness; and submissiveness comes to equal complete loss of control and total, abject surrender. The uncertainty associated with all relationships becomes unpredictability; then unpredictability becomes certainty: that of looming, inevitable, attack, destruction, and loss.

A Case Example

One of my avoidant patients developed his characteristic sensitivity to criticism because he redefined criticism as anything short of complete acceptance so that if you didn't love him completely, you condemned him totally. He developed low self-esteem because he viewed any slight imperfection on his part as a fatal flaw and came to believe that if he was not all good, he was no good at all. He developed a fear of losing his identity completely because he viewed closeness as merging and merging as engulfment so that any woman who liked him would, by definition, keep him from completely realizing his individuality by demanding that he submerge himself fully into her as an individual.

THINKING ACCORDING TO EXCLUSIVE (AND EXCLUSIVELY NEGATIVE) CAUSES

Avoidants who think this way become selectively blind to alternative explanations for their avoidant beliefs. Unable to think of any positive elements in, and so other explanations for, others' presumed negativity, they explain others' less than fully positive behavior toward them as strictly antagonistic and rejecting. Although they see the possibility of negativity in all positivity, they rarely, if ever, see the possibility of positivity in those situations that they at first perceive to be completely negative. Thus "he didn't return my phone call yet" becomes not "he wants to get back to me but he is busy," but "he does not like me enough to want to get back to me ever," or "he was talking to me when his cell phone rang, and when he picked it up he turned away from me" becomes not "he had to answer that call because it was his business," but "he prefers the person calling him to me." Self-punitive attitudes originate along similar lines so that instead of "my anxiety is somewhat off-putting, I better be careful," we hear a much more self-pejorative "I destroy anyone who wants to love me, and so I am not worthy of even trying to be loved."

OVERGENERALIZING FROM ONE SPECIFIC INSTANCE TO ALL INSTANCES

Avoidants who overgeneralize slide too easily from shaky hypothesis to incontrovertible evidence to irrefutable fact. For example, a patient viewing all new relationships as if they are repeats of old, traumatic ones becomes effectively blind to alternative possibilities so that because he fell in love with someone unreliable once, no one he loves can ever be trusted again.

Very frequently, avoidants negatively parentalize what are in fact positive relationships after basing their conclusions on trivial shared characteristics of new nonparental and old parental relationships, then emphasizing the inconsequential or inaccurately perceived negatively of the new based on a tenuous similarity to the less than satisfactory old. For some avoidant women, all men remind them of an abusive father, and for some avoidant men, all women remind them of a rejecting mother.

CATASTROPHIC (ALARMIST OR WORST POSSIBLE SCENARIO) THINKING

Catastrophic thinking involves histrionic exaggeration, leading to overcautiousness or to the taking of desperate (and unnecessary) protective measures, leading to serious personal and professional misjudgments or even to making a suicide attempt. Avoidants who think this way typically make "mountains out of molehills" as they indulge in "all is lost" or "for want of a nail the ship was lost" or "for want of a penny the kingdom was lost" thinking. They assign absolute rather than relative meaning to minor problematic events, then overreact to these as if they constitute major negative developments. They become unable to say to themselves "so what" and "big deal," then remain calm and unemotional about things that don't really matter, or even about things that do matter but not that much, or, if that much, are best overlooked for the individual's overall happiness and peace of mind.

Serious perfectionism is a kind of catastrophic thinking, where the avoidant discards a potentially or actually viable relationship because of perceived minor flaws, pulling back completely from a valid social/ sexual interaction just because the other person has merely made a single, insignificant transactional blunder.

Many avoidants make two, or more, cognitive errors simultaneously. For example, a patient's habit of taking criticism too seriously led him to feel too frightened and devastated to relate intimately to anyone. This serious fear of criticism started with *similar equals the same thing* distortive thinking so that if someone merely requested that he do something, that request became an intended criticism that that thing was not done. Also, *thinking catastrophically*, he perceived actual minor criticism to be a rejection and the rejection a warning that the relationship was in serious trouble, and that it, and his life, were going to end badly.

Cognitive errors do not develop or thrive in a vacuum; rather, they appear, take shape, and persist within a facilitating matrix of disruptive, often traumatic, developmental events; internal conflicts inadequately resolved by normative or pathological defensiveness; negative behavioral conditioning; distortive interpersonal perceptions first formed in childhood that persist into adulthood; comorbid emotional disorder; misguided existential and socially based philosophical beliefs; and ongoing real-life stresses.

In the realm of disruptive developmental events, often adults continue to think in an avoidant manner in the here and now because as children, they identified with parents who thought the same way, or as children, they long ago jumped to the only partly true conclusion that their parents were criticizing or rejecting them. For one guilty patient, his mother's getting even a little angry when she felt his behavior was out of line meant that she didn't love him at all. Now he believes that anyone who sets firm limits on him is, just as she did, furiously criticizing him and rejecting him completely.

In the realm of ongoing interpersonal stresses, a shy, hypersensitive avoidant patient carrying on the "great tradition" of early parental negativity felt uncomfortable meeting new people because he failed to distinguish making a minor social blunder from ruining himself completely socially. He believed that others' basic feelings about him could change, without warning, from positive to negative, just the same way his parents' basic feelings did change toward him when, as a child, he did something they disapproved of. He did not believe that adult interpersonal relationships had an in-built margin of error so that most peoples' basic feelings did not change from positive to negative over something trivial or even momentous. Instead, he saw everybody as a parental clone who would turn on him the same way his parents did when he made childish mistakes.

I could not convince him otherwise because his family actually did continue to reject him over nothing—by showing a clear preference for his brothers and sisters now, as they did then, and seamlessly, essentially from the day he was born.

CHAPTER 9

Development

EARLY PSYCHOLOGICAL ISSUES

Avoidant Disorder of Childhood and Adolescence

The *Diagnostic and Statistical Manual of Mental Disorders*, third revised edition (*DSM-III-R*), describes a syndrome it calls "avoidant disorder of childhood and adolescence," whose traits survive in the adult avoidant in the form of interactive problems that disrupt intimacy. This *DSM-III-R* syndrome is characterized by interpersonal anxiety manifest in a "desire for social involvement with familiar people, such as peers and family members," associated with "an excessive shrinking from contact with unfamiliar people" so that the child is "likely to appear socially withdrawn, embarrassed, and timid when in the company of unfamiliar people and will become anxious when even a trivial demand is made to interact with strangers," and may even become "inarticulate or mute."[1]

A Case Example

A 10-year-old has no friends of her age. Her only interpersonal contacts are her parents and a few of their adult friends. She never leaves her parents' side, partly because the mother never lets her out of her sight, and partly because she is unable to go more than a few feet from home because she fears loud street noises, being stung by bees, and riding on public transportation (she fears she will drown when the train she is on crosses a bridge and falls off the tracks into the water), and partly because she fears strangers. (Her preoccupation with details—she is able to list 256 breeds of dogs as well as all the birds ever found in Colorado—suggests that she might be suffering from an associated Asperger's syndrome.)

However, I have treated a number of patients who described their children as having emotional symptoms that seem to have been the *opposite* of those described in the *DSM-III-R*. In this non-*DSM* disorder, the child is both unable to relate outside the home and, while at home, makes the parents' life into a hellish onslaught of disagreements and fights.

A Case Example

A patient of mine describes a son like this:

Last night, I drew the line and asked my husband to draw it with me, too, but I am still reeling in a mother's desolation. There has been no movement in my eldest son's life since the last time I asked him to start looking for a job so he could move out; his presumption was that he should live here forever not talking to us, find intermittent clerical jobs, and play tennis occasionally, while going to bars nightly, stumbling in in the wee hours of dawn. I might have even put up with that, except for the fact that he never talked to me (or anyone), and when I talk to him, there is a particular anger toward me, which came out in full force yesterday.

The tension between us resurfaced Sunday night when he fed my dog a chicken leg (bone and all), and I was livid. He said I was acting crazy, all dogs eat chicken. Yesterday, when I was supposed to pick up my other son from school (he got out early that day), my electric garage door got stuck and wouldn't open, so I knocked on my eldest son's bedroom door (it was 10:30 A.M.; he usually gets up at 1 or 1:30 P.M. from his late nights) and said, "My garage door is stuck, would you go and pick up your brother with your car? He is waiting and there is no one there to give him a ride." He said nothing, so I asked him again and then went to the front yard to rake leaves to the street curb for the collection. Next thing I know, my little dog had been set loose and was running toward me out onto the busy street. This kid comes out in his underwear and pulls open the garage door, berating me for not being able to do it myself. Trying to grab onto my dog before she gets squished by traffic, I yelled, "Asshole." I felt terrible that that slipped out, but he almost seemed to be trying to harm the dog to get to me. His response was, "What a crazy bitch you are.

It's only a dog," and then, "If I'm an asshole, you go and get my brother yourself. Your door is opened."

I was a nervous wreck. I said, "Son, this isn't working. You don't respect anyone in this house, you don't pull your weight, I asked you to rake the yard because your father has been sick (he had a bad flu last week and couldn't move) and you refused to do it—this isn't how a family is supposed to work. I feel terrible that you walk right by me every day without talking to me, and when you look at me you are always so hostile. I didn't mean to call you an asshole, I was just nervous and trying to grab the dog while in the middle of traffic. I think it's time for you to launch your life now, this isn't working for either of us."

R: Are you throwing me out?

T: I told you before, you can stay until you have a steady job, providing you work toward getting one, and in the meantime, you either pitch in with the chores or pay rent *and* treat all of us like we are human beings. You don't need to be partying every night and staying in bed 'til 1:00 P.M. every day when you could be looking for a job.

R: What do you think I want to be, a hermit like you, a 45-year-old loser with no friends, no job, who sits on her ass all day in front of a sewing machine?

T: Is this what you think of me after I spent my life loving and caring for you?

R: You never did a thing for me except get on my back. You have three kids who hate your guts. Do you think that's us, or could it be you?

I called my husband and said, "As hard as this is, we need to be on the same page about it." When my husband comes home, he tells that kid that he would call the police on him if he ever acted like he did again. The kid then puts all his things into a large blanket, his computer and stereo into a box, and leaves. Said he would never come back and never wants to see us again.

I said I didn't want him to go like this, that I wanted him to build to a point where he was ready to go, when he could afford a place. I told him I loved him very much, but that I saw him floundering and this was the age he needed to be working toward something.

He said, "You both hate me," and started to cry. I said, "We both love you and want to try to make this relationship work while you stay here and work toward your independence. Can we try to be a real family who loves each other and helps each other out when we need it?"

He just shook his head. And cried. Then he left to go who knows where. And that is the last image I have of my son. I didn't sleep all night.

EARLY TRAUMA

Avoidants avoid new situations and relationships that resemble old, traumatic ones. Avoidants who experienced incestuous sexual seductions, or who underwent severe punishment for trivial manifestations of their sexuality, steer clear of activities, places, or people that arouse these recollections. Thus a patient who, at age three, was severely whipped for "playing doctor" with the little girl next door became, as an adult, a celibate avoidant—his way to keep himself from being "whipped" once more by those who might once again censure him for having and even wanting sex. I have had a number of patients avoid commitment because it makes them feel tied down and smothered, just as they felt when in their first years of life when they underwent unpleasant operative procedures such as a tonsillectomy and adenoidectomy.

EARLY PARENTAL RELATIONSHIPS

Millon speaks of how shyness develops out of early parental "rejection, humiliation, or denigration."[2]

A Case Example

A shy, hypersensitive, avoidant patient felt uncomfortable meeting new people because he failed to distinguish making an insignificant social blunder from ruining himself socially completely. His fear of ruination originated with his parents turning on him when he made childish mistakes, which, of course, he predictably made because he was, in fact, still a child. It also originated in his relationship with a rejecting father, who paid little attention to him, hardly played with him, and never took him to the movies or museums, and in his relationship with his mother, who demanded absolute "apron string" fidelity in return for giving him any love at all.

Benjamin notes that patients with "AVD began the developmental sequence with appropriate nurturance and social bonding [giving the avoidant-to-be] a base of attachment that preserved normative wishes for social contact." However, the AVD-to-be was "subject to relentless parental control on behalf of constructing an impressive and memorable social image. The opinions of others outside the family were given high value. Visible flaws were cause for great humiliation and embarrassment." At the same time, the message was sent that "those outside the family were . . . likely to reject the AVD." This led the AVD to be "concerned about public exposure" and to make "impression management" a priority. There was also "degrading mockery for any existent failures and shortcomings," backed up by "shunning, banishment, exclusion, and enforced autonomy." As a result, the AVD developed "strong self-control and restraint to avoid making mistakes that might be humiliating or embarrassing." "When internalization [occurred the individual became] very sensitive to humiliation," leading to defensive "social withdrawal in anticipation of rejection and humiliation" and an "unwilling[ness] to reach out unless there is massive evidence that it is safe to take the risk."[3]

Those who suffer early in life from excessive parental control may grow up feeling as if every new adult relationship is a trap—as one patient put it, "an involuntary commitment." Some of these individuals become excessively dependent avoidants, who give in, submit, and do exactly what they are told. But others become excessively independent avoidants who rebel and do only the opposite of what others expect of them. For example, though they want to get married, they refuse to do so just because it's what their parents want them to do (and they see everyone as their parents).

Bruising parental criticism for being overly emotional can lead a child to grow up remote and unfeeling to spare himself or herself such further assault, for example, criticism for being a crybaby. Children who are told that "it's bad to feel, and worse, to get at all angry" might, as adults, discourage all relationships in order to avoid subjecting their partners, and themselves, to their own angry outbursts. Children negatively compared to their siblings can grow up feeling devalued compared to everyone else and either retreat to avoid testing their unworthiness or attempt to feel more worthy by turning every new potentially loving relationship into a jealous, competitive, rivalrous situation, where winning to feel valued for the first time in their lives becomes the only thing, and all they care about.

Parents who infantilize their children in order to have them all to themselves can create an avoidant-to-be by keeping the child at home away from all his or her friends. In the case of the married couple, now separated, who lived apart in two connected houses (discussed in chapter 4), the mother would not let the daughter visit her father unaccompanied, even though they lived in a safe neighborhood and the father lived just down the porch. Instead, the mother insisted upon escorting the child from her house directly to the father's door and watching until the child got safely inside. Infantilized children like this often pay the price, when they are still children, in the currency of defective relationships with siblings and compromised relationships with others outside the home and family. When they become adults, these children often pay another price: they become avoidants who have regressive relationships marked by an isolating dependency (codependency) on one, associated with a disinterest in, fear of, antagonism to, often based in jealousy of, all.

Parents who are themselves avoidant often create an avoidant child in their own image. They can do this directly, by vocally warning the child about the dangers of getting close, or indirectly, by criticizing just about everyone else for doing normal, nonavoidant things. In one case, parents who vocally criticized their own friends' small indulgences, such as having cocktails each evening before dinner, helped create a child who avoided others because she believed that there was something "evil" about getting together with people, having a drink or two, and just enjoying oneself.

Paradoxically, early *positive* experiences can also lead to the development of avoidant personality disorder (AvPD). Healthy, nonavoidant parents can unwittingly create avoidant children should, as commonly happens, the child counteridentify with them to become a counterparental isolate. A child reluctant to break away from a pleasant home life and an early, pleasant, too-close relationship with the parent of the opposite sex can later in life develop an oedipal avoidant syndrome rooted in a desire to remain faithful to the parent, specifically manifesting as follows:

- staying single or picking a remote, unavailable partner to marry
- then having a poor or nonexistent sex life with him or her
- while longing to meet someone new and more romantic
- and seeking or having an affair
- yet picking a new partner who is equally avoidant, especially one who is also already married, so that the affair goes nowhere and leads to disappointment and regret, which is

- one's comeuppance for cheating on one's original partner and threatening to wreck or actually wrecking one's own and the new partner's marriage

A Case Example

I had a strange dream once when I was younger. My mother was young and maybe in her 30s. She was very beautiful, and always dressed to the nines, as she was in the dream. We were ready to go to the produce market with my father, but my mother (I was a kid in the dream) looked at me and said mischievously, "Why don't I go without him this time?" My father hadn't woken up yet, and I was afraid that he'd beat us if we went without him. Yet I wanted her to have her freedom, so I said, "Go, Mamma," and she did: right out the door, beautiful, in a dress, high heels, pearls, her hair and lipstick just so, and she looked back at me and disappeared into the crowd. Then my father woke up and demanded to know where my mother was. I realized I hadn't put my bra on yet; it was still in my hand for getting dressed, and I panicked trying to get past him, covering my chest, hoping he didn't grab me as I ran around him into the bathroom. Then I woke up in a panic.

I know, it's a Freudian field day. I just hope it is one of those false repressed memories. But I always was extremely afraid of him as a kid (he has mellowed now, thankfully) and always repulsed by the way he grabbed me and wouldn't let me go when he had a few too many. Which probably explains why someone like my asexual husband would attract me when I was young. At least in my dream, my mother broke free of her imprisonment. I believe I picked a remote man due to my fear that any close relationship would be incestuous, then, in response, spent my whole marriage blaming him for being that way, having affairs that went nowhere, and fantasizing dumping him if one of my affairs "clicked."

EARLY NONPARENTAL RELATIONSHIPS

Rosenthal, in the *New York Times*, describes studies that show how the early "interplay between young siblings exerts a powerful life-long force" as people "keep the relationships they had when they were young—such as rivalry or bossiness . . . color[ing] all their interactions in the adult world."[4]

Additionally, peers, teachers, entertainers, religious leaders, and the medical profession encourage avoidance directly or through the media by word and/or deed. Millon emphasizes the role played by peer group ridicule in the development of AvPD.[5] The media have a pro-avoidant effect on the adolescent when they extol the benefits of Zen withdrawal and do-your-own-thing philosophies that overstress the importance of freedom, independence, and individuality, while by implication, fully condemning that submission and deindividuation necessary to form close, loving relationships. Religious leaders who are excessively moralistic, and therapists who encourage and maintain avoidance through long, drawn out, harsh therapeutic regimens meant to ready the patient for having a full life that never comes, also belong in the category of "gurus," whose so-called expertise in fact involves "expertly" encouraging avoidance.

BIOLOGICAL FACTORS

Ballenger views avoidance as a way to deal with anxiety/panic attacks that appear when a "brain alarm system . . . fires . . . too easily"[6] so that the patient responds to the events of everyday life with excessive anxiety.

In some individuals, shyness is the product of constitution/temperament. Millon refers to "a genetic or hereditary . . . 'interpersonal aversiveness'" displayed in early "hyperirritability, crankiness, tension, and withdrawal behaviors" in "easily frightened and hypertense babies who are easily awakened, cry, and are colicky [and who] rarely afford their parents much comfort and joy [but who rather] induce parental weariness, feelings of inadequacy, exasperation, and anger [accompanied by] parental rejection and deprecation." Millon speculates that anatomical (an "'aversive center' of the limbic system") and hormonal-biochemical factors ("excess adrenalin and rapid synaptic transmission") might account for this genetic interpersonal aversiveness.[7]

Kagan, according to Ruth Galvin, says that at one time, he assumed that "timidity was acquired through experience, the repeated avoidance of challenge strengthening a childhood tendency to withdraw. Now he . . . wonder[s] whether he had overlooked something: temperament." He describes a "small group of people . . . who are born with a tendency to be shy with strangers and cautious in new situations," a temperamental quality Kagan calls "inhibition," which is related to shyness. He remarks how some children, like some puppies, are born inhibited and remain so throughout their lives. Kagan believes that this temperament is inherited. Kagan also notes that "although society sees [shy people] as underreactors, inhibited persons may actually have a *stronger*-than-normal response to novelty—too strong, in fact, for their brains to tolerate, with inhibition and shyness appearing as the self-protective result."[8]

EVOLUTIONARY FACTORS

Becoming a civilized human being entails a degree of loss of "animal" warmth, spontaneity, and connectivity. The cat that, knowing that its owner is aggrieved, sits on a foot to offer sympathy, companionship, and comfort, with evolutionary "refinement," becomes the human who responds to another's suffering with "grin and bear it," "cut it out," or "go get professional help." Thus a cat, after having lost her lifetime companion, another cat, became inconsolable, meowing all night, uncomprehending. When the cat's owner died, the cat, not the family, was the first to notice that she had passed. The others were all in the kitchen, eating. The cat was at her owner's side, howling.

Humans have normal primitive, protective "animal" avoidances such as a reflexive fear of mice and harmless snakes, a superstition of black cats crossing one's path, a tendency to curl up in the fetal position when one feels overwhelmed or depressed, and, what is perhaps the ultimate biological avoidance of all, fainting "dead away" due to fright or in disgust. Even in such of our everyday expressions as "badgering," "weaseling," "outfoxing," and "hogging," we are reminded of the jungle origins of some of the most interpersonally aversive human behaviors. Some avoidants in their self-protective behavior remind us of a stray cat who, however hungry it may be, thinks twice before accepting a handout, and some of a raccoon who strikes a compromise with humans—not bothering them as long as they don't bother it. Others remind us of dogs—pups who, thinking only of themselves, push others aside to get to an available teat; adult dogs who protectively roll over to beg for mercy, playing dead to retain life, or who retreat to a lair for safety, protection, and territorial advantage to avoid a fight; and older dogs who, when ill or about to die, remain transfixed within and become remote, perhaps to anticipate death—so that they can deny they love life.

One of my avoidant patients, a man with multiple social phobias, compared himself to his cocker spaniel, who developed a fear of blimps and had to scan the heavens for one before venturing out of doors—he speculated as a displacement from a fear of airborne predators. In her inability to walk near large objects like trash bins, he saw his own agoraphobia, and in her fear of walking over grates, he saw his own fear of being at the edge of a high cliff, in danger of falling, about to descend into nothingness.

PART TWO

THERAPY

CHAPTER 10

An Overview of Avoidance Reduction

I call my method of treating avoidants "avoidance reduction" to describe an approach to treating avoidant personality disorder (AvPD) that is dedicated, eclectic, holistic, and action oriented. My therapeutic approach is *dedicated* because it is focused on the distancing process in all its aspects. It is *eclectic and holistic* because it uses multiple therapeutic techniques to deal with the broad range of core issues integral to AvPD, including, but not limited to, its developmental, psychodynamic, cognitive-behavioral, interpersonal, and existential-philosophical aspects, which, when taken together, make up the "avoidant gestalt," as summarized in table 10.1.

My eclecticism is rooted in the work of Oldham and Morris, who suggest an approach that involves "desensitizing [avoidants'] anxiety, [helping avoidants learn] social skills, [helping avoidants] consciously change . . . some of their self-destructive thinking patterns, [and using insight] psychotherapy," which the authors believe "can be highly beneficial for the Avoidant person who has the courage to face—instead of running away from—his or her problems."[1]

It is also rooted in Millon and Davis's eclectic schema for treating avoidance, one that involves multitasking, that is, simultaneously using insight-oriented, interpersonal, cognitive-behavioral, self-image (self-worth)-enhancing, and pharmacological therapy.[2] Specifically, Millon and Davis suggest having avoidant patients (1) understand their avoidance developmentally and dynamically; (2) focus on increasing pleasure; (3) learn to understand others; (4) learn to differentiate between real, incidental, and imagined threats; (5) develop internal (and internalized) realistic reference points by which to judge their own

Table 10.1
Eclectic/Holistic Avoidance Reduction

The *analytic dimension:* the therapist obtains information about and imparts insight into the dynamic aspects of the individual's avoidances. The information is obtained from a study of the patient's past life and of his or her current avoidant fantasies and behaviors, including transference ideation/behavior.

The *cognitive dimension:* the therapist identifies and corrects illogical, inappropriate, and often paranoid interpersonal negative thinking, partly to help the patient recognize and acknowledge the positive aspects of relationships the patient currently views as all negative.

The *behavioral dimension:* the therapist, informally or formally, asks the patient to perform a series of graded, nonavoidant, connective interpersonal tasks of progressive difficulty in order to approximate nonavoidance in a gradual, stepwise fashion.

The *interpersonal dimension:* the therapist identifies and understands specific avoidant interpersonal anxieties and shows avoidants how the outer manifestations of anxiety (anxiety equivalents) such as shyness can make others uncomfortable, leading others to react by thinking not "he is afraid of me," but "she is too stuck up to talk to me."

The *educative dimension:* the therapist enhances motivation by enumerating the virtues of relating over being isolated and teaches the patient the social skills that can lead to pleasurable and rewarding experiences, which in turn inspire further attempts at fuller social mastery.

The *supportive dimension:* the therapist provides the patient with a warm, reassuring, healing holding therapeutic environment within which the therapist attempts to reduce relationship anxiety directly, e.g., with such reassurances as "you will get over your anxiety if you patiently persevere."

The *pharmacotherapeutic dimension:* the doctor prescribes selected patients antianxiety and/or antidepressant agents, always keeping in mind that many patients would prefer to at least try verbal therapy before taking medication.

---

behavior; (6) improve their self-image; (7) make cognitive corrections/rework aversive schemas; (8) use distraction methods such as positive social interaction; (9) increase contact to acquire critical social skills; (10) try new experiences, which can help by enhancing and maintaining motivation and providing the opportunity to monitor behavior and correct maladaptive, automatic thoughts and irrational beliefs; (11) learn to control fretful-expressive behavior while simultaneously establishing and improving friendships; and (12) use indicated pharmacotherapeutic agents, such as beta-blockers, monoamine oxidase inhibitors, or serotonin uptake inhibitors, to reduce anxiety. Millon and Davis further recommend that these different therapeutic modalities take place in a supportive setting, where the therapist counters apprehension with "freehanded empathy and support," the "therapist's only recourse."[3]

My approach is *action oriented* because it emphasizes doing as well as thinking. It goes beyond utilizing the more "passive" therapeutic techniques that rely exclusively on influencing and changing through understanding to emphasize the more "active" therapeutic techniques, particularly behavioral approaches where the therapist exhorts patients to convert from avoidance to nonavoidance by facing their fears now, as best they can, through exposing themselves directly to situations that make them anxious so that they can take that all-important leap from understanding what troubles them to actively doing something about it.

PSYCHODYNAMICALLY ORIENTED PSYCHOTHERAPY

Psychodynamically oriented (psychoanalytically oriented, insight-oriented) methods, a cornerstone of eclectic therapy, emphasize developing an understanding of the present manifestations of avoidance through identifying its anlage, that is, its developmental origins. Thus one avoidant's present-day shyness was partly due to guilt about relating that originated in excessive closeness to a mother who discouraged her from getting involved with men by promoting the nonsensical belief that it was unthinkable for any daughter of hers to marry a stranger. A source of another's shyness was a fear of humiliation originating in her early relationship with a father who went out of his way to spot when she accomplished something significant—just so that he could avoid keeping her from getting a swell head by paying her a compliment.

Psychodynamically oriented therapists also explore to relieve the patient's present turmoil through developing an in-depth understanding of his or her current associations and fantasies in order to be able to fully answer such questions as, "Why exactly does asking a girl to dance make you so anxious?" The answers often come from asking other questions such as, "Is it that you fear she will reject you? And, if so, why should a stranger's rejection matter so much?"

Most psychodynamically oriented therapists try to help soften their patients' guilt feelings. They do that both by helping them become more accepting of impulses they currently renounce and by facilitating their use of healthier defenses to cope with guilt they cannot reduce or fully eliminate. Thus patients might better come to deal with feeling guilty about hating others by relinquishing projection of their hatred ("I don't hate you, you hate me") and instead denying and suppressing the hatred so that it shows less and therefore has less of a devastating effect on connectivity.

Psychodynamically oriented therapists regularly identify and attempt to understand avoidances as they appear in the patient's negative actions with, based on transference to, the therapist, as when patients avoid an aspect of the therapeutic process, and even their therapist, by canceling appointments when something painful is about to surface.

How does understanding (insight) cure? In simplistic terms, patients make things right by learning to unlearn what went wrong. Though much of the literature about AvPD downplays the importance of insight, citing, as do Anthony and Swinson, the likes of the lack of evidence for the effectiveness of understanding (Freudian) dynamics,[4] I believe that insight-oriented approaches, while not sufficient, are necessary, and synergize well with other approaches, particularly with cognitive-behavioral therapy.

COGNITIVE-BEHAVIORAL THERAPY

Eclectic therapists also use a *cognitive-behavioral* approach focused on exposing and correcting the illogical thoughts that lead patients to distance themselves from relationships due to forming and maintaining excessively fearful notions about being criticized, humiliated, and rejected. Cognitive-behavioral therapists correct thinking directly by reframing negative into neutral or more positive cognitions following the rules of evidence. They also correct thinking indirectly by suggesting behavioral interventions that consist of asking patients to do what makes them afraid in small, incremental steps as a way to slowly but surely reduce their anxious thinking (while simultaneously stirring up new anxious thoughts that the patients can bring back into therapy for further analysis and subsequent correction/integration).

Too, they employ exhortation ("I know you can do it" and "try living around your need to distance even before the fears that lead to your distancing have been fully mastered") in order to goad patients into attempting successive approximations to healthy behaviors, hoping that they will gradually become habituated to the anxiety that predictably appears when they attempt to perform those very things that make them afraid.

Many therapists use a combination of psychodynamically oriented and cognitive-behavioral therapy.

A Case Example

A patient who complained about being afraid to go out on a second date benefited both from learning about how her past affected her in the here and now and from correcting her present misconceptions about dating directly so that she could feel calmer and act in a more productive fashion. For example, she once refused to have a second date with a man simply because he said that before making the next date with her, he had to check his schedule book. Correcting the cognitive error that "I will get back to you" equals "I have rejected you" was helpful, but not enough to change the emotional distortive thinking that came from deep within. To do this, we needed to go back to the beginning, when she first felt totally rejected over something similar, and equally insignificant. Now we discovered that her father was a man who, refusing to commit himself in advance to a specific time when they could get together, regularly told her when she asked him, "When can just the two of us have fun?" that, "I will get back to you about that," then did not firm up a date for months, if at all. Understanding that "you view all new boyfriends as your procrastinating father" helped her see present relationships for what they were in the here and now, not as what she imagined them to be through the "retrospectoscope" of her past interactions with this parent. This insight acted synergistically with her new cognitive learning, the two together freeing her up to form a relationship that ultimately led to her getting happily married.

Though advocates for cognitive therapy rarely speak of its downsides, there are shortcomings and complications of cognitive therapy that can interfere with improvement or make matters worse. Cognitive therapy is inherently critical, for by definition, the therapist, however unintentionally, sends the patient two implied messages: "your thinking is wrong" and "you personally are wrongheaded"—not messages avoidants, already notoriously sensitive to lack of support and feeling/being devalued, necessarily want to hear. Also, resistances appear to this as to every other form of therapy. Two of these are the positive resistance of falsely reporting progress to please/humor a therapist obviously trying to be of help and the negative resistance of stubbornly and even sadistically maintaining one's psychopathology to spite a therapist too obviously pushing for change along lines the patient sees as predetermined and so deems to be controlling.

THE INTERPERSONAL APPROACH

Eclectic therapists also use an *interpersonal* approach, where they study the dyadic causes and manifestations of avoidance with a view to resolving distorted interpersonal perceptions that lead to maladaptive interpersonal behavioral patterns such as those that are the product of anxiety over intimacy. These therapists focus on the central interpersonal avoidant patterns and problems I emphasize throughout such as fears of humiliation, criticism, and rejection at the hands of others; low self-esteem that makes it difficult for patients to confidently relate to other people; and the belief that serious closeness means completely losing, rather than only partially compromising, one's identity. Interpersonal therapists basically try to make it clear that avoidants' expressed and secret interpersonal fears are excessive and their perception of the dangers associated with relating are overblown. They usually attempt to interrupt cycles of negative feedback where avoidants actively create some of the criticism they feel passively victimized by after provoking others to mistreat them less out of dislike and more out of fear.

SUPPORTIVE THERAPY

Eclectic therapists also use a *supportive* approach involving positive feedback from the therapist ("you are too good to fail," "that's great that you have succeeded," "your low self-esteem is lower than by rights it should be") and reassurance ("you can handle and overcome your anxiety"). When indicated, they give fatherly/motherly advice ("there are other places where you will be happier/more welcome/ more popular than in the suburbs"). Also, they often advise avoidants to seek succor from others who are potentially in a position to help— secret sharers, counselors, friends, family members, and lovers, who can, it is hoped, help the patient cope and feel better. And they use relaxation techniques such as teaching the patient to breathe deeply and more slowly; meditation; and when indicated, antianxiety pharmacotherapy. They do all these things, and more, within a comforting, therapeutic holding environment that serves as a kind of protective bubble for the patient attempting to venture forth into old and new anxiety-provoking interpersonal adventures.

THE EXISTENTIAL APPROACH

Eclectic therapists use an *existential* therapeutic approach consisting of reshaping the patient's philosophy of life. Methods involve helping the patient rethink favored avoidant positions and goals through identifying with and emulating others the patient admires for their social prowess and reading self-help books that take valid nonavoidant positions such as "when looking for a partner, be flexible about type" and "don't compare yourself to others."

FAMILY THERAPY

Eclectic therapists might use a *family therapy* approach, hoping to resolve interfamiliar conflicts that interfere with an individual's outside relationships. For example, they try to convince a smothering family to let go and stop infantilizing the patient by discouraging him or her from going out of the house, other, at least, than to go to work to support the family.

Some Case Examples

Family therapy made it clear to a shy avoidant that she had become a remote, formal, rigid, and inhibited adult because she feared acting on her positive impulses without first getting "parental" approval, and because she feared losing control of her instincts in the heat of passion and saying and doing things that she would later be ashamed of because what "her people" thought or might think of her, that is, her reputation within the family, had become more important to her than what she thought of herself and than her personal growth, happiness, and satisfaction. We traced her excessive need for approval to her parents' continuing warnings that people frown upon friendly women for being sluts and look down on a woman who is at all outgoing as being "loose"—a warning that her parents, as it became clear during our sessions, continued to issue for their own selfish purpose: to keep her at home just so that she would always be around and available to take care of them in case they needed her.

She responded by entering a session wearing a T-shirt whose logo was "99% devil, 1% angel," her way to tell her parents and me that she had finally begun to break free from her inhibiting need to find out and buy into what her parents thought about and expected of her, and to obtain parental approval before she acted, instead of acknowledging her own feelings, then seeking personal direction. Next, having become less dependent on what her parents, and anyone who reminded her of them, thought, she was able to brave the inevitable criticisms and rejections that everyone gets in this world without becoming discouraged to the point that she couldn't do anything on her own without first having to ask for permission. Now she could try to connect with men without giving up easily, instead of fleeing out of a relationship at the first sign of closeness and, in retreat, figuratively going home again.

Family therapy made it very clear to one avoidant that he was threatened by closeness because he worried about what his parents thought of his romantic relationships. In treatment, he learned to ask of his parents, "What's the worst that you can do to me?" then to answer his own question by telling them, "If you continue in your old ways, I will simply have to stop talking to you." But still, his fear of parental disapproval persisted, making true intimacy with others impossible. So we next worked on helping him collect evidence on how the parental disapproval he so feared was less directed to him than it was the product of his parents' own distortive thinking, and therefore being relevant to them only was not an indication of how he should view, and treat, himself.

In short, avoidant symptoms yield best to multiple approaches involving, first, getting to the bottom of things, then patching things up by making a variety of repairs. Though diverse approaches might at first appear to be mutually inconsistent, or even mutually exclusive, they can (and should) be used together, either alternatively or simultaneously. Because of the complex personality of the avoidant, a satisfyingly complete solution to the distancing problem can only be obtained through combined, multilayered therapeutic interventions.

Of course, not all avoidants should be treated exactly the same way. Different avoidants will need, desire, welcome, and respond to different treatment plans created to fit the individual's specific problematic interactive anxieties. The presence/absence of comorbidity, particularly the presence of paranoid and depressive tendencies, must be taken into account. Also important in formulating a treatment plan are the individual's personal preference for intellectual versus practical approaches; current circumstances and needs (patients with big supportive families often need less hand holding than patients whose avoidance has left them all alone); and the degree of desire to change, as determined by personal aspirations and individual goals and ambitions and ultimately influenced by therapist availability and cost.

In the realm of the patient's personal problematic interactive anxieties, avoidants who are less fundamentally shy than fearful, such as commitment-phobic avoidants who would be outgoing, except for their long-standing, deeply ingrained interpersonal anxiety about becoming fully intimate, may benefit the most from exposure techniques combined with emotional support as they venture forth trying to overcome their all-the-world's-a-stage fright. But patients who are temperamentally more shy and retiring than scared may benefit the most from an ongoing, long-term supportive relationship with a therapist meant to tide them over—as the therapist acts the part of a healer who the patient can rely on long term and cling to, as improvement, it is hoped, takes place, however slowly.

The more intellectually oriented avoidants do best developing insight first, then acting on what they learned next, while the less intellectually oriented avoidants do best first "doing," with "understanding" coming next, if at all. The first group of patients likes to contemplate a journey before, during, and after embarking on it. The second group of patients is satisfied just to be handed a road map. While the first group often does well being told, "Face your fears of parties so that we can analyze those fears as they arise," the second group often does well simply by being urged: "Go to parties for progressively longer periods of time in graduated 'doses' so that you will be able slowly but surely to get used to mingling." Patients who tend to intellectualize do not take well to approaches that are exclusively total push, while patients who are more doers than thinkers feel stalled and cheated by therapists who seem only to want to talk first and expect action next, if at all.

In the realm of differing individual goals, many avoidants are content to work around, rather than attempt to fully overcome, their anxiety. Just as social phobics afraid of being trapped in the theater can simply go through life happily sitting on the aisle in the back row, and social phobics afraid of heights who cannot sit in the theater balcony can, if they can afford it, simply buy a comfortable seat in the orchestra or give up going to the theater altogether; patients with AvPD can seek a lifetime of partial, rather than full, relationships, such as relationships with friends rather than lovers, paid strangers such as waiters or prostitutes, or relationships organized around impersonal gratifications they make subsidiary to interpersonal pleasures such as the gratifications to be gotten from hobby clubs or group therapy. The therapeutic approach must also be geared to the individual's style of relating. Some avoidants really like being isolated. Others are comfortable with a single codependent relationship, hopefully one that promises to last for a lifetime. Still others look forward to only moderate connectivity so they can have the best of both possible (avoidant and nonavoidant) worlds. And some look forward to leading a normal life with only modest compromise or, if possible, none at all.

As to what approach to use first, avoidants who are very anxious or depressed about their lives, especially those who have experienced a series of losses, need support and sometimes pharmacotherapy in the beginning of therapy, with uncovering reserved for later, when the patient's realistic difficulties have become less, or less urgent, so that what suffering there is has now become primarily of an existential nature—not a matter of "what do I do to survive?" but of "how can I look at things differently so that I can feel more alive, connected, and joyful?"

My sessions fall naturally into the following pattern. We develop insight in one session; use the next session to develop a game plan for putting what we just learned into practice (via intersession exposure); have a session or two where we develop further insight, particularly into the anxiety aroused by this new exposure, with all sessions taking place in a setting of continuing support and reassurance along the lines of "you can do it" and "you will not faint or die when going out in public"; have another practice-oriented "game plan" session or two; and so on. A full working-through process comes later. Here we cover the same ground repeatedly and in different contexts, until it all "sinks in," not only intellectually, but also affectively, that is, emotionally—and practice makes perfect.

Simultaneously, I attempt to handle the avoidant's negative and positive resistances to therapy. Most avoidants start off wanting to be helpful to the therapist and to cooperate with treatment. At first, they work with the therapist in a joint endeavor meant to overcome their avoidance. They plead with the therapist to tell them what to do to meet people and how to overcome their relationship anxiety. Later in treatment, however, they almost always begin to balk. *Positive* transference resistances develop where they use the therapist as too much the substitute for a real relationship. *Negative* transference resistances develop where they test the therapist, often to the extreme. They disregard proffered advice and sometimes even deliberately disrupt viable outside relationships in order to make the therapist look defective and impotent. They seek self-understanding only to misuse it. They say, "I will change when I learn," but either they never learn so that they don't have to change, or they learn intellectually but not emotionally so that they can continue to get the gratification that comes from complaining, "See, I've got insight, but it doesn't work." Laboring in therapy under a poor self-concept, feeling guilty about, and fearful of criticism for, their thoughts and feelings, and constantly worrying about whether or not the therapist approves of what they say or do, they become overly cautious and hesitant to discuss important matters openly. Afraid of all closeness, they begin to distance themselves from the therapist by being vocally negative about therapy and about the therapist. Coming to see the therapist as a parent, they refuse to "get married just because you want me to, like my mother did" and otherwise fearfully turn an opportunity to grow into just another occasion to rebel. Finally, as Benjamin suggests, as easily injured individuals who readily "feel degraded or put down by any therapist suggestions [they often] boil . . . over and abruptly quit . . . therapy."[5]

In short, they use therapy as just another opportunity to become avoidant. Therefore therapists must undercut their resistances both directly and indirectly. Undercutting resistances directly means working them out on a conscious level by pointing out who the therapist actually is and is not, for example, "I am not a controlling parent or rival sibling," and by frequently and pointedly reminding patients that they should work with the therapist toward a common goal, not against the therapist toward developing just another avoidant relationship. Undercutting resistances indirectly means analyzing their unconscious origins with the goal of uncovering how present-day resistances are repetitions of old avoidant difficulties now reappearing with the therapist, and so not a thing to be accepted, tolerated, or condoned, but something to be subjected to the same corrective scrutiny as any other manifestation of avoidance occurring not only outside of, but also in, the treatment room.

CHAPTER 11

Psychodynamically Oriented Psychotherapy

The Quality Assurance Project asserts that "individual psychoanalytically oriented psychotherapy is the treatment of choice for [avoidant personality] disorder."[1] This is in contradistinction to most contemporary writings that advocate cognitive-behavioral therapy over all other forms of treatment for avoidant personality disorder (AvPD).

THE BASIC TECHNIQUE

In contrast to cognitive therapy, which emphasizes *correcting*, psychodynamically oriented (psychoanalytically oriented) psychotherapy emphasizes *understanding*. Psychodynamically oriented psychotherapy recognizes that the inner life of avoidants determines a good deal of their outer behavior. Its goal is to help avoidants understand the inner workings of their current removal behaviors through and through so that they can replace withdrawal with new, more comfortable, adaptive, satisfying, and mature interpersonal contacts, free of irrational, unconscious fear. As Millon notes, its method consists of "reconstructing unconscious anxieties"[2] at the roots of the avoidance and exploring the avoidant's anxiety-provoking fantasies as they occur in the patient's present life as well as in his or her transference to the therapist.

INCULCATING INSIGHT

Psychodynamically oriented psychotherapists emphasizing the central role insight plays in attaining a cure focus on strengthening old and inculcating new self-awareness. Many avoidants do not discern that they are avoidant or the extent to which they suffer from AvPD.

A Case Example

An avoidant patient, though aware that he suffered from AvPD, was unaware of the extent to which he was inhibited and of how his inhibitions affected his life, compromising his own functionality and troubling those around him. In the realm of how his avoidance affected his life, he said he was pleased with the way his life was going, even though his fears kept him from leading a full, connected existence and instead forced him into the shadows of dark, anxiety-laden remoteness. But he failed to recognize how masochistically he was acting when he attempted to relate only in circumstances where he was assured that no relationship would develop, and how destructively he acted when he used the Internet not to meet someone, but to act out his avoidances: not advancing his case, but presenting his case history, putting himself in a negative light by offering bad presentations of his good qualities, as when he painted his preference for fidelity as clinging and his flexibility as desperation. Ambivalence of the "caring sharing, no one over 25" sort appeared in his Internet ads as his way not to expand horizons, but to eliminate good possibilities. Rigid preferences and the making of nonnegotiable demands led him to insist that for him, it was crucial that others have identical interests—something he called "compatibility," though for him, it was a reason not for inclusion, but for exclusion. Particularly unwelcoming in his ads was his overemphasis on preferred age and body habitus that amounted not to suggestions about what he would like in someone, but to criticisms of what he disliked about everyone. Not surprisingly, few responded to his ads, and those who did made a date, then broke it, or kept the first date just so that they could break the second—sadistically building up his expectations now, the better to disappoint him later.

In the realm of how his avoidance affected the lives of others, he suspected that his perfectionism troubled and hurt other people who otherwise might love him. He knew, "When it comes to relationships, I hurt my chances by being so demanding." But he failed to recognize how much he had become, to use his last girlfriend's words, a "perfect snob," who hurt others as he dropped someone already good enough, just to look for someone even better.

Other avoidants, though they discern that they are avoidant, deliberately, if unconsciously, downplay and cover up the extent of their avoidance and the degree to which it limits them socially. They paint this distorted picture of themselves to the therapist because they are terrified that the therapist—the very person from whom they seek help—will criticize them like everyone else, ridiculing and humiliating them by dismissing their problems; calling them "lazy losers, wallflowers, and wimps"; condemning them as bad instead of treating them as troubled; and rather than helping them get better, punishing them for being ill. So they censor crucial intimacies out of embarrassment and shame, or they reveal them but simultaneously excuse them as "not me," closing off an in-depth discussion of their psychological problems by blaming their circumstances or other people, as when they present their inability to connect not as an emotional problem of theirs, but as a natural, expected, "anyone would feel that way" response to externals beyond their control. So we hear "you can't meet anyone in this hick town/in a big city like New York," or "none of the bars in this dump are any good," or "my boyfriend is the problem," or "my boss makes me work so hard that I am always too tired to socialize after work," or "everywhere I go villains harass me sexually," or "my parents defeat me at every turn," or "my wife's only goal in life is to torture me." Often citing contemporary "do-your-own-thing" or "me-ism" philosophies, they blame the society in which they live for being a place where everybody encourages them to be avoidant. Frequently, they blame not their psychology, but their biology, and we hear "it's inherited," "I was born this way," "it's not me, it's my chemical imbalance," "I'm ugly," "I have physical problems," "I'm too old," or "my genes hold the real secret of my inability to connect." They also rationalize their avoidance as *healthy*, typically disguising it as a *preference* or *taste*. As an example, one avoidant who nightly dreamed that he wanted to, but was afraid to, meet people, daily rationalized his avoidance as follows: "I prefer to live alone because I can fill the refrigerator with what I want to eat, drop my clothes wherever I want to, play my sound equipment when and how loudly it suits me, and when I go to work and leave a can of soda cooling behind know it will be there just waiting for me when I return."

REDUCING GUILT

Psychodynamically oriented psychotherapists focus on understanding and reducing guilt that creates withdrawal due to rigidly prohibitive, critical, self-unaccepting and self-destructive attitudes, especially those relating to success and survival. Thus an avoidant believed that she should not marry until both a favorite aunt and all her sisters found themselves a husband. Unconsciously, she saw the world as a zero-sum place where getting something for herself necessarily meant hurting others by outshining them—and where getting anything at all meant taking an equivalent something away from someone else.

EXPLORING THE CHOICE OF EGO-IDEALS

Psychodynamically oriented psychotherapists also focus on discovering if avoidants' relational ideals (ego-ideals) are chosen not by, but for, them, that is, if they originate in freewill or are determined by unconscious forces. In my experience, few people are avoidant, and hence alone, by choice. Even those avoidants who swear that they are truly happy in their loneliness and isolation, who insist that their isolation is splendid, and who affirm the wonders of being able to come and go as they please without that proverbial ball and chain around their ankle, really desire closeness and healthy dependency, not the complete freedom that they say they want. Instead, their desire to be free is, in fact, a compunction to remain unattached, and that is, in turn, largely the product of a rigid, self-punitive morality that leads them to be so preoccupied with matters of good and evil that they find themselves forced to squelch their human feelings in order to angle for sainthood and martyrdom, their way to deal with the shame they feel about their anger and to reduce the self-humiliation they put themselves through for having even the most modest of sexual desires.

DEALING WITH UNHEALTHY DEFENSES

Psychodynamically oriented psychotherapists focus on identifying unhealthy defenses so that they can help avoidants first, to relinquish them, and second, to put healthier defenses in their place. Healthier defenses include *counterphobic* defenses, to master anxiety by facing and meeting it head-on, "damn the torpedoes"; and *resignation* defenses, where avoidants learn to tolerate a small amount of anxiety and relax into their fears, instead of resolutely meeting them head-on, only to find that they have made things worse for themselves by trying to fight what is predictably going to be a losing battle.

DEALING WITH SECONDARY GAIN

Psychodynamically oriented psychotherapists routinely ask avoidants to relinquish the secondary gain they harvest from avoidant symptoms once formed. As I ask agoraphobic avoidants to relinquish the pleasure they get from always having a companion on street outings, and social phobics to relinquish the gratification they get from lazily avoiding giving a speech, I ask mingles avoidants to relinquish the gratification they obtain from sex good and plenty and instead seek greater gratification from closeness and commitment: quality over quantity.

DEALING WITH TRANSFERENCE RESISTANCES

Psychodynamically oriented psychotherapists are ever alert to the avoidant negative transference resistances that by highlighting their patients' problems in microcosm serve as useful grist for the analytic mill. Avoidants often resist therapy by avoiding the therapist, the same way they avoid everyone else. They fail to show up for an appointment, call to make another one and break that, come late—calling to say, "I am just leaving from home" about the time their appointment starts or coming at the right time but on the wrong day—all the while apologizing, yet continuing to repeat their actions. Too often, they respond to eureka insight by becoming critical of the therapist who imparted it. Thus, one patient, each time she learned something meaningful, responded by devaluing the teacher (me) to render the teachings less troubling by damning them, and me, into insignificance. Another patient responded to interpretations that made her anxious by reviling me as a know-nothing, damned-if-you-do and damned-if-you-don't doctor. Feeling I pushed her too far, too fast, she complained, "You are making me anxious," yet feeling I was too accepting of her reluctance to try to meet people, she complained, "You aren't doing your job." She then attempted to reduce her anxiety by intensifying mine: by criticizing me personally, first for being lax, and then for being incompetent and unethical. Thus, on the days she thought that I was married, she accused me of having extramarital affairs and trying to seduce her, while on the days she thought I was single, she accused me of being a priestly celibate or a homosexual disinterested in her because I was disinterested in all women.

SUPPLEMENTAL TECHNIQUES

Psychodynamically oriented psychotherapy is rarely fully effective unless accompanied by supplementary methods employed to put the understanding obtained to use. Exposure techniques do more than just habituate the individual to anxiety directly. They also simultaneously facilitate the psychoanalytic process by releasing anxious thoughts that can then be brought back into therapy for discussion. Pharmacotherapy can help subdue fear and reduce guilt, and meditation and deep-breathing exercises can help the avoidant relax, putting him or her into a better frame of mind to work on understanding what went wrong in preparation for doing something to make it right.

A Case Example

A patient, an avoidant in both his professional and his personal lives, entered therapy complaining that he was too shy to meet old and make new friends, and certainly to meet someone to become his partner. At work, he volunteered for night duty so that he would not have to interact with too many coworkers or spend too much time with his family. In his personal life, he had one love affair when he was very young and never had another. Many years ago, when he was a teenager, he fell in love with the girl next door, but he was too shy to speak to her directly. The best he could do to make contact was to tie a romantic message for her on an arrowhead and shoot the arrow over the fence and into her yard. He thought that that was just the right flourish. Instead, he was surprised, and chagrined, to discover that the next phone call wasn't from her, but from the police.

As an adult, he kept one or two old friends to satisfy his (minimal) attachment needs, and on those rare occasions when he agreed to go to parties, once there he stood in the shadows in a corner of the room looking longingly at, but unable to join in with, the people having fun. He scared off what few people he managed to approach, or who approached him, by putting them in no-win situations, rejecting them both if they acted friendly (because he feared people who got too close) and if they acted unfriendly (because he disliked people who kept their distance). Then he would leave for home early, and all by himself, to return to his small apartment, where he could watch television with the phone pulled and the intercom turned off (using a special switch he installed), accepting only e-mail because that way, "instead of being the passive victim of anyone who decides to call and bother me, I can pick up my messages when, and only when, I choose."

On occasion, later in life, he was able to start a serious romance, only to pull back early in the game after telling himself that it would not work out. First, he brooded about all the mistakes he might make that, as he was convinced, would turn the other person off. Then he would perversely actually make those mistakes so that he could ensure that his gloomy predictions would come true because nothing could ever work out for him. Then he would think, "I already ruined things, so why bother continuing?" and in anticipation of complete disaster, he would become protectively remote and distant and bolt before a potential partner could, as he soon became convinced would happen, lose interest in him.

In reality, other people did not much take to him. His appearance made it difficult for him to connect with the very few people he felt comfortable knowing. As he said, "They call me 'Skull' because of my sunken eyes and cheekbones, 'weird' because my face is asymmetrical, and 'peculiar' because as I walk, I keep one shoulder higher than the other." However, instead of doing what he could to improve his appearance, he confined himself to checking in the mirror from time to time—assessing flaws, overlooking virtues, and not really thinking about making those repairs that were both indicated and possible. Unconsciously, he held himself back because he actually wanted to look strange to others—so that others would continue to remain complete strangers to him.

Over the years, he developed a number of social phobias relating to different specific trivial prompts symbolizing a variety of deep, interpersonal terrors. In part, he had installed these phobias so that he could avoid getting close to people, his way to live out his motto, "If you fear visiting them, you won't go, and if you don't go, you won't have to invite them back." He could drive over bridges when he was not going to a date's house, but when he was, he could not make it across due to the fear that he would faint, lose control of his car, hit an abutment, and have a fatal accident. Additionally, he was unable to take the train because he feared it would crash. He also developed a phobia of being in church. During the service, he had to sit near the exit door so that in case he should feel weak and faint, he could get out without calling attention to himself.

Eventually, he began to have some difficulty venturing out of doors at all. During the day, he had trouble going out because he feared being stung by flying insects, particularly wasps, and because he feared a repetition of an incident where a policeman had stopped him for no reason at all and asked him, in what he thought was an accusatory fashion, where he was going. Next, he completely stopped traveling from his home town to the city for all the reasons just mentioned and because he had become convinced that the second he got off the train, someone would approach him, pick his pocket, and strand him by taking the money he needed for the return trip.

In spite of these limitations, and the considerable suffering attendant upon them, he claimed that being an avoidant had many advantages.

As he, in essence, put it, "It's great keeping my positive emotions in check. That way I can avoid humiliating myself by expressing feelings that I consider to be both so passionate as to be embarrassing and so common as to be trite. Besides, I do not really need other people. All I need comes from within. I enjoy my own company best. I like being isolated and get a great deal of pleasure from being able to go home, sit there surrounded by the things I love, and come and go as I please. I enjoy collecting things so much that I feel that the worst day at the flea market is better than the best day at the meat market, and anyway, my cat is my best friend, someone I can always count on—unlike everybody else I have met up to now."

Our therapeutic work consisted in part of understanding in depth how his avoidances began. For example, we learned that his fear of criticism partly originated in his early relationship with a mother who savaged him when he did things wrong, without also complimenting him when he did things right, to the point that, as he put it, with a sort of humorous resignation, "She actually died before she could say even a single nice thing to or about me."

We also uncovered, clarified, and analyzed the here-and-now fantasies that made up his current avoidant symptoms. We discovered that his shyness partly consisted of his staying away from people out of concern that he would take anyone he met away from someone else, much as his siblings took his mother away from him. An intense moral scrupulosity also led him to fear that others might criticize him for his sexual feelings. Too, he wanted to be a good role model for others he believed should, when it came to sexual relationships, follow his lead and be just as Spartan and abstemious as he was. As he described it, his was an advocacy for the highest level of morality, whose means of getting rid of temptation was not, as Oscar Wilde said, to yield to it, but, as he said, to get rid of the people who tempted him.

We discovered that for him, stinging insects symbolized his critical mother, as did the preacher in church and the policeman on the street. We further learned that he could not take the train because the moving train symbolized his impulses and train crashes the dreadful consequences of having and expressing them. Driving over the bridge symbolized his fears of forward movement and success—reaching the pinnacle, only to be mauled physically (i.e., castrated) as a consequence of soaring.

We analyzed his church phobia as due both to a fear of being submissive ("controlled by the proceedings") and to a fear of being embarrassed publicly should he get too emotional about the service and lose control. The latter fear had some basis in reality, for on more than one occasion, just a small amount of alcohol released his inhibitions to the point that he acted aggressively in public and said nasty things to people he hardly knew—mostly, but not always, under his breath.

Such understandings gleaned over several years of therapy helped him deal with his relationship anxiety enough to form tentative, partially intimate relationships. He kept his old friends and developed a few new ones. He moved in with a woman he felt comfortable with, partly because she was an avoidant herself: an unassuming, undemanding person who desired little closeness and intimacy from him or from anyone else. They fought a great deal and threatened to leave each other on a regular basis, but that was only their way to reassure themselves, and each other, that neither was engulfing, or being engulfed by, the other.

On follow-up, he said that now was the happiest time of his life, although he recognized, "As my therapist, you are probably disappointed in me, thinking that the adjustment I made is somewhat less than ideal, at least according to what I consider to be your overly rigorous standards: particularly what I perceive (and you know that I am right!) to be your belief that everyone should get married, and that anything less than marriage represents an unsatisfactory adjustment to life, because by definition it represents a lesser way to live."

CHAPTER 12

Cognitive-Behavioral Therapy

COGNITIVE THERAPY

Cognitive therapists identify, illuminate, and challenge avoidant logical distortions with the goal of correcting specific errors of thinking (avoidant ideation) likely to generate avoidant behavior. The therapeutic goal is to help patients think and act more rationally and productively so that they can more readily connect with others, and even commit to a long-term, lasting, loving relationship with someone special.

Along these lines, Beck elicits, challenges, and attempts to correct automatic thoughts, such as "others view me as socially inept and undesirable," that lead to avoidant withdrawal, that in turn leads others to counter with "unfriendly . . . behaviors and actions."[1] Beck reality tests these thoughts by asking avoidants to "apply . . . rules of evidence," "consider . . . alternative explanations," and solve interpersonal problems by "putting aside the subjective meanings they attach to a communication and focusing on the objective content"[2] so that, for example, avoidants can recognize that someone, merely by expressing a personal need, is not per se blaming them for not having gratified it.

Along similar lines, scattered throughout his book, Rapee offers cognitive-reparative approaches to treating shyness and social phobia. These can be paraphrased and summarized as follows:

- learn how to interpret and think about situations and other people more realistically, for example, through learning that feelings and emotions are directly caused by thoughts, attitudes, and beliefs, not by the things going on on the outside

- identify and change basic beliefs and unwritten laws such as "everyone must like me, and if I am not liked, I am worthless"
- identify and challenge basic fears—the things that make you anxious
- don't overestimate the likelihood that bad things will happen in social situations
- ask, "What is the evidence for my alarmist expectations?" and reassuringly tell yourself, "If the worst should occur, so what?"
- Practice attention-strengthening exercises to help pay strict attention to the task at hand.[3]

A Case Example

A shy patient hesitated to leave the house because some of his neighbors did not say hello to him on his morning walk—he believed because they did not like him. I helped him reframe his conclusions about the supposedly noxious behavior of his neighbors so that he could become more realistic about this and other similarly terrifying interpersonal situations. I suggested that he apply the rules of evidence, consider alternative explanations, and pay strict attention to the task at hand—which involved focusing on the objective content of what his neighbors were saying, not on the subjective meaning he was attaching to their communications. I clarified that while some of his neighbors might dislike him, others were simply caught up in their own little world, thought *he* didn't see *them*, or, if they did, did not want to call out his name because it was early in the morning and they were afraid of waking up the whole neighborhood. I clarified that his neighbors did not reject him because they thought that they were superior to him, and would not reject him even more when, getting to know him better, they saw his flaws more clearly. I also suggested that when making contact with people, he should monitor his anxiety to make certain that it does not exceed bearable limits, and if it does, he should pull back and try again the next time. For example, I suggested that to avoid creating internal unpleasantness, he should not, as was his habit, discuss politics and religion, but instead promptly switch the discussion to neutral issues such as the weather, or impersonal, unthreatening matters such as the real estate values in the neighborhood.

Some cognitive therapists stress the importance of spotting, identifying, and correcting cognitive errors as they arise in the transference. To illustrate, an avoidant who learned that her therapist was not being critical of her simply because she was correcting her cognitive errors thereby learned that her husband still loved her, even though he didn't always agree with everything she said.

Some cognitive therapists use role-playing, where they ask patients to put themselves in others' places for the purpose of developing truer assumptions about what others have in mind. In one case, a patient who felt he was being rejected because he didn't get an immediate reply to an e-mail he sent was able, after putting himself in the (over-worked) recipient's place, to understand that the response was delayed simply because the person who received the e-mail was currently busy. (I describe role-playing, a predominantly behavioral technique, further later.)

Avoidants, especially those who snap at others in retaliation for imagined criticism, can also benefit from empathy enhancement, a technique that involves reducing transactional negativity through understanding where the other person is "coming from."

Some Case Examples

Shortly after a man's wife died, she received a notice from the internist who took care of her asking her to please come in for her annual physical examination. Her husband was outraged at first, but when I asked my patient to put himself in the doctor's place to explore the possible reasons for the doctor's confusion, the patient recognized that it was nothing personal and that the doctor, however misguided, was ultimately primarily concerned about his wife's welfare. So instead of getting mad, and even, he called to tell the doctor's office that his wife had died, to thank her doctor for treating her, and to commend the doctor for his continuing concern, however misguided, for the state of her health.

A psychiatrist felt passed over when an internist called not on him, but on a psychologist colleague, for a consultation with the internist's patient. The psychiatrist remained angry until his own therapist pointed out that he, the therapist, knew (for personal reasons) that the internist was merely living out a positive relationship with his own psychotherapist, also a psychologist.

An avoidant vendor out of the morning newspaper reacted to the question, "Do you have any more of these newspapers?" with "It's not my fault that I am out of them—why is everyone bugging me?" As his therapist, I suggested that he put himself in the place of his customers and see that they were expressing not a criticism of him, but a need of theirs, so that he should instead try a shorter, sweeter, less interpersonally divisive, more accommodating reply: "Sorry, no."

Some therapists actively suggest positive thoughts patients can install to counter their negative cognitions. For example, a therapist first helped a patient who feared public speaking because he feared he would faint think less catastrophically about what might happen if he actually did faint, however unlikely that possibility. He next suggested that the patient hold a countervailing, distractive, reassuring thought while giving his speech: "my anxiety always dissipates a few minutes after I get started."

Therapists often help patients think less catastrophically by supportively, soothingly reassuring them that anxiety almost always subsides shortly after a feared activity, such as going to a party or driving over a bridge, begins. What happens is that patients crest over what I call their "phobic hump," at which time their anxiety diminishes or disappears, to be replaced by positive feelings of mastery, pride in accomplishment, joy in activity, and elated feelings both pleasurable in themselves and a source of motivation and courage to try again.

Therapists can help their patients think less catastrophically about being criticized, humiliated, and rejected by helping them enhance their self-esteem. They can do that by helping them develop reference points independent of their need for and the results of impression management. Patients can more clearly see the evidence for and against dark forebodings and disjunctive fears if they stop the self-spectatoring involved in attempting to constantly improve upon the grades they bestow on themselves in their own continuously self-administered interpersonal "report cards." Avoidants can also helpfully ask themselves what it is about other people that makes it so necessary for them to actually hand out bad grades, trying to see, as is almost certainly the case, that "it's their problem, not mine, because people these days only talk about themselves." Avoidants can profitably ask themselves if the people actually humiliating, criticizing, and rejecting them are really important enough for their negativity to matter and take seriously to the point that it takes hold. And avoidants who have actually been personally "downgraded" and rejected can reassuringly tell themselves, when applicable, that "it's their loss, not mine."

Unfortunately, "illogical" cognitions can be resistant to corrective logic when there is enough reality to the so-called illogic to make full reality testing and reassurance difficult or impossible. Because planes do sometimes crash, it is not possible to offer blanket reassurance to phobic patients that flying is completely safe. Similarly, it is as impossible to completely dismiss the appropriateness of opening night jitters when performing before critics as it is impossible to completely dismiss the possibility of rejection when meeting new friends and lovers.

Because cognitive therapy inherently involves challenging how patients think, and because all challenges by their very nature are invariably critical, therapists should always do cognitive therapy in the context of a supportive holding therapeutic environment, where they offer patients countervailing comfort, reassurance, and understanding. They might repeat something supportive such as "most people share your anxiety and fears, at least to some extent" and "don't blame yourself for making the thinking errors you make, for while it might be necessary for therapeutic purposes for me to speak as if you are entirely responsible for making the cognitive errors we discuss, we both understand that even your most unrealistic negative cognitions are, to some extent, particularly in a person as sensitive as you, set off by the antagonistic cognitions, and provocative behaviors, of others."

BEHAVIORAL THERAPY

Social Skills Training

Social skills that do not develop automatically as a consequence of changing one's self-destructive thinking can be taught, leading, as the Quality Assurance Project notes, to "areas of increased social activities with decreased associated anxiety, a lessening of social isolation with diminished depression, and the loss of many irrational social beliefs."[4] Scattered throughout Anthony and Swinson's book are direct suggestions to patients as to how they can better interact and communicate effectively with others. To paraphrase these authors, they suggest avoidants learn to listen, modify off-putting nonverbal communication, and develop conversational skills. They teach them how to go on job interviews; how to communicate assertively instead of too passively (hesitantly, shyly) or passive-aggressively; how to meet new people, make new friends, and date; and how to develop public speaking skills. They help them learn to control avoidant fretting in settings in which these behaviors are brought to the fore and lead to less than satisfactory human transactions.[5] For example, they might teach them not to offer others a limp hand for an introductory handshake and to look people directly in the eye when they speak to them, instead of looking off into the distance, ostrich-like, thinking, "If I don't see them, they won't see me either."

GRADED EXPOSURE

As noted throughout, behavioral therapists suggest patients perform individual tasks of graded difficulty geared to overcoming specific avoidant inhibitions. Thus Benjamin suggests that therapists help
avoidants block maladaptive patterns with "desensitization to avoided
social situations [by having the patient try out] successive approximations to more sociability." She also emphasizes that therapists can best
accomplish this if they give their avoidant patients "much reassurance
in a context of competent, protective instruction."[6]

Avoidants doing what makes them afraid in small increments must
not let temporary setbacks unduly discourage them. As Rapee suggests, to become habituated to anxiety, avoidants need to "stay in a
situation until [they start to] calm down," and they must not let themselves "be discouraged by bad days."[7]

Here are some ways a representative sampling of my avoidant patients underwent gradual exposure to feared situations:

They got out of the house and talked to strangers, saying hello to
just one new person a day.

They responded to a stranger who said hello, instead of questioning
the stranger's intentions, then averting their eyes.

They stopped walking by people they saw, acting as if they didn't
see them.

They discussed a problem they were having with the person they
were having it with, instead of retreating from or ignoring that person as "difficult."

They went to work even when they didn't feel like it, instead of calling out sick in order to have a "mental health day."

They broadened their horizons, for example, by answering the
phone, instead of letting the answering machine pick up the call.
Though they did not have a partner, instead of staying home and
eating all by themselves, feeling sorry for themselves, they went
out to dinner alone. They bought a computer so that they could
get e-mail from their friends, modified favored hobbies to do them
with other people—collecting stamps in a group, instead of by
themselves, or buying a book in a real bookstore, instead of in the
remoteness of cyberspace. At work, they forced themselves to join
in group conversations and sit with others in the cafeteria, instead

of sipping coffee alone or taking their lunch to a park bench and eating it there in isolation.

They went to bars or onto the Internet for networking, meeting as many people as they possibly could, then slowly but surely winnowing relationships down perhaps to one significant other.

They accepted dates arranged for them, instead of protesting based on preconceived notions that reflected preexisting avoidances, turning "blind dates" down for purported philosophical reasons that were little more than rationalizations of self-defeating motives.

Patients can expose themselves not only to uncomfortable *external*, but also to uncomfortable *internal* sensations (interoceptive exposure) so that they can learn to better tolerate their inner anxiety experiences. For example, they can learn to tolerate dysphoric feelings by conjuring up frightening fantasied situations in their mind, starting with the mildest anxieties and ratcheting up to the most frightening, letting these all work their way through their thoughts and emotions. The self-analysis of their dreams can provide new and helpful self-discoveries.

Exposure therapy works in part because it helps avoidants achieve minor successes, which reduces full despair about complete social failure. Success breeds success because real accomplishment enhances self-esteem by promoting self-pride that increases self-confidence, which leads to improved functionality that further enhances motivation (for motivation comes as much from doing as the other way around). Avoidants who relate at all successfully discover that relationships make them feel good about themselves; feeling good about themselves makes them feel more worthy of relating; and feeling more worthy of relating helps them relate even better. Additionally, actually being in a positive relationship helps reduce negative symptoms—as the positive energy from real-life friendships flows back into reducing underlying maladaptive, automatic thoughts and irrational beliefs, allowing fuller, more satisfactory human transactions to occur, while providing support and structure that predictably reduce avoidant anxiety. For example, a patient was unable to ride on a train until she decided to force herself to visit a potential partner she met on the Internet. Now, feeling enveloped in his protective warmth, she was able to make the trip and to do so virtually anxiety-free.

This said, avoidants who are both patient and highly motivated can bypass the need for incremental, step-by-step exposure and deal with the worst first in an attempt at instant mastery, deliberately increasing their anxiety to a painful (but supportable) level, hoping to break through to health all at once, instead of gradually, and before all their deep fears of closeness have been definitively resolved.

MANIPULATION

A phobic pass or other talisman can help those avoidants who are impressionable enough to believe in magic. Some therapists give an avoidant afraid of going to a party a signed slip of paper that reads, "Pocket and hold on to this and you will be okay on your date tonight." Others give a social phobic afraid of public speaking a slip of paper that says, "You will be able to get through your speech without having your voice crack, or passing out."

ROLE-PLAYING

This helps patients spot specific relationship problems so that they can begin to relate in new, less tentative, more effective, less self-destructive ways. Videotapes of avoidants interacting with others with the avoidant speech and behavior patterns edited out to create a new, more nonavoidant performance can show avoidants what exactly they can do now to act less avoidant in the future.

INJECTING THE THERAPIST'S PERSONAL NONAVOIDANT PHILOSOPHY

Once, hoping to teach a patient how relationship difficulties can be overcome through yielding, compromise, and positivity, I quoted W. H. Auden's 1957 poem, "The More Loving One": "If equal affection cannot be / let the more loving one be me."[8]

PARADOXICAL THERAPY

Jay Haley's *paradoxical therapy* is a form of behavioral treatment that is, in some ways, the *opposite* of exposure therapy. Here patients are asked, or told, *not* to do the very thing that they should be doing—that very thing that makes them most anxious. The therapist counts on the patient's native stubbornness and oppositionalism to surface and lead to fearless counterphobic and hence healthy action.[9] For example, one therapist suggested a patient take a vacation from relationships, anticipating that as a stubborn, resistant avoidant, he would do exactly the opposite of what the therapist advocated—relate to others, just to defy the therapist!

Paradoxical approaches are particularly helpful for sexual avoidants because they almost predictably lyse inhibitions by evoking the lure of the forbidden. Sexual avoidants often experience an enhancement of sexual desire plus an urge to actually have the prohibited sex they were formerly unable to have simply because now, told to cease and desist, they feel tempted to sneak around and start having it against the therapist's wishes and behind the therapist's back.

Enhancing Motivation

Therapists can enhance an avoidant's motivation to relate by enumerating the benefits and rewards of relating, hoping to convince the patient that such rewards are sufficiently great to make it worthwhile to experience the discomfort involved.

Urging Patience

I remind patients that they will not be better by tomorrow because they did not become avoidant overnight. Also, most avoidants both like and need the way they are and fear the alternative too much to become instantly nonavoidant just on a therapist's say-so. For in one sense, avoidance is a philosophy, an entrenched, much-beloved, personal value system, and in another sense, patients need their avoidance because it is a defense that reduces anxiety, if only by offering breathing room in interpersonal crises—an opportunity to regroup forces in preparation for making the next, terrifying move. Too, nonavoidance, like almost all new behaviors, requires practice before it can become perfect and second nature. Finally, pushing oneself too far, too fast into feared encounters can lead to such intense anxiety that in response, avoidants may quit therapy or stay in treatment but, therapeutically speaking, drag their feet to reestablish their comfort level.

Journaling

Journaling/workbooking can clarify and critique one's avoidant positions and firm up what needs to be done to better reposition oneself interpersonally. Journaling is discussed further in chapter 20.

RELAXATION TECHNIQUES

Deep breathing and muscle relaxation can help induce a state of calm and control the hyperventilation that often accompanies interpersonal anxiety.

CREATING RIGHT-BRAIN ACTIVITY

Right-brain activity (the product of emotions) can blot out left-brain activity (characterized by faulty, worrisome thinking). For example, an avoidant anxious about public speaking can blot out stage fright by thinking about a joyous celebratory dinner to come "if I get through this."

HAVING JOINT/GROUP EXPOSURE

Avoidants can get together with ex-avoidants to consult with them to find out how these ex-avoidants became nonavoidant. They can also join in with other active avoidants to egg each other on as powerful allies in a joint program to conquer relational panic.

Of course, certain avoidant problems are more amenable to behavioral therapy than others. The shy patient who fears meeting someone new at a party can attempt trial connecting, but the more outgoing patient who can start but not see a relationship through to its conclusion cannot be reasonably expected to attempt trial committing.

Behavioral cures can unfortunately backfire, leading to increased isolation. For example, although avoidance can be made more tolerable with hobbies, it is usually a better idea to make hobbies more tolerable with nonavoidance so that avoidants don't while away lonely hours keeping busy, instead of busying themselves making the hours less lonely. So often, solitary hobbies increase isolation by acting as reminders of how much one is missing. So the often given behavioral remedy "get a hobby if you can't relate" should be corrected to "relate, so that you don't have to get a hobby."

CHAPTER 13

Interpersonal Therapy

Sullivan places the focus of therapy on interpersonal anxiety[1]; that is, he studies old and new interpersonal distortive fantasies in order to correct resultant transactional removal behaviors that keep patients from getting close and developing anxiety-free intimate relationships. Frieda Fromm-Reichmann describes the goals of treatment as a "potential freedom from fear, anxiety, and the entanglements of greed, envy, and jealousy . . . actualized by the development of [the] capacity for self-realization, [the] ability to form durable relationships of intimacy with others, and [the ability] to give and accept mature love."[2] Millon and Davis emphasize having "a 'corrective emotional experience' with the therapist," with the therapist serving as a mirror for everyday relationships and offering a positive experience that it is hoped would "generalize to [other] contexts outside of the therapy hour."[3]

I focus on the dyadic unit as a way to understand one or both of its individual members. I identify avoidant interactive behaviors, bring them to the patients' attention, and study their conscious and unconscious meanings. I try to learn about the special circumstances under which interpersonal withdrawal actions appear, that is, the "when," or the exact moment, that the avoidant begins to pull back from others, and to learn about the "why," that is, the reasons for the retreat. Do avoidants become anxious in some situations but not in others, and withdraw from some but not from all people? Do some feel comfortable with a person "of their own kind," but withdraw from people who are significantly unlike themselves, for example, "beneath them" or "better than I am," or of a different color, race, religion, or social status? Or is it just the reverse: do they feel uncomfortable with a person

of their own kind and seek, almost compulsively, someone as much unlike themselves as possible?

I also correct interpersonal cognitive errors, for example, I suggest
avoidants stop exaggerating relational dangers so that closeness equates
to commitment, entrapment, and fatal smothering. I ask avoidants to
stop overestimating the degree to which others are being negative to
them, turning a cancelled dinner date into a catastrophic signal that
all relationships will henceforward be troubled and doomed. I ask
avoidants to try only to react fully positively in safe situations with
family, chums, and potential or actual partners who are warm, yielding, permissive, and available, and to react with at least some caution
in dangerous situations such as those where the possibility of fulfillment is weak. I especially warn them not to attempt to get close to
others who are by nature distant, unfeeling, forbidden, and unavailable
such as people who are already taken, like "almost divorced" men who
promise to leave their wives but have no intention of ever doing so.

I teach avoidants specific interpersonal skills. In particular, I ask
them to identify and reduce the contribution they make to the distancing process, where they create relational negativity by behaving
in a way that others will predictably find off-putting, if not openly
insulting.

I strongly suggest that avoidants routinely exercise their power of
positivity—striving to be nice and generous to, and less overly demanding of, others so that they come to act in the same healing way
toward other people that they would want other people to act toward
them. Being nice is always good practice for avoidants, and that usually involves becoming less critical and demanding of, and more for-
bearing toward, others, and failing that, if they must feel and behave
negatively about and to others, doing so in as restrained a manner
as possible so that they can at least leave the door open to making
amends—apologizing after the fact, then going back. Being nice also
involves being generous—giving others something without expecting
to get something in return. That often starts with reducing excessive
expectations of others to avoid disappointment that can lead to punishing those who have done one a good-enough good deed.

A Case Example

A student wrote to me asking how he could get a copy of my book
on writer's block, which he wanted to read but couldn't afford on his
small allowance. I guided him, I thought graciously, on how to get the
book out of the library, only to have him criticize me and the library

as follows: "I'll order a document copy mailed out (I don't fully understand what the hell this is, to be honest; you'd think they'd make it clear, operating a service and all . . . I mean, they won't loan me the book by mail order, but they'll photocopy every page and mail them to me? I mean . . . seriously, who would do that?). I've read your book on paranoia, by the way, not because I'm paranoid. It just seemed interesting, and I like to read a lot, y' know. I'm not really interested in self-help stuff, to be brutal, I tend to think things come and go, are what they are, so to speak, and if you've got a pretty good handle on yourself, you know when to turn a page—forward or back. Y' know what I mean?"

I also suggest avoidants, such as the student I just quoted, be empathic: not getting sidetracked onto how others make *them* feel to the extent that they lose focus on how they make *others* feel, as they address only their own emotional needs and not those of the people around them. I advise avoidants that they can best be empathic if they appreciate the good in others, and they can do that by better understanding others' feelings, needs, and motivations as well as by seeking benign explanations for others' presumably bad behaviors, forgiving their small transgressions, and thus giving others an opportunity to save face, and themselves the opportunity to retain the possibility of making repairs.

Finally, I ask avoidants to give up their need for full identity maintenance. I remind avoidants afraid of relinquishing any aspect of their identity to a significant other that as the singer Joni Mitchell said, when it comes to love, "some loss of self is inevitable."[4] I also emphasize that new and often more pleasurable identities emerge in close, intimate relationships, particularly the identity of being a happily partnered/happily married individual. I also point out that avoidants can, if they like, compensate for any loss of personal identity they will probably incur in a relationship by developing a new and stronger professional identity independent of, and supplemental to, the personal identity that they are so often highly terrified of losing completely.

CHAPTER 14

Supportive Therapy

Supportive therapy for avoidant individuals consists of what Benjamin calls "generous doses of . . . empathy and warm support . . . delivered without a hint of judgmentalism or rejection . . . provid[ing] evidence of a safe haven" where acceptance rules. Benjamin also notes that in therapy, "the AVD's [avoidant's] pattern is an especially intense version of the 'generic' patient position. He or she wants to be accepted and loved, and 'holds back' because of poor self-concept and fears of humiliation. The 'generic' therapist position addresses this 'generic' patient position," gradually helping the AVD share "intimacies and feelings of inadequacy or guilt and shame," while the therapist's "benign and nonjudgmental acceptance of the AVD helps the AVD begin to accept himself or herself [and] as the therapy relationship strengthens, the patient can begin to explore his or her patterns."[1]

Following are three important cornerstones of my own supportive therapy approach to avoidants.

LIKING AND RESPECTING THE PATIENT

Patients who perceive that their therapist likes and respects them feel that the therapist truly wants to help, leading them to feel accepted, rather than rejected—a healing therapeutic response that can persist long after psychotherapy is over, as the patient carries the therapist's positivity around inside, with the therapist having become at least the one person in the avoidant's life different from rejecting mother, emasculating father, and all the other hurtful and cruel people that inhabit the world of the avoidant's scary past, frightening present, and dreaded future.

OFFERING THE PATIENT REASSURANCE

Here are some reassuring messages that I give my anxious avoidant patients.

EVERYONE EXPERIENCES A DEGREE OF SOCIAL ANXIETY

Avoidant patients who feel uniquely troubled, or uniquely bad, often find it reassuring to learn that they are not alone—because almost everyone gets anxious in social situations. Indeed, a big difference between a healthy and an avoidant response is the willingness to accept and tolerate a degree of social anxiety and continue to function in spite of it.

SOCIAL ANXIETY CAN BE OVERCOME

Avoidant patients almost always benefit from hearing that their prognosis is good, for they have the gift of relating already inside, and "all" they have to do is unwrap it.

ALL OF US (EVEN AVOIDANTS) HAVE SOME CONTROL OVER WHAT WE ALLOW OTHERS TO DO TO US

Avoidants, like everyone else, have the option of staying away from, or getting out of, relationships with difficult *avoidogenic individuals* (those who would make anyone anxious and drive just about everyone away) without feeling guilty or being criticized or stigmatized for doing so.

CRITICISM IS RARELY FATAL

Most of us survive the criticism that all of us get from time to time, no matter who we are or what we do. For example, most of us get through being put in can't-win situations similar to that of the woman who was criticized for being a slut for showing her sexual feelings, then criticized for being cold, unavailable, and unresponsive for hiding them.

THERE ARE WAYS TO MAKE EVEN DEVASTATING CRITICISM MORE TOLERABLE

Avoidants can find strength and approval from within by refusing to calculate their self-worth by their so-called reputation. It helps to recognize how often not us, but our critics, are the ones who deserve censure for elevating their own self-esteem by lowering the self-esteem of others. Furthermore, there is often a bright side to being criticized, as people identify, sympathize with, and move in to support the underdog. Dealing with criticism is discussed further in chapter 17.

Fears Are Worries, Not Realities

Avoidants can be reassured that there is little or no justification for many of their fears. Flooding by and depletion of one's life force due to letting strong feelings loose can occur, but it is almost always mild and transitory, consisting of a mere passing sensation of fatigue. And while there are documented cases of grooms and best men passing out during a wedding ceremony (but with few to no real consequences), I know of only a relatively few documented cases of public speakers actually fainting (at least for emotional reasons) while giving a speech or appearing on TV.

Guilt Is Almost Always an Overresponse

Guilt over minor peccadilloes is mostly the product of distortive thinking about one's past and present behavior, leading to inappropriate low self-esteem that breeds self-criticism and hence even more guilt.

Anxiety Almost Always Subsides Shortly after Starting an Activity

Cresting over a phobic hump occurs as a result of denial and habituation so that anxiety disappears, to be replaced by a feeling of mastery, pride in accomplishment, joy in activity, and sense of general elation—all of which are both pleasurable in themselves and a source of courage to try again.

A Case Example

A patient afraid to drive over a bridge at first refused to try because he was generally too anxious to leave home and because of specific fears that something terrible might happen if he got behind the wheel: he would faint, lose control of his car, and, bumping and crashing into other cars, die and kill others in a fiery crackup. One day, he nonetheless forced himself to drive over a bridge. Predictably, anxiety began as soon as he got near the base of the bridge and increased as he ascended; then, as he crested, his anxiety turned into a feeling of euphoria due to delight in accomplishment—happiness about his triumph both over the obstacle bridge and his need to avoid it, and ecstasy over his having successfully mastered his bridge terror. (However, the entire cycle began once again the next time he tried to drive over the same bridge.) Things were much the same for him when he forced himself to attend a party. He felt anxious at the beginning of the evening. The anxiety worsened as the evening progressed. However, after an hour or so, the anxiety peaked and began to diminish, to the point that he was able to introduce himself to one or two people. Now he felt quite pleased and delighted with himself and began to function almost normally. This feeling lasted for the rest of the evening (once again, only to restart the next time he went to a party).

GIVING THE PATIENT GOOD ADVICE

Pinsker generally discourages giving patients specific advice. He tells them that "for $11.98, you can buy books that tell you what to do."[2] Instead, he prefers to outline general principles. I feel that outlining general principles, while an excellent idea for treating most patients, may be wrong for those avoidants who misinterpret hands-off approaches as a lack of caring on the part of an unconcerned therapist.

This said, therapists who give advice should explain that taking it does not make one a dependent pushover. They should also caution patients to do what works for them, and not to do something simply on the therapist's say-so (or on the basis of myths currently in circulation). They should also avoid too specifically telling patients exactly what to do in situations where different reasonable options exist, for here individual choice must reign. I personally feel most comfortable giving avoidants advice on how to develop social skills and overcome specific avoidant pathology. For example, I feel comfortable suggesting that Type I avoidants try to overcome their shyness by "getting out there and meeting new people," while listing some places they might actually go to do just that. But I believe it would be presumptuous of me to decide who among those they actually meet are right, and who are wrong, for them.

Not all avoidants are candidates for the same advice. Therapists giving advice should respect the level of nonavoidance a given individual wishes to achieve—how much closeness and intimacy he or she wants out of life and is capable of attaining. Some so-called avoidants truly want to be loners. Still others long for a close but not a fully intimate relationship. For some, marriage is the right and only goal; others fear it will ruin their and their partner's lives. Each avoidant has to determine for himself or herself what, on a continuum from social isolation to full closeness and intimacy, is desirable and possible and suggest the therapist intervene accordingly. And the therapist should always ascertain how much sacrifice an individual is willing to make for relationships in the way of the inevitable negative accoutrements of meaningful connecting: some loss of self and a diminution of autonomy and independence.

Here are some examples of advice I have given to avoidants that they subsequently told me they found to be helpful.

DEVELOP A NONAVOIDANT OUTLOOK

Avoidants should recognize that the downsides of being alone are far greater than the anxiety associated with closeness, intimacy, and commitment.

SEEK CONSENSUAL VALIDATION

Avoidants can benefit from confiding how anxious they feel to others. Doing so avoids their seeming to reject others, for most people predictably mistake personal shyness for disdain targeted at them, leaving others less sympathetic and more antagonistic.

LEARN THE ART OF POSITIVITY

As emphasized throughout, avoidants should try to act as positively as they can toward others, becoming kind, generous, and forgiving, instead of being testily unwilling to extend themselves halfway and refusing to negotiate and compromise. They should become empathic as they eschew narcissistic self-preoccupied pulse taking, thinking only of "my anxiety," without also considering others' feelings, needs, and motivations. Sensitively addressing others' emotional needs, not only one's own, consists of being as apologetic, supportive, generous, and unsadistic as one's anxiety and need for withdrawal will allow, while whenever possible offering others an explanation of one's avoidance: "I am not being antagonistic; I am simply feeling afraid."

THINK TWICE BEFORE HOOKING UP WITH TRULY ANTAGONISTIC INDIVIDUALS

Examples of individuals best avoided follow:

- those who serve as bad examples because they themselves are seriously avoidant and proud of it, such as people who put things before people, like fussy housekeepers who won't invite anyone over to the house because they fear that they will ruin the furniture
- rationalizers of their own inappropriate aggressiveness as mere assertiveness
- pessimists who tout tragic fiction and sad songs to affirm their belief that few, if any, relationships ever work out—one reason why "life sucks"
- paranoids who can neither trust nor be trusted
- hypermoral individuals who condemn as sinful anything spontaneously and characteristically human, especially human sexuality
- infantilizing individuals who encourage staying home all of one's life to devote oneself completely to taking care of faltering children, needy siblings, or elderly parents
- friends who attempt to act as substitutes for romantic relationships—particularly devastating are "close" companions who, when they find their own intimate relationship, dump the avoidant suddenly and without warning. For example, a psychiatrist leaned heavily on and formed a codependent relationship with a psychologist friend who willingly listened to her troubles for many years. Then, when the psychiatrist got married and no longer felt so needy, she told the psychologist, "I am out of the shrink realm and into the art realm, so because now we no longer have anything in common, I won't be seeing you anymore."
- jealous individuals who ensnare then guard avoidants, luring them into isolating groups, like therapeutic support groups, whose members too readily substitute themselves for individual relationships, then demand group cohesion at the expense of individual freedom and group loyalty before personal achievement and fulfillment. Thus in a group house on Fire Island, whenever the members of the house sensed that one of the roommates was about to connect, the other members suggested that they all go to the local ice cream parlor and look for men: a place significantly called "Unfriendly's." Other isolating groups are those whose members es-

pouse a Zen-like philosophy of removal as the best or only way to reduce interpersonal anxiety; advocate antisocial behavior, as do some rumbling motorcycle club members; or advocate bigotry by word or deed, for example, putting seriously exclusionary by-laws into place to keep out others they deem unacceptable because of their race, religion, ethnicity, or sexual orientation.

Don't Stay Overlong in a Relationship That Isn't Working

Doing that is a particularly bad idea when it is being done out of an excessive sense of guilt about leaving and a masochistic need to change the minds of those very others who are most set against one.

Never Use Sex as a Vehicle for Expressing One's Avoidance

Hypersexuality should not become a way to display one's fundamental unrelatedness or a way to rebel against a society believed oppressive.

Never Use Sex as a Vehicle for Overcoming One's Avoidance

Sex should not be a masochistic, self-punitive begging, where one reluctantly submits sexually just to retain a relationship along the lines of "I'll do anything you want me to if only you will love me and not leave me." Nor should avoidants make "good sex" the sole criterion for pursuing a given relationship, especially if they are planning all along to abandon the relationship when the sex loses its luster.

When Involved in a Committed Sexual Relationship, Try to Practice 100 Percent Fidelity

Especially for avoidants, cheating tends to be more an avoidant problem than a nonavoidant solution—something that puts distance between people by creating personal guilt and partner resentment, even in partners who at first seem willing to go along. Therefore avoidants should confine their "extramarital relationships" to incomplete relationships selected to supplement, not replace, "spousal" relationships: a relationship with a pet (where the nonhuman aspect makes the closeness both acceptable and tolerable); a nonsexual relationship with a friend (especially a member of the same sex in a heterosexual marriage/opposite sex in a homosexual marriage); a nonsexual relationship where, additionally, age differences are reassuring (so that homosexuals/heterosexuals may more comfortably adopt an older man/woman as a close companion than a younger one or one of the same age); and close family relationships as distinct from equally close relationships with strangers. To avoid distancing, avoidants who have any strong outside relationships should always emphatically reassure their partners that "I will not allow this person to come between us or take me away from you."

Avoidants often ask me as their therapist whether they should try to meet people in singles bars or attempt to connect over the Internet. I advise avoidants that, used appropriately and in moderation, these places of approach can help the avoidant find a lasting relationship—but only if avoidants first overcome their avoidance enough to "mingle" and work any contacts creatively—looking not for quick sex or a merger, but trying to network with the long-term view in mind. Networking involves slowly but surely, and patiently, making as many acquaintances as one can, deliberately spreading oneself thin in the beginning, making multiple contacts, developing a circle of acquaintances, then narrowing the newly developing wide band of relationships down to one significant other, the most important individual in one's new life: Mr. or Ms. Right.

Needless to say, avoidant behaviors can be as disruptive in singles bars, or on the Internet, as they can be anywhere else. Thus an avoidant man I finally convinced to go to a bar to try to meet women "accidentally" negated my advice by carelessly saying loudly and convincingly, "There isn't anyone in this bar that I would sleep with"—thinking he was just talking to one of his friends, only, as he knew from experience might happen, to find that as he spoke, everyone else fell silent so that "the whole world heard what I said."

Because all contact is by nature nonavoidant, avoidants desiring to network need only begin somewhere, almost anywhere, for starters forming distant relationships in anticipation of gradually getting closer as their anxiety subsides. Avoidants can start by being nonavoidant in some small respect, such as by saying hello to strangers. They can also form experimental "practice" (transitional) relationships that serve the purpose of loosening up, conditioning themselves not to fear rejection, advertising their availability, and getting a nonavoidant reputation via showing others "I want, and am willing, to accept people."

Avoidants should take care not to fall for the come-ons of dating services that offer miracles in the form of alluring advertisements virtually guaranteeing to provide them with suitable mates. Disappointment and an unwillingness to try again is their fate, as it is of the avoidants who buy into books and embrace gurus that tell them how to succeed relationally, effortlessly, and in short order, promising an immediate and easy solution to a complex problem that will almost certainly take time and effort to solve.

AVOID GIVING PATIENTS BAD ADVICE

Bad therapeutic advice includes advice best reserved for non-avoidants such as "do your own thing"; "get your anger out"; "play hard to get"; "don't say yes when you mean no"; and "make complete honesty your best policy." Avoidants need to become more, not less, connected by keeping their anger in to develop and cement relationships; by generally playing easy, not hard, to get; by sometimes saying yes when they mean no—being cooperative, compromising, and even submissive, if only to temporarily reduce tension; and instead of always expressing themselves and speaking freely and indiscriminately, by being very careful of what they say and do in the recognition that most times they are only one of many hypersensitive people in any given room.

As mentioned earlier, therapists should not routinely give avoidants advice about who specifically is right or wrong, good or bad for them, leading the avoidant on to condemn specific relationships prematurely, and on some trivial and principled but unhelpful grounds. Along similar lines, an avoidant should seek not a *compatible* partner based on his or her answers to an Internet questionnaire, but a *simpatico* partner, who, whatever his or her specific personality profile happens to be, is motivated to make a relationship work, willing to change if necessary, and especially loath to validate avoidant fears of being rejected by others by actually being rejecting.

SUPPLEMENTAL APPROACHES

At times, I refer my avoidant patients for an appearance makeover, to an exercise guru, or to another physician for needed medical care for physical ailments.

I sometimes suggest tricks avoidants can use to master the anxiety associated with giving a speech or meeting people at a social gathering.

Public speakers can help deal with the fear of fainting associated with stage fright by reassuring themselves that they are not losing consciousness by moving about in place, wiggling toes, tightening the thighs and buttocks in a symbolic attempt to get the blood to flow back to the brain, sucking on a mentholated cough drop or sugar candy to refresh themselves, or having a sip of ice water to "shock" themselves back into focus. They can also make their audience seem less frightening by demeaning them, for example, by imagining them in a ridiculous pose so that the audience looks as ridiculous to the speaker as the speaker feels he or she looks to the audience.

I often recommend the following "healthier" defenses as potentially salutary substitutes for defensive withdrawal (healthy defenses are also mentioned in chapters 11 and 20):

- *Healthy avoidance*, which allows patients to retreat from unimportant, uncomfortable relationships in order to prevent discomfort in these relationships from spreading to contaminate and destroy potentially productive social and personal contacts (healthy avoidance is specifically discussed in chapter 3)

- *Healthy denial and counterphobia*, to cope with criticism and rejection and to overcome anxiety about becoming intimate—short of becoming an extensively frantic, gregarious hypomanic who pushes too hard and acts too precipitously to master his or her terror of doing anything at all

- *Healthy projection*, involving an "it's you, not me" philosophy (particularly useful in an emergency where one's self-esteem has fallen and badly needs a temporary lift through a reduction of self-blame via blaming others)

- *Healthy identification*, becoming like others who are less fearful and less guilty, more self-tolerant, and more self-assertive. While this is controversial, therapists can, in selected cases and in a limited way, become identification figures through sharing personal experiences by telling their patients how the therapist warded off or actually resolved his or her own problems with avoidance, doing this in the hope of encouraging his or her patients to identify with the nonavoidant therapist. However, sharing experiences, life stories, life problems, and personal triumphs, while likely to be effective with *dependent* avoidants, who hang on a therapist's every word, and with *obsessive-compulsive* avoidants, who are so paralyzed when it comes to making any interpersonal progress that they beg to be told what to do (even though, at their most resistant, they plan not to do it, or to do the opposite), is likely to be a bad idea for *paranoid* avoidants, who suspect their therapists of wanting to steal their money by talking about themselves on their time, and "dime," and for alarmist *histrionic* avoidants, who see any signs of avoidance in the supposedly healthy therapist as indicative of the *complete* hopelessness of their own situation, and as a bad sign for the outcome of their therapy.

CHAPTER 15

Other Forms of Therapy

VIDEO

Bandura has described a process that he calls "observational learning," a form of modeling through which avoidants and others can learn how to form healthy interrelationships by imitating people who are interacting with the appropriate level of intimacy.[1] Buggey uses a special method of observational learning that employs video self-modeling (VSM)—a relatively new technique for modifying behavior using positive examples of interactions created through the editing of videos, where avoidants can view themselves performing a task just beyond their present functioning level.[2] In VSM, the therapist videotapes avoidant patients interacting with others, then edits out the problematic interactions so that the avoidant patients can watch themselves doing better. This has been found to be an especially powerful way to learn nonavoidance since people imitate models they are similar to, and who is more similar to us than ourselves?

MARITAL/COUPLE THERAPY

Marital or couple therapy is a form of interpersonal therapy dedicated to helping two individuals basically committed to each other repair their relationship.

A review of the literature and an informal sampling of therapists reveals that marital therapists do not always agree on the best way to help couples in which one or both members of the dyad are avoidant work out their problems. Possible methods include the following:

- reducing unilateral or mutual avoidances through abreaction and other techniques meant to relieve contributory emotional tension and pressure
- undergoing psychodynamically oriented psychotherapy to resolve marital problems through the development of insight into what is going on individually and interpersonally
- simply agreeing to disagree in a relationship where change is unlikely, so that one or both partners can, through forbearance and compromise, live comfortably with dissention
- having an affair to solidify a marriage
- having an affair to rescue oneself, at least emotionally, from a difficult situation
- deciding to split up, ending a relationship with a partner who is too remote, too uncaring, and too unwilling to change

As an example of an expert advocating having an affair to solidify a marriage, Beavers says, "I believe that affairs can hold stuck marriages together probably as often as they rip them asunder. If reasonably gratifying, the affair may avert emotional illness in the involved spouse."[3]

GROUP THERAPY

Benjamin recommends group therapy for some avoidants, noting that "new skills can be developed in the group [and] normal social development can follow."[4]

When group therapy is done properly, avoidants undergo an encouraging and motivating experience in a nonpunitive setting, where, not feeling criticized and humiliated, they are comfortable relinquishing at least some of their shyness and remoteness. Unfortunately, I have never come across a therapeutic group specifically dedicated to treating sufferers from avoidant personality disorder (AvPD).

PHARMACOTHERAPY

Specific schema to help the physician determine which medication is better for which avoidant are beyond the scope of this text. Generally, I find pharmacotherapy most helpful for two groups of avoidants: shy avoidants who cannot initiate relationships and social phobic avoidants such as those afraid of attending a group gathering (an effect evident to those who have successfully palliated themselves with alcohol before entering a crowded room).

Medications found to be helpful for selected patients with AvPD include beta-blockers for stage fright, benzodiazepines, and two classes of antidepressants: serotonin reuptake inhibitors (SRIs) and monoamine oxidase inhibitors (MAOIs). Gabbard specifically advocates diminishing *anger* and *guilt* chemically.[5] Marshall specifically recommends beta-blockers, MAOIs, and benzodiazepines as being most useful in the treatment of social phobia.[6]

Rapee, dissenting, discourages the use of all pharmacotherapy. He suggests, I believe irresponsibly, that with cognitive therapy, medication becomes unnecessary, and so "if you are taking medication that was prescribed by a doctor, you need to go back to that doctor and ask him or her to help you stop taking the medication."[7]

Unfortunately, many of the medications recommended for AvPD have unwelcome side effects. They can variously becloud an avoidant who needs to concentrate on attaining nonavoidance, imparting a fuzzy feeling to an individual who functions better when bright and fully alert; sap energy needed for making friends and lovers; and make avoidants feel too well to sustain the motivation they need to solve problems: imparting a false sense of comfort that decreases the chances that they will work through their avoidance (and go out and meet people).

Therapists should not prescribe drugs just so that they don't have to interact with their patients. One doctor, instead of talking at length with his avoidant patients, gave them all an activating medication for their withdrawal and a sedating medication for their anxiety and the anxiety-based somatic symptoms that often appeared when they tried to socialize. Another favored avoidant psychotherapists at his clinic by screening job applicants with the questions, "What drug do you give to an elderly lady who wants to leave a retirement community because she feels hemmed in there?" and "What drug do you give to a patient who wants to break away from his mother but cannot because should he do so, he would fear for her emotional health?" (In my opinion, in such cases, psychotherapy is likely to be the main, and often the only, mode of intervention.)

A TECHNIQUE OF LAST RESORT

Avoidants can, right from the start, simply accept their avoidance and decide to live with it, as if they can't do any better. These avoidants can be helped to build their avoidance into their daily routine. They can willingly, voluntarily, give up the pleasures and rewards of non-avoidance in exchange for remaining relatively anxiety-free. This, a solution of last resort, is best reserved for those situations where a realistic assessment of the patient's possibilities and progress to date suggests that because some pessimism is indeed indicated, the therapeutic goals should be kept modest.

CHAPTER 16

The Ideal Therapist

Avoidants often contact me to ask if there is a central referral source for therapists treating avoidant personality disorder (AvPD). I get letters such as the following:

> Hello, Martin. For many years I am spiraling deeper into isolation, and only yesterday I read about avoidant PD and discovered I fit on all counts. I am not sure what to do about it. I am 47, live in California. I decided to write to you and ask if you can recommend a group in our area I can join to work on this problem. I am scared to talk to people and my memory is weak. Thank you, JG

There is no such group that I am aware of, and of even greater concern is that while many therapists specialize in treating social phobia, few, if any, therapists specialize in treating AvPD. Therefore finding a satisfactory therapist generally involves vetting the therapist one already has, as you determine for yourself to what extent he or she is competent to treat you, and act accordingly, while at the same time trying to make his or her job a little easier by being as much the ideal, and as little the difficult, patient as possible.

The following are ideal ways for a therapist to deal with an avoidant.

RECOGNIZE THAT PUSHING AVOIDANTS TOO HARD, TOO FAST TO BECOME NONAVOIDANT IS COUNTERPRODUCTIVE

The ideal therapist recognizes that exposure to feared impersonal and interpersonal situations has to go at a rate that is comfortable for the individual. Becoming nonavoidant can take months or even years of stop and start movement toward that goal, for reasons (already discussed) I summarize (for purposes of convenience) here in table 16.1.

Some Case Examples

I told an avoidant patient, a man who was actually in satisfactory physical health, to "get out more, go to new places, meet new people, and get to know your son once again." Instead of following any of my suggestions, he replied with a letter full of excuses:

Your prescription I cannot follow. In the first place, you are obviously not aware of my physical disabilities. My energy reservoir is very low, and just a few hours out simply exhausts me. Added to that is the fact that the severe arthritis in my left foot makes it impossible just to walk around the block. Furthermore, my urinary tract problems require frequent emptying of the bladder (anywhere from every 10 minutes to every half hour). So, besides the fatigue factor, I cannot consider long trips. But possibly the

Table 16.1
Why Becoming Nonavoidant Takes Time

Avoidants both like and need the way they are and fear the alternative too much to yield their problems up easily and immediately and just on the therapist's say-so. For avoidance is in some ways like a favored philosophy, part of an entrenched and even somewhat beloved individual, very personal, value system. Avoidance is also a psychic mechanism that is treasured because it reduces anxiety. That means that unwelcome anxiety will predictably reappear when the therapist starts "tinkering" with the avoidant defense.

Between sallies toward mastery, avoidants, like anyone else, need to rest and regroup their forces in preparation for making their next move.

Nonavoidance, like all newly acquired behaviors, requires practice before it can become perfect and second nature.

Avoidants routinely perceive excessive therapeutic zeal as an attempt to dominate and control them. Therefore pushing them prematurely into feared encounters can make them anxious, depressed, and negativistic to the point that they bridle and may either leave treatment in order to reestablish comfortable distance from the therapist or stay in treatment but resist it to restore their own sense of being in control and their feeling of personal mastery.

severest problem is my unpredictable physical instability (dizzi-
ness, loss of balance, etc.). This is due to a cerebral deterioration,
the onset of which I expect will be proved on the CAT scan I am
to have shortly. While it is true, as you suggested, that I would
like to live on the Upper West Side of Manhattan, because of the
easy access to many cultural events, a goodly number of them
free, such as the Juilliard concerts and the weekly library concerts
at Lincoln Center, a hop skip and a jump there and back would
have no benefit for me, even if it were physically possible. Furthermore, my contact with the son you suggest I see regularly is,
to say the very least, tangential. So even if he were inclined to eke
out a couple of hours for a visit, the event would be both superficial and painful.

The following is my comeuppance for pushing a patient with AvPD
too far, too fast to get married.

A patient who complained that she couldn't meet men and get married said she had begun to meet them, but "forgot" to tell me that they
were all already married. When I discovered and exposed this avoidant
ploy, instead of meeting married men, she met a single man and actually married him—someone, though, sadly, she had selected for being
close to death from cancer.

Generally speaking, the ideal therapist reserves total push techniques
for shy and phobic Type I avoidants, who, already pushing themselves,
accept others pushing them as well, and even welcome being urged to
expose themselves to situations that make them anxious. However, the
ideal therapist uses these techniques with caution, if at all, for ambivalent Type IIa avoidants who one day wish to be pushed "to get out and
meet people" yet another day, resenting that, resist and rebel, and for
seven-year-itch Type IIb avoidants, who need not be urged to form a
new relationship but to stay where they are in the old one—for what
such individuals require is not more, but less action, and not less, but
more reflection.

DO NOT PRESENT TRIVIAL OR UNHELPFUL REMEDIES AS EFFECTIVE

Simple behavioral conditioning, such as "make a list of all the things
that frighten you about people, then master your fears by tearing up the
list," or more complex behavioral interventions, such as videotaping
the patient and confronting him or her either with the raw results (to

illustrate what needs to be changed) or with the results edited to make him or her look better (to illustrate goals) often makes more supplemental than effective primary therapeutic modalities, for several reasons. First, a characteristic of mental illness *is* the inability to learn from experience. Second, as I discovered from having treated many veterans with posttraumatic stress disorder, few avoidant individuals can, through conscious effort alone, rid themselves of the traumatic imprints that figure heavily in their fearful withdrawal. Therefore I make a point unlike the one made by behaviorists who criticize all psychoanalytic approaches as unproven: *some* behavioral approaches, while proven, are simplistic, and while they do lead to change, it can be trivial and often gradually wears off as conflicts return and once again take hold, making it difficult to get therapeutic results to satisfactorily and permanently generalize outside of the "lab." Third, approaches that use videotaping overlook how difficult it can be to convince some avoidants to be filmed in the first place. This is partly because avoidants imagine a critical implication to filming that threatens the more sensitive, more paranoid avoidants, who interpret being filmed as being watched, and being watched as being criticized and humiliated—as one avoidant put it, "rubbing my nose in my misbehavior."

DO NOT TREAT AVPD
AS IF IT IS SOCIAL PHOBIA

As discussed throughout, the ideal therapist differentiates these two disorders as having different therapeutic requirements. He or she treats social phobia as a phobia/confluence of phobias, but treats AvPD as a personality disorder.

DO NOT GIVE AVOIDANTS PREMATURE,
ILL-ADVISED REASSURANCE

Creating too much hope can lead to excessive disappointment later on. However, the ideal therapist does not foster too little hope either. Too often, therapists, in an attempt to be reassuring, tell their patients something like, "Being alone, being by yourself, isn't so bad, there are worse things than being alone, I even envy you your going alone to camp out in the country under the stars." But without realizing it, they are thus implying that avoidance is so chronic and untreatable that their patients will never improve. They are also coming across as belittling, for by reassuring their patients that "things as they stand are not so bad after all," they are effectively saying, "You are entitled to very little, can expect even less, and anyway your problems aren't that momentous in the first place."

DO NOT BE CRITICAL OF THE PATIENT

A number of observers point out how often therapists criticize their patients in the guise of treating them and suggest that all therapists, not only analysts, instead respond to patients in a consistently positive way, instead of being rejecting, disapproving, and controlling.

DO NOT CREATE MORE AVOIDANCE
THAN YOU CURE

Sometimes avoidance creation is an unavoidable complication of even well-done psychotherapy. Often treatment has to be so lengthy and involving that it cannot help but encourage the patient to let current relationships deteriorate and put forming new ones on hold. Treatments like short-term psychodynamically oriented psychotherapy and cognitive-behavioral therapy (the latter is, by design, almost always time limited) help solve the problem of overinvolvement, for as short-term interventions, they do not act so much the substitute for real living and do not tend to encourage the patient to waste good years of his or her life in the therapist's office on the couch, preparing for a future that may never come. However, so often avoidance creation is not due to the length, but to the content of therapy. For example, too often therapists create more avoidance than they relieve by siding with the patients' interpersonal antagonisms after hearing only their one side of the story. Thus one therapist encouraged a patient to have her alcoholic husband not let off on psychiatric grounds, but sentenced to jail for a behavioral peccadillo, reasoning that "it isn't wise for him to constantly evade the consequences of his behavior." The therapist said that what she did was a good thing, but it was only good in theory. For it is true that alcoholics must face the consequences of their alcoholism—but in this case, the patient's real intent was to rid herself of her husband, and her husband knew it. So as a result of this "therapeutic" intervention, the husband started drinking again and, unable to forgive his wife for being heartless, filed for divorce.

Therapists often encourage/create avoidance by telling avoidants to "keep busy" as a way to deal with their lonely isolation. For most avoidants, "get a hobby (or a pet, particularly a dog) and you won't miss not having friends" should be changed to "get a friend or partner and you won't miss not having hobbies or a pet." Like pets, hobbies are suitable for supplementing, not for replacing, relationships with other human beings. Although avoidance can be made more tolerable with hobbies, it is usually a better idea to make hobbies more tolerable with nonavoidance so that avoidants don't while away lonely hours keeping busy by themselves, instead of busying themselves working toward making the hours less lonely. Solitary activities can also increase the distress of isolation by acting as constant reminders of how much the patient is missing. The next "hobby" in such cases can become increasing preoccupation with one's own body, leading to further isolating somatic symptoms/hypochondriasis. (Besides, the therapist who tells the patient to get a hobby is often perceived to be a defeatist, whose true unsaid message is "since that is the best you can do.")

The most untherapeutic therapists create more avoidance than they relieve by offering themselves up as substitutes for real relationships. A therapist who needs to fill his or her practice and bring in enough money to live on might unconsciously discourage "outside" relationships in very subtle, almost creative ways. For example, one therapist, advised by a patient that she planned to marry a man her junior and stop therapy, replied, "Men that much younger than you are only interested in your money"—in this case, clearly a projection.

DO NOT BE OVERLY INTELLECTUAL AND IMPRACTICAL

What some avoidants really need is a directive, nuts-and-bolts lecture on what the therapist believes constitutes being avoidant and how and why to change that. Therapists who avoid "lecturing" their avoidant patients, whether they do so by overanalyzing; overcorrecting thinking; overmodifying behavior; overgiving drugs on the assumption that the problem is biological, not psychological; or doing bio, instead of giving positive feedback, should consider the avoidant's cry of "I'm afraid of rejection" as an opportunity to say something trite but true, like "it's better to have loved and panicked than to have never loved at all."

DO NOT DO FAMILY THERAPY WHEN INDIVIDUAL THERAPY IS INDICATED

With avoidants, the advantages of family therapy are often outweighed by the disadvantages. In particular, in family therapy, it is difficult for the therapist to take the family's side, even when indicated, since avoidants regularly misinterpret the therapist's in any way siding with family members in interfamily disagreements as a criticism of or an abandonment of them, the primary patients.

DO NOT BECOME IMPATIENT
WITH AVOIDANTS

Some therapists find avoidants frustrating. Perhaps therapy is going too slowly and the therapist is tempted to lower expectations in a rush to see some movement and terminate. Perhaps the patient is deliberately being stubborn in order to provoke the therapist to declare, "Impasse, let's take a vacation from therapy" or "Let's quit, I've done all I can do for you." The therapist suggests marriage is the goal and the patient counters that he or she instead prefers a long-term committed relationship because marriage isn't right for everyone; or the therapist suggests a long-term committed relationship before, or instead of, getting married, and the patient counters either that all he or she wants is a circle of friends and acquaintances, not anything more intimate, or that marriage is his or her goal, and that by suggesting otherwise, the therapist is trying to humiliate and defeat the patient. Impatient therapists at best cut corners, cow patients into saying they feel better, dismiss ill patients from therapy before they are better, or, at worst, as happened in one case, essentially "throw the patient out of treatment" without notice, and in the middle of a session, because "we aren't getting along very well and it's better if we cut our losses and I don't waste your money; but I will ask you to pay for this entire session since I can't fill the time on such short notice."

DO NOT TAKE AVOIDANT
NEGATIVITY PERSONALLY

Too many therapists come to dislike and become overly critical of avoidants as their response to taking the patient's negative transference personally. Patients who, with very little justification, complain, "You are criticizing me" make some therapists uncomfortable because they make them feel like a critical parent or an errant child. Patients who disagree with everything the therapist says, damning it into oblivion by responding with faint praise, foot dragging, or lack of movement to brilliant, apt, insightful, and decisive formulations, make some therapists feel like misguided fools wasting their time and the patient's money. At times, avoidants' guilt about their sexual instincts arouses like feelings in the therapist, enhancing the therapist's sheepishness about having a body and sexual desire. Some therapists feel that all avoidants are too distant and remote for their taste; and I have even spoken to therapists who view the avoidant patient as a "cry baby" because "most of them are unable to suck it up and tolerate even a little social anxiety."

Therapists often act out their feeling critical by using deep interpretations to hurt, as in "You are as hostile to others as your mother was hostile to you." They blame the patient for actively causing every rejection he or she in actuality experienced passively. Too often, they refer to avoidant "misanthropy" when it would be less confrontational, and truer, to refer to avoidant "fear."

DO NOT BECOME OVERLY SYMPATHETIC TOWARD THE AVOIDANT "PLIGHT"

Overly sympathetic therapists view avoidants solely as the innocent victims of less than ideal inner and outer circumstances and even conceptualize the patient's avoidance as a "disease over which you, the sufferer, has no control." They should instead ask avoidants to take some responsibility for themselves and their actions. Blaming early trauma exclusively for the avoidant's present plight is common, but it has the effect of excusing avoidants for being avoidant. That, in turn, supports their desire for the world to change when they are the ones who need to work on making many of the changes in their world.

CHAPTER 17

Helping Avoidants Overcome Their Fear of Criticism

As the *Diagnostic and Statistical Manual of Mental Disorders*, fourth edition, suggests, avoidants hesitate to look for interpersonal intimacy because of an extreme sensitivity to criticism that leads them to fear being "exposed, ridiculed, or shamed" and subject to "mockery or derision."[1]

Avoidants do not feel criticized only when they haven't been; they also deny that they have been criticized when they have been. In the latter case, instead of registering criticism consciously, they perceive it, but subliminally, or suppress it completely, thus allowing it to fester to the point that it leads to unmanageable, seething anger, and stuck just below the surface, it causes ongoing divisive resentment, ultimately outing to wound or destroy their interpersonal relationships.

It helps if avoidants recognize that so often, when it comes to being criticized, the problem lies not with something that they, but something that their critics, did wrong. To this end, avoidants can profitably understand what motivates their critics to be critical: their presumptuousness, their prejudice, and their distortive cognitions, all of which render their criticism too impersonal to be taken personally. Thus most critics

- are judgmental people prone to getting easily upset and, when upset, to hurling random epithets that predictably hit avoidants, individuals already guilty and hypersensitive, particularly hard

- are in an irrational transference to their subjects, mistaking them for a prying mother, controlling father, or competitive sibling

- have identified with their own shrill, harsh, hurtful parents and now are abusing people in the present the same way their mothers or fathers abused them in the past

- are basically talking about themselves, that is, criticizing themselves in the act of criticizing others. For behind all criticism of others lurks a self-criticism as critics routinely project onto, then humiliate and demean, others for traits they dislike in themselves. Therefore avoidants should reframe the negative things critics say about them as negative self-statements on the part of the critics, displaced outwardly, with criticizing another being just the critics' way to criticize themselves, with the "you" being a "for example," and so the formulation "it takes one to know (and criticize) one" here holds a special truth.

- are suffering from mild to severe psychopathology. Most avoidants find it comforting to spot specific pathology in their critics. As Keating suggests, avoidants can lessen their "difficult feelings . . . by understanding some of the syndromes of difficult people [who] may be feeling depressed, guilty, fearful, etc., and refus[ing] to admit such feelings even to themselves."[2]

Such understanding helps avoidants affirm themselves, develop a semiscientific method of self-defense, and even, if they like, improve their relationships with their critics by responding to the critics' emotional ranting in a therapeutic fashion, as a therapist might respond, say, reassuring fearful histrionic critics that all is not lost, or suspicious paranoid critics that the danger they believe themselves to be in is minimal to nonexistent.

Avoidants should also attempt to understand where they themselves are coming from, in the sense of what motivates them to respond so fearfully and negatively to criticism. Why, for example, do they value others' negative opinions about them over their own more positive opinions about themselves, and continue to do so even when they *know* that their critics are misguided? Perhaps it is a combination of submissiveness to almost everyone, plus a global self-punitive, self-negating attitude that leads them to be a "sucker for authority"—parentalizing critics, and everyone else, as omniscient, good, and omnipotent mother or father clones, while simultaneously treating themselves as unknowing, bad, little children too small and weak to even consider challenging others' negative views. Perhaps they have become "compliment junkies" because when they were children, they were either criticized too much or loved too extensively and now as adults need to sustain a compensatory or harmonizing, habitually unflawed self-image that can only come from always getting 100 percent positive feedback from others, without which they respond in a predictably negative way, and as predictably, catastrophically.

Perhaps it is jealousy that causes avoidants to become overly sensitive to criticism. In his 1922 paper "Certain Neurotic Mechanisms in Jealousy, Paranoia, and Homosexuality," Freud divided jealousy into *competitive or normal, projected,* and *delusional* types. The first is connected with a sense of loss and narcissistic wound as well as enmity against the successful rival; the second involves a projection of one's own temptations (that may have been repressed) with flirtations as a safeguard against actual infidelity; and the third is associated more specifically with projection of repressed homosexuality.[3] Competitive or normal jealousy leads avoidants already sensitive to feeling as if they are second best to too readily feel that they are being criticized and rejected because they don't match up; projected jealousy leads avoidants already feeling sheepish about being amoral to too readily feel that they are being criticized and rejected because they are sinners; and delusional jealousy leads avoidants already questioning their sexual orientation to too readily feel convinced that they are being criticized and rejected because they are queer.

Avoidants can be taught to respond to criticism in a healthier way. They can learn to

- ignore as much as possible those negative people who reject them
- remind themselves that no matter who they are, not everyone is going to like them or approve of what they do
- harden themselves to criticism they cannot avoid, developing a thick skin, turning off that alarm bell in their heads, and always remembering that being criticized is rarely catastrophic and that what seems so important today often turns out to be unimportant tomorrow, for most matters in life are not matters of life and death
- develop a sense of humor, putting both unjustified and justified criticism into perspective by lightening up and seeing the amusing and, in the infinite scheme of things, unimportant side of what at first looks to be an interaction of tragic proportions. Thinking macrocosmic thoughts can help. For some avoidants, looking up at the stars and realizing what is a big and what is a

small thing puts passing ill-considered or even justified criticism into perspective.

- tell themselves when they do get criticized and rejected that it is not the end of the world, but a part of, not an unfortunate complication of, being involved in a relationship

This said, there are times, to be determined by the individual, when avoidants should meet criticism head-on, mustering as much strength as possible to respond to criticism not like a turtle pulling back into its shell (flight), but like a lion turning on those who trouble it (fight). Now having in effect "identified with the aggressor," they turn tables and, instead of cowering, become as aggressive to the critic as the critic has just been to them. Too often, avoidants are the recipients of advice along the lines of "just let it pass, don't become so defensive; I wouldn't even give them the time of day, it just encourages them." As a result, they have (wrongly) come to fear that being assertive with their critics, for example, aggressively setting limits on them, will predictably ensure further criticism and rejection. In truth, assertion can help avoidants reduce criticism and rejection and develop and retain a more positive self-image. Avoidants who tell their critics straight out, "You do not know what you are talking about," or "You are one, too," or "You did it first," or "It is not a matter of who will accept me, but a matter of who I will accept" at least won't withdraw from their critics after saying or doing nothing in response. They will instead respond forcefully, actively, and productively, effectively neutralizing the attack on them with a valid, effectual counterattack. Thus a patient of mine remembers a stranger telling her not to let her dog on the beach when in fact the dog was on the sidewalk bordering the sand. She felt less cowed when, instead of replying "sorry" then seething in retreat, she said, "I haven't given you permission to talk to me." Avoidants can profitably plan their repartee in advance of an anticipated attack. I often advise my avoidant patients to make and hold on to a list of their positive points so that when they are actually attacked, they are prepared to reel these off along the lines of, "This is what I like best about myself."

Those avoidants who have difficulty responding to their critics assertively need to discover the reasons why. These are, with remedies implied, as follows:

- the belief that submissiveness offers protection along the lines of exposing the underbelly as a sign of abject, protective surrender

(in fact, submissiveness gives many critics, who are invariably sadists, carte blanche, then a second chance, condoning and encouraging them, for most critics, as sadists, perceive submissiveness as weakness, implying vulnerability, which inspires further attack)

- an excessive need to develop and maintain a positive self-image based on being nice and cooperative at all times, even in the face of intense, unjustified, and irrational negativity from others
- low self-esteem that leads avoidants to feel too unworthy even to attempt to mount an effective self-defense
- a fear of failure: "It won't work"
- a fear of success: "I will go too far"
- some = all thinking characterized by the inability to distinguish setting limits from getting annoyed, getting annoyed from getting angry, and getting angry from committing murder
- an excess of empathy and altruism, where, after putting themselves in their critics' shoes, they use their own terror-stricken responses to others' criticism to judge how devastated others would presumably feel in response to criticism coming from them

Particularly helpful is aggressively living well as the best revenge: having an extremely pleasurable life to spite all those who seem to want one to be miserable.

Sometimes avoidants can actually have a rational discussion with their critics. They can start by simply refusing to accept global criticism—roughly the equivalent of name calling—and instead ask for details, telling their critics, "Only if I know exactly what I am being criticized for can I respond in a meaningful, considered way and so adopt the best possible defense, point-by-point, with facts, not out of my emotions."

Avoidants can also learn how to manipulate their critics to get them to lay off. They can make their critics feel guilty by acting as if they love them back, no matter how harshly they treat them, saying something like, "That's OK; the negative things you say about me don't cause me to feel less positively about you," however ingenuous that statement might be. Alternatively, they can make their critics feel guilty by beating them over their heads with their own bloody bodies ("Look what you have done to me"), or they can successfully disarm their critics by saying, "Mea culpa," that is, "getting back" with a self-criticism, as in "you are right, I know that's the way I am, but, pity me, what can I do about it, I don't seem to be able to change." Manipulations work especially well with those critics who unconsciously want to be loved but go about getting that love in a paradoxical way, via criticizing others as a test to see if, nonetheless, they still love them, with all their heart, under the most inauspicious circumstances.

Avoidants can almost always reduce the negative impact criticism has on them by putting third parties between them and their critics. Third parties can support avoidants by advising them how to avoid criticism in the first place and how to cope with and recover from criticism that they were unable to escape. As supportive confidants, third parties can take the avoidants' side at times of stress—offering them a retreat, a place where they can go to be reassured that they are not as bad as their critics say they are, while being reminded, when applicable, that it is the critic, not the avoidant, with the big problem. E-mail support from friends can be particularly valuable for avoidants who otherwise might have to face their anxiety completely alone. And as Benjamin Franklin said, applicable here, at times of stress the best things to get you through are "three faithful friends—an old wife, an old dog, and ready access to cash."[4]

Having *private* demeaning fantasies toward their critics can also help avoidants feel less cowed. Thus avoidants can help overcome a fear of public speaking by thinking of the audience as fools, perhaps in the nude.

Sometimes the best idea is to just walk away from criticism physically and emotionally, completely shunning troublesome people and instead focusing on one's most fervent admirers and one's truest and most loving friends.

Avoidants should certainly lose interest in meeting only the difficult challenges of life, in only winning the hard games, and in only meeting and making the tough conquests, as they make the difficult, critical people in their lives the very ones who count the most and only set out to appeal to, by changing the minds of, those that are most set against them.

Some Case Examples

One artist reacted to criticism with the thought, "They criticize me with such conviction and knowledge that they must be right." He spent his early years depressed, hoping "for the big reward, more important than the Tonys and the Oscars—having the *New York Times* say something nice about me." His mental state improved when, instead of hoping to get the *Times* to reverse its position, he developed a healthy disdain for its opinion and went about his business, closing the eye formerly always open to what "Daddy thinks of me."

A doctor's megalomaniac colleague continually put him down. For example, once he confessed to this colleague, "I don't like this person," only to be told, "I happen to know that the feeling is mutual." Another time, after he bragged to this colleague that "if I wanted to, I could always get a job at a certain organization," the colleague told him, "What makes you think *they* would want *you*?" This colleague also put the doctor down medically, no matter how accurate and clever the doctor's formulations. Indeed, the more accurate and clever they were, the more he challenged them. The doctor felt that his ideas were being quashed or ignored. Yet he kept trying, and kept failing, to please and impress. Each night, he would go home feeling depressed, his self-esteem lower than the night before, and each morning, he would go back for more, trying to get his depression to lift by bringing this man around in an attempt to feel supported and accepted, instead of attacked, humiliated, and rejected. Finally, he realized the senseless nature of this commitment and sensibly simply stopped talking to the colleague—beyond a curt good morning and a discussion of any business that had to be transacted. His therapist, in supporting his new approach, added, "Don't think you are supposed to get along with someone just because you work with him." Now the doctor's self-esteem returned, his depression lifted, his creativity and cleverness reappeared, and his work performance improved markedly.

Of course, avoidants should not completely harden themselves to ignore or minimize the utility of *constructive* criticism. Instead of becoming automatically and reflexively defensive in the face of any and all criticism, they should distinguish constructive from destructive criticism, then reexamine themselves to see if any constructive criticism is deserved, accept it if it is, and change accordingly. That doesn't mean seeing themselves as bad. It just means trying to be and do better the next time by turning the criticism into a positive, creative, growth-enhancing experience, making the criticism work for them by taking it somewhat to heart, doing better, and most important, making certain that their critics hear all about how well they have done, are still doing now, and plan to do in the future.

CHAPTER 18

Helping Avoidants Overcome Their Low Self-Esteem

Beck notes that "in anxiety the dominant theme is danger"[1] and that the "person with an avoidant personality simply minimizes . . . social interactions in order to protect [himself or herself from a specific danger, the danger of developing low] self-esteem."[2]

Avoidants' low self-esteem consists of a low self-approval rating originating in an inability to meet self-expectations due in part to self-imposed, excessively high self-standards, along with a hypersensitivity to the criticism of others, leading to a highly critical self-attitude. As a consequence, the avoidant individual concludes, "I think as little of myself as they think of me," or even "I am worthless." The resulting negative self-image then leads to withdrawal meant to self-protect—improving one's self-image through avoiding a test of that self-image by avoiding large aspects of living through isolating social rituals. These involve giving up the seeking of interpersonal gain to avoid experiencing interpersonal losses. That, however, decreases functionality as escalating defensive disengagement creates the very losses that the avoidant is attempting to avert. These losses create a further diminution of self-esteem, for the avoidant now feels, and often is, alone, and predictably tends to think, "I must be a defective person, for why else wouldn't I have a single friend in the world?"

Elevating an avoidant's self-esteem therapeutically can diminish his or her need to withdraw defensively. This process starts with distinguishing low self-esteem that is *rational and appropriate* from low self-esteem that is *irrational and inappropriate*. Low self-esteem that is *rational and appropriate* originates in self-criticism and criticism from others that is all too well deserved. When this is the case, enhanced self-pride has to come not from altering one's thinking, but from doing things differently. Low self-esteem that is *irrational and inappropriate* appears when avoidants, for little or no reason, come to dislike themselves or begin to feel that others dislike them. Here enhanced pride has to come not from changing one's behavior toward others, but from changing one's mind about oneself and treating oneself better, as a more worthy object of one's own affections. Following are some ways (adaptable for self-help) therapists can help avoidants do just that.

UNDERSTAND THE ORIGINS OF THEIR INAPPROPRIATELY LOW SELF-ESTEEM

Avoidants can better recognize the distortive nature of their low self-esteem if they comprehend its origins in what is often their no-longer-relevant past. Developmentally speaking, low self-esteem often starts with parental deprivation of love and even physical abuse that the parents tell their children they deserve. Now their children, lacking a standard of comparison, and believing their parents are both fair and omniscient just by virtue of being both adults and parents, buy into that. Then, as adults, these children continue to seek out, or actually beg for, parental approval, but now from people other than their parents. They form present-day relationships with negative-thinking parental substitutes just to try to reverse their negativity. They seek to be made whole again by creating positivity in people who, by their very nature, can only feel negatively toward them. Of course, the devaluation continues anyway. Then they view the continuing disdain as a further reason to self-blame and withdraw because, as they conclude, it's not that these people don't love them for reasons of their own, it's that nobody can love them because they are completely unlovable.

INTERRUPT SELF-PERPETUATING VICIOUS CYCLES

The therapist interrupts low self-esteem-creating/enhancing vicious cycles such as "I can't do this because I am deficient, and I am deficient because I can't do that," for example, "I can't socialize because I don't feel worthy enough to attend social events, and I don't feel worthy enough to attend social events because I can't socialize." Effectively interrupting vicious cycles allows the avoidant to experience satisfying small successes that ultimately break the impasse through incremental achievement, leading to less withdrawal and enhanced motivation to go forward. A simple supportive therapeutic statement meant to interrupt low self-esteem-inducing vicious cycles might be "in my eyes you are a worthy person," and a typical behavioral intervention might be our familiar "habituate yourself to avoidant anxiety by acting more and more nonavoidant each day, and doing so in small increments."

REDUCE EXCESSIVE
AND INAPPROPRIATE GUILT

An excessively guilty conscience, a crucial element of low self-esteem, takes multiple forms: excoriating self-criticism; excessive "don't make trouble" submissiveness; painful brooding with depressed mood; and pathological, self-destructive acting out.

Speaking cognitively, avoidants develop a guilty conscience because they

- view a few of their negative past actions/present attributes as constituting the entire, inadequate, valueless, or evil self
- think catastrophically, guiltily overreacting to their minor peccadilloes as if these are major sins, then withdrawing, feeling sheepish, ashamed, and shattered by thoughts that they are "stupid" or actual criminals
- see any sign that they are not fully accepted as evidence that they have been completely rejected and feel thoroughly bad, even if one person reacts badly to them
- unfairly judge their behavior in similar = the same thing terms along the lines of assertion = aggression = murderous intent = homicidal action, so that simply thinking bad thoughts becomes the equivalent of doing bad things
- think projectively, changing anxious, self-punitive attitudes into feeling disliked by external malevolent forces and people

Avoidants need to engage and talk back to their guilty, critical, punitive conscience and demand that it be less critical of and more positive toward them. They need to continue to affirm their humanity in spite of their imperfections. They need to accept their reasonable sexuality without suppressing it due to an unreasonable, rigid, all-pervasive, crushing hypermorality. They need to accept their anger, recognizing that everyone, even avoidants, has some justified annoyances toward some people, such as those who are troublesome, scary, and rejecting without even being provoked. They need to permit themselves to be successfully competitive without undue survivor guilt accruing from the belief that the world is a zero-sum place where because there is a finite quantity of X, anything they get by definition they get by taking it away from Y so that instead of experiencing guilt over doing well when others are doing comparatively poorly, they can come to view themselves as separate entities entitled to fulfill their own destiny regardless of whether others fulfill theirs.

Avoidants also need to reduce their guilt over being avoidant. They might do this by making creative excuses for themselves. For example, they can tell themselves not "you shouldn't be that way," but "I am that way not because I am bad, but because I am different. That is who I am, and I am being true to myself." They can soothingly remind themselves that they, like anyone else with an emotional problem, can't always control their anxiety and so shouldn't blame themselves unduly for becoming frightened, especially in situations where many people would feel a bit scared such as upon entering a room crowded with strangers. Emphasizing the bright side of what others perceive to be their flaws, they can tell themselves, "Many people like distant, remote people." They can excuse themselves for being modestly neurotic, "for everyone is." They can allow themselves to make relational mistakes without necessarily viewing one relationship peccadillo or major failure as a sign of full personal deficit. They can lighten up enough to accept some relationship anxiety as integral to, not an unfortunate or catastrophic complication of, connecting, so that now they no longer masochistically respond to partial relational failure with complete, self-destructive, apologetic, self-protective, across-the-board withdrawal.

For avoidants, the two magic words of guilt reduction are "so what." These words can help avoidants recognize that all is not completely lost just because all is not entirely well. Now they can stop thinking "I ruined myself completely" over the slightest, and often entirely imagined, interpersonal "misbehavior."

Finally, avoidants can profitably allow healthy avoidance to become part of their defensive repertoire. They can and should stay away from people who make them feel guilty, or guiltier, recognizing that these people have problems of their own and that it's better to withdraw from them than to socialize with them—and stop going back, convincing themselves that they are returning for satisfaction, when they are just going back for more.

REDUCE PARANOIA

Avoidants can become less suspicious of others by countering distortive empathy, a process where they jump to the conclusion that others are judging them negatively because they assume that others are using the very same rigid, unfair, and excessively self-punitive yardsticks avoidants use to judge themselves.

DO AN EVIDENCE-BASED SELF-STUDY

Therapists should encourage avoidants to make a two-column list where they identify their positive features in column A and inscribe these beside the negative features they go on to document in column B—then do the math to see if, overall, they are "OK as is" and, if not, see what they can do to develop a more balanced, more positive self-view, one they newly create and maintain independent of what others seem to, or actually do, think about them. Avoidants who do this remedial exercise often collaterally decrease their need for impression management as they stop grading themselves based on what they believe others are thinking about and how others are responding to them. Instead, they develop internal strong, independent, unvarying self-standards that allow them to view themselves as viable individuals after asking themselves not "do I have what he or she expects of me?" but "do I think well of myself?" Now they refuse to calculate their self-worth entirely by what they assume their reputation to be with others. As a result, they start finding strength and self-approval from where it counts: mostly, or even entirely, from within.

CHAPTER 19

Treating Sexual Avoidance: An Overview

Treatment of sexual avoidance consists of an approach that I call "sexual avoidance reduction." This approach involves a combination of psychodynamic, cognitive-behavioral, interpersonal, educational, and pharmacotherapeutic therapies. The goals are to generate improved performance indirectly through understanding the problem, in particular, relieving sexual inhibitions by reducing inhibitory responses, and to generate improved performance directly through learning the sexual "ropes" ("sexual skills training"), ideally enhancing motivation (the will to act) and increasing emotional expressiveness by reviving desire, improving confidence, and resolving conflict. Here presented in outline form for easy access and maximal utility are the main components of sexual avoidance reduction.

TECHNIQUES

PARTNER INVOLVING: PREVENTION

Sexual avoidance between partners can often be prevented by making a good match in the first place. Thus a man with a Madonna complex is well suited to a woman who is Madonna-like. Men and women who are gay need to admit it to themselves as soon as possible to avoid trying to succeed heterosexually, losing valuable time, getting into a failed marriage, and harming their partners by promising them more than they can deliver.

A Case Example

After a few years of marriage, the husband of one of my patients moved out of their shared bedroom permanently. Initially, his wife had pushed for marriage and he had acquiesced, although he really wanted to be a priest. His telling her exactly that when they first met should have given her a hint of what was to come, but she had had a very sheltered upbringing and knew nothing about such matters. She wished she knew that the husband's disinterest in her sexually was not a fixable thing, but she was too young to realize that, and she just assumed that he wasn't attracted to her as an individual—because something was wrong not with him sexually, but with her personally. Therefore she concluded that repairs could be easily made if only she somehow took some action.

STIMULATION ENHANCING

Sexual avoidants need to identify the location of, and learn ways to stimulate, the erogenous zones. Sexual avoidants can learn about the mechanics of better sex through the use of sex manuals. Learning the principles of intimacy is different, and more complex, but it can be done through therapy or by using the many good intimacy guides readily available in bookstores such as books on the topic of "how to get closer."

GUILT REDUCING

Sex education has a collateral effect: reducing guilt by implying approval of the thing being taught. For sex education, among other things, effectively gives the individual permission to feel sexual and actually have sex. Sexual phobias respond especially well to permission giving through sex education. Its healing mantras stick with the learner, countering negative inhibitions by undoing negative parental and societal messages that have been internalized and crop up at the most inconvenient moments to intrude into and disrupt one's bedroom activities.

INSIGHT DEVELOPING

Improved performance can come from understanding the psychodynamics of sexual avoidance, particularly the role played in sexual conflict by the inhibitory factors discussed throughout. Therapists can impart this understanding through psychodynamically oriented therapy, for example, by analyzing masturbatory fantasies and transference distortions and through interpersonal treatment focused on how dyadic relationship problems express themselves sexually. Sexual avoidants can, on their own, use the dynamic formulations found throughout this book to help emerge from those destructive intrapersonal and interpersonal inhibitions that keep them in, or force them back into, their sexual cocoons.

A Case Example

A patient with multiple sexual performance difficulties was often unable to get an erection. If he got one, he would soon lose it. If he kept it for any length of time, he would sometimes experience premature ejaculation and sometimes suffer from ejaculatio tarda.

Through therapy, we discovered that his sexual symptoms were partly his (unconscious) way to tell his fiancée that he wasn't planning to marry her or anyone else. Speaking of his trip to visit his fiancée in a foreign country, he said, "I never had an orgasm the whole time I was there. That's because I wanted to let her know that she was getting too attached to me, and so I can't go back to Europe for she has already planned a life for us when I return. As I always say, 'If I want sex, I'll find sex,' but who needs a relationship for that?"

His sexual inhibitions were also a product of his intense fears of connecting and committing arising out of a conviction that being tender with a woman signified merging the intimate and sexual feelings he longed to keep separate. For being tender meant becoming feminine and sissified as well as inevitably being swallowed up by women to the point of losing his identity. Coming to orgasm meant yielding, and yielding meant becoming vulnerable to a woman's hurting him— the wages of his sin of letting her up close to him and into his world.

We also learned that his sexual inhibitions were due both to a fear of success and a fear of failure. Erectile and ejaculatory functionality signified success, and success signified vulnerability to loss, and even meant punishment by death. A fear of failure took the form of compulsive self-spectatoring like that due to what the *Psychodynamic Diagnostic Manual* calls "feeling unsure of [oneself and being] preoccupied and worried about [one's] general adequacy."[1] So when he was having sex, what went through his mind was, "Boy, she is sexy, and she's brand-new, and we're going at it top speed, and I'm almost there, and almost there, and almost there, but, oh boy, I am losing it, and I'll never get there, and it's another ruined attempt, and I wanted it to go so well, and what is she going to think of me, and what is going to happen to our relationship, this is awful, she will hate me and never see me again, it's the end of my world." As a result, he was unable to just let the sex be and, too focused on whether sex would work, and what was going to happen in the future if it didn't, he became unable to just enjoy what he was doing in the here and now. For he had made every sexual act into a momentous test of how valuable he was both as a person and as a man, and thus into a commentary on what fate might hold in store for him in the immediate and far distant future.

PERSONALITY CHANGING

Sexual avoidants can enhance their sexual desire and performance indirectly by overcoming inhibiting personality problems. To illustrate, *obsessively* high expectations associated with excessive resolute perfectionism relating to sexual performance lead to easy disappointment and ready retreat. Often a personality buffered by *posttraumatic stress* experiences performance inhibition based on anticipation of partner abuse originating in intrusive past accurate and/or retrospectively distorted memories of experienced sexual traumata.

ENVIRONMENTAL ENHANCING

Improving unfavorable, sexually negative surroundings is a simple, direct way to enhance desire and performance, for example, sound-proofing a bedroom that is close to where the children sleep.

EMOTIONAL CHARGING

Strong and persistent stimulation involving nonsexual touching, such as massage, can act as an instrument both of immediate release and of release over time. That, along with regular sexual contacts without forcing things or expecting too much, can cumulatively relieve sexual strictures by ultimately breaking through self-induced, compulsively turned on inhibitory sexual "cold showers."

BEHAVIOR CHANGING

Behavioral therapy can lead to performance improvement and enhanced enjoyment. For example, a therapist might suggest that a man treat his ejaculatio tarda by increasing his thrusting force and speed and reducing the frequency of his sexual encounters. For some men and women, monogamy without masturbation is a particularly powerful aphrodisiac achieved through focusing on one object, improving quality by reducing quantity. One man's sexual performance improved markedly when he merely stopped encouraging himself to have intrusive, wild sexual fantasies about third parties and instead forced himself to focus entirely on sex with his wife.

Calm can be enhanced and anticipatory brooding and the anxiety associated with spectatoring reduced through the use of such relaxation techniques as Zen removal and specific breathing exercises, the details of which are beyond the scope of this text.

COGNITIVE RESTRUCTURING

Identifying and correcting cognitive distortions such as "no orgasm = no life" can help individuals stop their panicky viewing of each and every sexual encounter as the sole test of whether they are or are not a full man or woman who will or will not be punished, rejected, and exiled for their sexual thoughts, desires, and performance.

MEDICAL CURING

Symptoms of sexual avoidance can often be relieved directly through the use of medical "magic bullets" such as drugs that treat erectile dysfunction, antidepressants that retard ejaculation, and sexual aids that enhance sexual pleasure (but should not become a substitute for the greater goal of attaining full sexual psychological adequacy without them).

PARTNER INVOLVING: REMEDIATION

Partners of sexual avoidants can be encouraged to aid the healing process. Instead of leaving it up to chance, partners should tell each other what they really want sexually, and do so without shame. The power of positivity—especially sexual altruism that makes not one's own, but one's partner's comfort/pleasure/orgasm the main thing—can be helpful, especially if the other partner, becoming appreciative, develops new and more loving feelings that feed back to increase the first partner's desire, ultimately enhancing both partners' performance.

Partners should stop doing anything they might be doing to thwart each other's sexual performance/enjoyment. They should avoid allowing themselves to become unattractive. They should not humiliate their partners by making hurtful jokes either about them or about their sexual performance, either directly or indirectly, privately or publicly, and instead, even when feeling negatively, try always to display at least a degree of positivity. They should not express disgust by asking their partners to shower before sex, or come across as disinterested or disdainful the way a patient recently did when he told his straight girlfriend how it was really dykes on bikes that most turned him on. In many of my patients, sex improved when one partner stopped creating the very distancing in the other that he or she complained of. A woman getting paranoid about her boyfriend devalued him by complaining that he was trying to get her pregnant just so that she would stay with him. Another, also becoming paranoid, accused her husband of having an affair when he was actually being faithful, and a third, instead of letting sexual encounters go at their own spontaneous, healthy rate, deaffirmed and invalidated his wife by constantly pushing her for sex even when he knew, but didn't care, that she wasn't interested because she was otherwise preoccupied.

OTHER INVOLVING

It can be helpful to do what one can to stem the influence of parents, in-laws, coworkers, and uncomprehending members of society who make things worse by intruding into a relationship, for example, by making negative passing comments or giving bad advice. In one case, the bad advice consisted of telling a couple to "make the break" when it would have been better to stay, and in another, telling a couple to "stay with the known devil out of a fear of illness and old age" when it would have been better to go.

OPTIONS OF LAST RESORT

The following options exist for resolving a situation where one or both partners are resolutely and incurably sexually avoidant:

- both agreeing to separate or file for divorce now
- both agreeing on an open marriage, staying together, and relating as friends without becoming enemies, enjoying the partner without being sexually demanding and threatening divorce, accepting the partner as is and living with things the way they are rather than responding negatively to diminished or nonperformance
- one agreeing to lovingly help the other find someone else more suitable

- saving oneself by bettering one's life, say, by taking trips to no-where/anywhere just to get away
- staying faithful and becoming sexually avoidant/inactive oneself
- helping a partner by compromising and agreeing to have a certain amount of sex anyway, yielding even when one doesn't really feel like it, even modifying one's sexual preferences to give the partner what he or she wants to avoid being rejected

Sometimes partners who married sexual avoidants who performed in the beginning then never again have children and feel stuck in, and are actually trapped together for, a lifetime of child rearing. Partners have to decide how to raise children in this environment. That often involves making important decisions about therapy, including about whether, as individuals, they should make the rounds of personal therapists and work out their problems one on one, or go together visiting marriage therapists to work out their problems in couple therapy. Since there are few to no fixed rules on how to proceed, the answers so often depend on personal preference as well as on therapist availability and cost.

FOR THOSE WHO ARE PARENTS

Parents have a job to do to prevent sexual avoidance in their children by staying out of their children's bedrooms. Figuratively or literally "looking through the peephole" can only cause the child's sexuality to become not an exercise in having fun oneself and giving pleasure to others, but in spending one's life avoiding displeasing and shocking mother and father.

Parents whose children have become so sexually avoidant that they are hanging around the house with little or no motivation to go forth and find someone for themselves have to learn how to handle a child reluctant to move on because he or she has few or no outside relational needs.

PROGNOSIS

The effectiveness of treatment of sexual avoidance often depends on the patient's motivation to change. That, in turn, may or may not be enhanced by increasing isolation from the partner. The prognosis often improves when organic causes, such as alcoholism; prescription medicine overusage or drug usage; testosterone deficiency; liver disease; diabetes; an endocrine, circulatory, or neurological disorder; or genital-area pathology such as penile phimosis or genital warts can be ruled in and effectively treated.

THERAPEUTIC ERRORS

As one of my patients related, illustrating how therapists often mistreat sexual avoidance, "The first marriage counselor we saw, back in the 1990s, told us to read performance manuals when what we needed was intimacy guides, then to read intimacy guides when what we needed was performance manuals." As the husband of the couple reported, much of the time, the therapist just sat there and laughed, while his wife sobbed away with a box of Kleenex because he wasn't having sex with her. The therapist said to him, "Are you *kidding*? You mean you really don't have sex?" The final therapist this couple saw (after that, they both gave up and gave in to someone else—as the wife said, "You could see how effective the therapists all were!") told the husband, "You're gay, right?" to which the husband honestly replied no, only to have the therapist respond with a most unhelpful, pedestrian, "Then get off the pot."

PART THREE

SELF-HELP

CHAPTER 20

Overcoming Shyness and Withdrawal

As an avoidant individual, that is, as someone who suffers from avoidant personality disorder (AvPD), you are shy, scared, and lonely. Fortunately, you can generally help remedy this state of affairs through your own efforts consulting with guides such as my action-oriented, step-by-step reparative guide on self-interventions you, as an avoidant, can use to overcome your relational (social) anxiety over attachment, intimacy, closeness, and commitment and get closer to your family, make more friends, and possibly even form an intimate reciprocal liaison with a significant other in a long-term, lasting, loving, fulfilling, committed relationship.

The following protocol, much of which is based on earlier material here repeated and recast for self-help purposes, offers specific delimited activities useful for preventing and overcoming AvPD—focused tasks that, in my experience, have helped avoidants go from retreat to connectivity. I break this protocol down into small, one-day-at-a-time steps to offer a laddered approach involving going a little forward each day, allowing the avoidant to make continual progress without feeling overwhelmed due to taking relational plunges that are excessive, only to panic, give up, and avoid the cure the same way he or she gives up and avoids so much else.

Of course, not all avoidants need to make changes that are minimal/incremental. Some can boldly truncate the process by facing what makes them anxious all at once, perhaps by combining some of the steps and skipping others where mastery is not necessary or has already been achieved. And obviously, not all of my daily exercises will be applicable to or needed by a given individual. Each avoidant person is different, for avoidants are encumbered to lesser or greater degrees by their avoidances; diverse in their fears; living under different external, variously more accommodating or less supportive circumstances; and individually more or less prone to backsliding. Also, completing each day's exercises is only a start. Selected exercises often have to be repeated more than once until practice makes perfect. What is important is developing a comprehensive, ongoing, personalized game plan adapted specifically to the individual's preferences and needs, taking into account one's personal, often unique, situation.

PREVENTION: SELECT YOUR PROFESSION WISELY

Those who recognize in a timely way that they are potentially or actually avoidant should consider selecting a profession that allows them to earn a living should their avoidance persist or worsen. These professions include post office mail sorter, writer/indexer, mountain climber, grave digger, philosopher/poet, psychotherapist who substitutes living vicariously through patients for real-life encounters, animal trainer/pet shop worker, or circus performer. Some avoidants-to-be might even consider selecting a profession that can help them become less avoidant. These professions include working in a charitable organization such as a homeless shelter or being a greeter in a funeral home, real estate broker, host on a cruise ship, sports instructor in a gym, politician, medical healer, salesman, and cab driver. An example of a profession that should be avoided would be a professional critic, for professional critics cannot help but acquire personal enemies because of their inevitable need to professionally eventually say something bad about someone's work.

PREVENTION: AVOID INTENSIFYING PREEXISTING AVOIDANCES AND KEEP NEW AVOIDANCES FROM APPEARING

Avoidants should try not to worsen their avoidance by doing the following:

- pushing themselves too far, too fast to become nonavoidant
- associating with avoidant companions, especially those who newly traumatize them in ways that revive old, unintegrated traumata
- self-traumatizing by compulsively and self-punitively reviving and trying to integrate early traumata, repeating them or their

equivalent in the here and now, over and over again, in an attempt, typically futile, to master the past

- settling in to endless punitive therapy with a therapist who revives old and creates new emotional traumata by being confining or making hurtful technical blunders
- going off medication they should stay on

Particularly onerous are actions that actively court rejection like those of my patient who was just too scared to meet a man she liked in person, so on New Year's Eve, she stood at his window, called him on her cell phone, told him she was down there (in the dark—he couldn't even see her), asked him to wave back, then disappeared before he could even make that simple gesture to, and unthreatening connection with, her.

ACCEPT AND LIVE BY YOUR GOOD PROGNOSIS

As Oldham and Morris suggest, "People with Avoidant Personality Disorder are luckier than they may think,"[1] for unlike schizoid individuals, who suffer from a fundamental inability to relate, avoidants have the ability to relate, but have difficulty realizing it until it is released through formal therapy or self-help (strength of will, singularity of purpose, and persistence toward achieving one's goal required!). Also, many avoidants get better spontaneously or should external circumstances improve—even when their AvPD is so chronic and severe that they have isolated themselves from most or all human relationships. Another fortunate aspect of AvPD is that unlike many other disorders, AvPD doesn't leave crippling residue or permanent scars, especially when avoidants have retained a few crucial relationships that they can use as the basis for revival and repair.

DETERMINE TO WHAT EXTENT YOUR AVOIDANCE IS HEALTHY AND PREFERENTIAL AND SO CAN, AND EVEN SHOULD, BE RETAINED

Avoidance can be healthy when it is not a sign of an emotional disorder, but of a preferential, reasonable, rational desire to be alone or to be left alone. Avoidance is preferential when avoidants, solitary by choice, have built their aloneness comfortably into their lives. They are not rationalizing when they say that they like being self-sufficient and self-contained, independent of others, and their own master, and speak eloquently of how they enjoy the peace that comes with removal and detachment. These are the avoidants we see in public comfortably eating dinner in a restaurant by themselves reading the Sunday newspaper on Saturday night, or fishing by day, day in and day out, alone by the seashore—welcoming the escape from inner turmoil that comes from pulling back from a world they feel is too much to bear. (Often they want to remain aloof but are too embarrassed to admit it, so they say not "I want to disconnect," but "I am too fearful even to attempt to make connections," that is, out of guilt, they say that "I am not an independent individual, but a pathologically avoidant person.")

Avoidance can also be healthy when it is limited and small scale, creative, appropriate to the circumstances, and for the ultimately greater nonavoidant good of allowing the individual to retreat from uncomfortable, unimportant relationships in order to prevent discomfort in these relationships from spreading to contaminate and destroy potentially important social and personal contacts or one's entire life.

RETAIN HEALTHY/NORMAL AVOIDANCES

Avoidants should not change simply because others expect them to. They should only make those changes that are right and necessary for them. A husband shouldn't enter therapy for being an avoidant when the real and only problem is that his wife, the one pushing for him to get help, is a passive-aggressive.

DETERMINE AND ENHANCE
YOUR MOTIVATION TO CHANGE

Change, even though possible, is time consuming, difficult, and painful. Therefore avoidants should not attempt to relinquish entrenched avoidant patterns before determining for themselves if the comforts of limits are greater than the discomforts of their limitations.

Motivation is enhanced by focusing on the advantages of nonavoidance (see table 20.1).

Do at Least One Nonavoidant Thing Today

Each day, avoidants should try to think and act in at least one nonavoidant fashion. That might involve just picking up the phone instead

Table 20.1
The Advantages of Nonavoidance

Potential freedom from relational fear

leading to the ability to form durable relationships of intimacy with others so that one comes to

savor pleasurable and rewarding interpersonal relatedness, which also involves

having pleasurable sexual relationships while

firming up a newly developing capacity for the self-realization that comes from forming durable relationships

leading to developing self-pride about one's new and improved personal and professional achievements, ultimately being able to

leave a meaningful personal, interpersonal, and professional legacy behind.

---

of letting the answering machine take the call. It might involve keeping one eye always open for who might be looking at and trying to make contact with them so that they can react appropriately to the positive overture. It might involve starting saying hello to strangers, even or especially the ones who probably won't say hello back. It might mean meeting relational challenges head-on, that is, not with their usual fight/flight responses, but by staying put and resolving relationship problems in place.

SET SPECIFIC GOALS

An important aspect of setting specific nonavoidant goals involves contemplating what it will be like when they are achieved. Avoidants can ask themselves, what will being nonavoidant feel like? Will things be better when I am connected than they are now with all my disconnects? What will my nonavoidant future be like, one where I am better able to relate, get close, and commit to relationships with friends, and even one significant other? What exactly will it be like to move out of my parents' home and face the world? Will it be worth all the trouble and anxiety predictably involved? Will I lose my nerve when my parents, as I can expect, respond negatively to my leaving? There are downsides of translating my new nonavoidant philosophy into meaningful action. But what reassurances can I give myself that I can tolerate any or all of them, and what reminders can I give myself about the many upsides that do exist?

Different transactional goals and their underlying causal anxieties require different specific remedies. For example, *exposure anxiety* has to be resolved if the main goal is to comfortably attend parties and other social events, while *anxiety over criticism* has to be resolved if the main goal is to become less remote at work by not allowing oneself to be cowed by unsupportive, openly critical superiors, peers, and underlings.

SET PRIORITIES

In setting goals for themselves, avoidants need to determine which avoidant behaviors cause them the most trouble and create the most havoc. Then they have to decide if they want to try to relieve their greatest fears first (even though those are the most difficult to master) or work first with their more moderate fears because though these are not necessarily the ones whose resolution will provide the most comfort, they are at least the ones that are easiest to resolve.

BE PATIENT

Avoidants must set themselves a realistic accomplishment/achievement timeline based on rational, not irrational (emotional), desire and practical need. That means recognizing that avoidance reduction takes time. Because avoidants didn't get to be avoidant overnight, they will not become nonavoidant tomorrow. Also, avoidance reduction requires persistence, which is time consuming, and vigilance, which is emotionally draining—with both needed to avoid backsliding should, as often happens, the same fears recur and need to be mastered all over again.

IDENTIFY RESISTANCES TO IMPROVEMENT

These include the questionable assumptions and shaky rationalizations listed in table 20.2.

JOURNAL/SCRIPT YOURSELF AS SUCCESSFUL

Journaling involves recording why one wants to change, including enumerating in writing the virtues of relating over being isolated and the rewards of relating over the acknowledged discomforts of getting close and undergoing commitment. It also involves recording one's emotional responses, and distinguishing these from one's realistic

Table 20.2
Resistances to Improvement

I don't have the time to meet people.

The world is a fearsome place, full of frightening, rejecting people, so why even bother trying to get better?

I have nothing but bad luck, so there is no sense in even attempting to meet anyone good, or good for me.

There aren't any people worth meeting where I live.

I can't help my shyness, and no one else can help me become less shy either.

My anxieties and fears are absolute, not relative, based on reality, not on fantasy, therefore I am incurable, for my problem is irremediable.

It's not my fault that I am an avoidant, it's my upbringing.

It's not my fault that I am an avoidant, it's my chemical imbalance.

My loneliness is preferential. I *like* to be alone; I value my privacy and independence above all else.

Marriage isn't right for everyone, and it's not right for me.

The grapes are sour, for relationships are not all they are cracked up to be.

Some of the best things in life are only available to the isolate, like being able to sleep without being awakened by a partner's snoring, being able to stay in bed as long as I like, being able to drop my clothes on the floor without anyone complaining about the mess, not having to pay for my partner's financial excesses, and being able to travel without compromising my itinerary just to give in to someone else's demands.

---

anxiety responses, that is, distinguishing what I *do* fear from what I *should* fear, then responding accordingly.

Journaling also provides avoidants with an opportunity to review their progress as they ask themselves and write down the answers to such questions as "what have I done to avoid whom today?" After they answer such questions, they should write down possible areas of improvement and change accordingly. For almost certainly they have done something that they should not repeat. They have looked right by someone good then retreated to remain invisible. They have overlooked someone who would like and even love them if only they would have let them. They have shied away from someone who is right for them using a flimsy excuse—because "he is a longtime friend and so we can't get romantic; because you shouldn't mix business (getting close to people at work) with pleasure (having friends and even meeting partners through the job); because she is someone I met on one of those 'stupid blind dates'; or because he has some (all too human) frailties and misfires from time to time." They have not listened hard enough to others' *positive* feelings mixed in with their *negative* feelings toward them. Having heard their words without listening between the lines, they have taken the expressed negative arm of another's ambivalence too seriously and, having also overlooked the good in the other person, failed to rescue a relationship they could have formed and sustained if only they had been a little more charitable, and a lot more understanding.

Avoidants should consider using the methods of Kelly, a psychologist, who, in the 1950s, used a technique called "fixed role therapy" to change people's perceptions of themselves and help them break through their self-imposed limitations. In a clinical setting, using a technique applicable to avoidants, he had clients write a self-characterization describing their strengths, values, weak areas, and the like. Then Kelly would "rewrite" the script, using much of the original, changing what the clients wished to alter. Then he would ask the clients to become this new character, in other words, to act "as if" they were the star of a play featuring the new, improved version of themselves.[2] (Of course, avoidants can rewrite their relational scripts on their own and give them the happier, more satisfying endings of which they dream.)

MAKE HELPFUL REAL-LIFE CHANGES

Avoidants who feel exposed/trapped in the small town they live in might try traveling to a big, anonymous city to meet old friends and make new ones. Avoidants who feel isolated in an unfriendly, large city might try visiting friends in a small town and ask them to introduce them around in the new surroundings.

MASTER YOUR ANGER

Avoidants should try to avoid getting angry in the first place. They need to spot exactly when they get angry; understand why they get angry; question if their anger is appropriate to the circumstances or is coming more from within than from without; and stop using anger as a defense against relational anxiety—getting angry to thwart loving and being loved. For example, they should not do what one of my patients did when she first sought blind dates, only to then look for something about the individual that would allow her to express her preconceived negative notion about how most blind dates are "bad news."

Many of those avoidants who were unable to avoid getting angry in the first place had some success changing their anger style from aggressive to passive-aggressive, with the goal of minimizing the even greater harm to their relationships that can come from hurting others' feelings less in subtle and more in open and direct ways.

FACE AND OVERCOME SHYNESS

Overcoming shyness starts with recognizing that shyness, and the withdrawal that accompanies it, is an active, dynamic, not a passive, static, condition. Avoidants shyly withdraw not passively, but actively, because they withdraw defensively—taking motivated steps to pull back from and even give up on looking for new relationships. Individuals should determine for themselves if they shyly withdraw for one or more of the following reasons, with, in each case, remedies implied.

Low Self-Esteem

Avoidants with low self-esteem are shy because they feel that they don't deserve to meet anyone because they feel too unworthy to form/ enjoy relationships, and even wish to spare others the pain and perils of having to relate to someone as unworthy as they believe themselves to be. They are also shy because their low self-esteem leads them to lack confidence to the point that they do not feel sufficiently comfortable relating unless their relationships meet a number of reassuring conditions in advance, particularly those involving the certainty of constant and unconditional approval and the promise that the relationship will not sour in any way in the foreseeable future, or ever.

A Pathological Need to Meet Others' Expectations and Impress Them

Avoidants are overly attuned to and sensitive about what others think of them. The opinions of peers, teachers, entertainers, religious leaders, and the media count for too much. They overworry about their image, convince themselves that others think poorly of them, think poorly of themselves, then shyly withdraw as their way to pass negative judgments on themselves—judgments that are even more negative than the ones others pass on them.

An Inability to Master Inner Fears by Harnessing Soothing, Reassuring Defenses

Shyness is due in part to the absence of reassuring defenses, which include *denial* defenses that say, "That is just the way some people are, it's their problem not mine, and I will simply refuse to let them bother me or get me down," and healthy *projection*, where avoidants blame others for scaring them, instead of acknowledging their own responsibility for being anxiety-prone.

A Surfeit of Unhealthy Projection

Here, after viewing the world as their personal inkblot and attributing their inner anxiety to external fear, they come to see the universe as a place full of frightening potential or actual adversaries, whom they shyly retreat from as their only possible response to what they imagine to be their personal difficult or impossible environmental circumstances.

ENHANCE SELF-ESTEEM

Self-esteem enhancement in great measure involves becoming more permissive toward oneself. This involves allowing oneself to be simply human—permitting oneself to make some mistakes, without constantly self-spectatoring and criticizing oneself for being imperfect, and instead, in a balanced way, congratulating oneself for doing some things right—although not necessarily for doing all things perfectly.

RELEASE THE HOLD OF PAST TRAUMAS

Avoidants can prevent past old traumas from becoming present post-traumatic stress disorder by discriminating between bad past and good present relationships so that they do not generalize from old bad past experiences to sully new, unrelated, potentially satisfying involvements. This tendency to generalize is exemplified by the cat that, burned by jumping on a hot stove, fears and avoids not only hot stoves, but cold ones as well. Avoidants need to regularly remind themselves that just because, as children, they experienced ill treatment at home does not mean that everyone outside the home will treat them equally badly so that as a consequence, they must avoid all men and women in the here and now as "hot stoves," when in fact, as "stoves," they are safely "cold." Not all new acquaintances are old, fearsome, problematic parents, siblings, or friends who once demanded that they impress others favorably as the only important thing, then rejected and deprecated them if they didn't; parents who double-binded them by criticizing them no matter which way they felt and whatever they did; peers who bullied them; people who stifled their humanity, especially their rational anger and perfectly acceptable sexuality; or people who told them, in their controlling fashion, "Either be exactly like me, or be gone."

It helps if avoidants keep in mind that contiguity between past and present is so often illusory and simply coincidental. For since humans can behave in only a few really different ways, everyone in the present is unavoidably, and in some respects likely, to remind all of us of someone from the past.

DEVELOP TRANSACTIONAL INSIGHT

Avoidants need to document why exactly they fear opening up and getting close to others. Table 20.3 summarizes some of the possible reasons for easy self-help access.

Table 20.3
Problems with Getting Close

They fear they will reveal something they don't want to feel, know about themselves, or display to others.

They fear being overwhelmed and tied down emotionally.

They fear being controlled and dominated.

They fear merger and need to maintain their identity fully intact.

They are too self-absorbed to be "just" one part of a couple—this though successful relationships, by definition, lead to a *positive*, often maturational, change from "me" to "us."

They are reluctant to make the personal sacrifices that relationships require.

They fear being hurt again in the present and future in the same way they were hurt in the past.

They are jealous individuals convinced that anyone they love will only betray them and leave them for someone else.

They are competitive individuals who feel guilty due to the zero-sum belief that what they win, others must therefore lose.

They fear success in all areas, and especially in the area of relationships.

(continued)

They have a masochistic need for failure, especially when it comes to relationships.

They have bought into social messages about the wonders of splendid isolation.

They actually like being loners, meeting nature by themselves in a test of strength and mettle, one that, if they win, they believe will make them strong and powerful enough to be able to endure and survive, no matter what.

ROLE-PLAY

Through role-playing, avoidants can put themselves in the place of others so that they can see exactly how they come across to people, then make necessary repairs to harmful interpersonal trends and fix potentially off-putting character traits such as obsessive rigidity and paranoid suspiciousness. Videotaping themselves and showing the results not only to themselves, but also to their significant others, can provide them with feedback as to how they can improve their appearance and behavior in a way that will lead others to become more accepting of and welcoming to them.

MAKE TRIAL FORAYS INTO NONAVOIDANCE

Becoming less avoidant requires actually giving nonavoidance a try. Too often avoidants decide implicitly (by only thinking about it) whether they do or do not wish to remain avoidant. Instead, they should embrace the simplistic but true principle "Try it, you might like it." Then they should say to themselves, "I will focus on, and single-mindedly make, relationships my ongoing concern. I will not allow myself to be sidetracked in my quest for nonavoidance. I will fix on my nonavoidant goals and head for my nonavoidant objectives in a straight line, with as few side trips or time-outs as possible, while not letting anyone or anything get in my way." They should then take themselves in hand and force themselves to act less shy and be more related, telling themselves, "You can do it, and you can do it now," even though they find themselves at the start behaving in an inadequate or embarrassing fashion.

TAKE CONSULTATIVE ACTION

Avoidants can profitably share their fears with others. Instead of retreating in silence to save face they should own up to their interpersonal anxieties, bringing them out into the open not only in order to expose them to the cleansing light of day, but also to get others to understand and sympathize with, instead of reflexively reacting negatively to, them. Asking others not to mistake their shyness for hostility makes it clear that they are not bad, but fearful, people, not individuals who dislike, but men and women who are afraid of, others. This effectively throws avoidants on the mercy of a, it is hoped, understanding "court" that will give them credit for their honesty and appreciate, understand, and respond positively to their frankness.

SEEK OUT HELPFUL FRIENDS AND FAMILY

At some point, avoidants should try to become sufficiently non-avoidant to be able to approach friends and family they can enlist to help them cope with and master their avoidance. These third parties can

- exhort avoidants to at least try to relate.
- act as good companions who provide avoidants with practice relationships and therapeutic corrective emotional experiences that can generalize, for relational successes with familiar, accepting people spread to facilitate or actually become relational successes with strangers, who, in their turn, likely will become more accepting and less difficult to approach
- promote healthy identification, leading by example—the example of model people who are less fearful, less guilty, more self-tolerant, and more self-assertive
- provide the avoidant with a warm, reassuring, healing holding environment in which there is less or no reason for anxiety; evidence that patient perseverance will lead to relief; positive feedback that says "you are too good to fail," "that's great that you have succeeded," and "your low self-esteem is lower than by rights it should be"; and good nourishing fatherly/motherly advice such as "there are other places where you will be happier/more welcome/ more popular than in the suburbs."
- introduce avoidants to others, hoping that potential or actual rewarding relationships with them might result
- offer avoidants constructive, not destructive, criticism, as tolerant friends giving avoidants a fair and balanced ongoing assessment of the effect they are having on others, and as amateur life coaches offering avoidants specific suggestions about what needs

to be done to make future improvements, without repeating past mistakes

- Offer younger avoidants-to-be (children and adolescents) an avenue of escape from parents, countering extant unhealthy parental attitudes by offering the young people a positive view of their true worth and a place of escape, saving them, it is hoped, from becoming more seriously troubled than they otherwise might turn out to be

Avoidants can profitably consult with ex-avoidants to discover how these others got over their avoidance. They can do this one-on-one or through joining therapy groups (if they can find the right one) composed of group members who are also having problems with avoidance.

Of course, avoidants, already too highly impressionable and sensitive for their own good, need to be very careful in picking third-party assistants. They should not ask for help from people who infantilize them with their own avoidant philosophy of life or who keep them in tow because they do not want to let them roam free. They should challenge gurus who advise or recommend avoidance in subtle ways—such as through advocating Zen-like removal philosophies, which, though useful for nonavoidants, are ultimately bad for avoidants, who are already too removed for their present and future good.

LEARN ACCEPTANCE: TO FORGIVE ONESELF AND OTHERS

Avoidants need to learn to be kinder and more forgiving both to themselves and others. In the vernacular, they need to cut themselves and others some slack, using a "so what?" approach that involves relinquishing that uncompromising, perfectionistic, all-or-none attitude about relationships that causes them to pull back if they or others make even one little mistake, and without giving all concerned a second chance. Avoidants should remind themselves that most relationships are neither all good nor all bad, but somewhere in between those two extremes, and strive to get relationship grades that, though not perfect, are at least passing.

INTERRUPT VICIOUS CYCLES

Avoidants need to interrupt vicious cycles characterized by the following:

- A given relationship doesn't work out, intensifying their self-critical tendencies, lowering their self-esteem, leaving them even more hypersensitive to criticism, predictably increasing their self-critical tendencies, and thus lowering their self-esteem even further.
- Their fear of rejection leads them to distance themselves protectively, resulting in their actually being rejected, leading to more fear of rejection and further distancing, as displays of unreasonable fearful timidity and shyness create negative feedback in others, who think not "he is afraid of me," but "he doesn't like me," or even "she hates me," prompting further withdrawal and further retaliative rejection from others.
- They avoid because they are depressed, and they are depressed because they have avoided.
- They do not seek interpersonal gains for fear of experiencing interpersonal losses, leading to defensive disengagement that creates the very losses they are attempting to avert.
- They feel shame that leads to avoidance, which leads to more shame about having been avoidant.

INURE YOURSELF TO CRITICISM

How to do this is discussed at length in chapter 17. I find a helpful mantra consists of reminding oneself that behind every criticism of another is a self-criticism, which is not surprising considering how people, especially these days, are mostly, if not only, talking about themselves, which they are doing even when they seem to be referring to/addressing others.

IDENTIFY AND CORRECT SPECIFIC COGNITIVE ERRORS ABOUT RELATIONSHIPS

This process is discussed in detail in chapters 7 and 11. Perhaps the most common cognitive errors avoidants make is to confound some with all, for example, ambivalence (he has mixed feelings about me) with rejection (she rejects me totally and completely).

ANALYZE YOUR DREAMS

Avoidants should analyze their dreams to see if they shed light on their dysphoric feelings and irrational negativistic beliefs. An example of dream analysis is offered in chapter 7.

CHANGE YOUR RELATIONAL PHILOSOPHY

Lonely individuals who consciously complain about relationship difficulties but unconsciously remain aloof from close relationships offered, or rupture actual close relationships that promise, really threaten, to work, often do so because philosophically they believe that isolation is splendid. Instead, they should make enemies with their avoidant value system before "I like being alone" becomes "and besides, I have no other choice." They must convince themselves once and for all that isolation, rarely splendid, is rather mostly an unpleasant and even dangerous condition. They should refuse to allow themselves to be carried away by siren songs about the pleasures of being alone. They should put intellect before passion, putting the recognitions that "it's not better to be alone than to be in a relationship" and "relationships are worth whatever trouble it takes to sustain them" in place like a helpful alarm, warning them that such beliefs as "the single life is for me," "I can get along better without you from now on," "life will be better after you've gone," and "I will be in great shape when you die and leave me your armoire" are not satisfying personal mantras, but self-destructive personal constructs. In other words, avoidants should follow Freud's advice—"where Id was, there Ego shall be"[3]—and distinguish preference from compulsion: their true ideal, and what they really want out of life, from their automatic thoughts and behaviors that effectively order them to be anxious.

Keeping all this in mind, avoidants should try to answer the following questions truthfully, and, depending on whether the answer is nonavoidant or avoidant, remind themselves of the answers daily:

- Do I *want* to be alone or do I *fear* commitment and intimacy?

- Do I really believe that isolation is splendid, or does something inside warn me of the terrors of connecting and strongly suggest that I stay out of a relationship because my dreams of intimacy will never come true, or actually be nightmares?

- Do I really want to "do my own thing," or am I afraid of "doing my thing with you"?

- Do I truly like my fantasies of walking alone into the distance through swirling mists, or am I conjuring up those mists in order to hide from myself and others, to keep myself from getting into a close, warm, loving relationship?

- Do I truly identify with songs that speak of being a rock and an island, tell me I should be glad that I am single, and proclaim that never, never, will I marry, so that I really want to be insular, or am I really afraid of "singing another tune,"' by analogy, leaving my avoidant island, taking the nonavoidant plunge, and swimming to shore?

Avoidants can help distinguish preference from compulsion by looking back over their lives to see if they can spot the exact (historic) moment when approach became avoidance, as desire to relate turned into a fear of closeness and intimacy due to beginning, and still active, conflicts between approach (desire) and avoidance (fear). Avoidants should identify present-day wish-fear/desire-guilt/ rebellion-submission conflicts within themselves in order to determine if it is these, not freewill, that are prompting their so-called philosophy of splendid isolation, one that is in fact the product not of a search for desirable splendor, but of the taking up of heroic, defensive measures to meet the, for them, avoidant irrational threat of welcoming others into their lives, homes, and families.

Avoidants can better relinquish their avoidant value systems and resultant avoidant positions if they

- identify with others whose beliefs and ways are less avoidant—emulating people they admire for their social abilities and successes, whose nonavoidant philosophy has led to real-life social connectivity

- take a more sanguine view of human nature, one that emphasizes the positive and welcoming aspects of people they presently view in a mostly negative and forbidding light

- disentangle themselves from overly repressive family relationships that are the product of and lead to/enhance/fix their avoidant beliefs such as the belief that family always comes first, and newly break as free as they can from families who won't let go, but instead resolutely infantilize and smother them

- become more willing to give up something to get something and so make the necessary sacrifices for relationships, as they accept some anxiety in exchange for a degree of accomplishment; willingly sacrifice a degree of self-pride, autonomy, independence, and the need to express oneself completely and honestly to a newly developing closeness; relinquish the pleasures of getting revenge on those who have presumably been rejecting of them; and give up at least some of their treasured identity, and instead of being "me," become "us," along the lines of Joni Mitchell's reminder that when it comes to love, "some loss of self is inevitable."[4]

MASTER DISSOCIATION

Avoidants need to stem dissociative flights from the possibility or actuality of acceptance where they fail to respond to positive gestures and laugh off a serious approach—as they become defensively aloof in order to reflexively squelch feelings they perceive to be dangerous and forbidden, doing so by the pathological expedient of distancing themselves from the people who elicit those very feelings.

OVERCOME BOREDOM
AND RESULTING NEOPHILIA

Avoidants need to relinquish protective boredom that, in effect, says not "I am afraid you find me uninteresting and reject me," but "I find you uninteresting and reject you"—one of those negative responses that disrupt intimacy along the lines of "don't say hello once and it will be overlooked; don't say hello twice and you will be overlooked."

HELP OTHERS BECOME LESS AVOIDANT

Helping others become less avoidant is a royal road to helping oneself along similar lines. Avoidants might try each day to convince one previously avoidant person to stop rejecting and to accept people instead. Avoidants might also consider working to create a less avoidant society—for example, supporting or joining groups dedicated to overcoming such (always avoidant) bigotry as gay bashing, and spousal abuse.

MAINTAIN YOUR PHYSICAL HEALTH AND
IMPROVE YOUR PERSONAL APPEARANCE

I often recommend a complete cessation of smoking, limiting one's use of alcohol, and using only prescribed medications in as low a dose as one's physician will agree to. When necessary, I refer my avoidant patients for an appearance makeover, perhaps to an exercise guru or cosmetic expert, and suggest that patients watch makeover TV shows such as those on what to wear.

EVALUATE AND REEVALUATE YOUR NEED FOR THERAPY OR ANY THERAPY YOU MAY ALREADY BE RECEIVING

Since avoidance is an interpersonal problem, the solution may require not only self-help, but also supplemental professional help from a flesh-and-blood therapist.

Avoidants need to be certain that their therapists have made the right diagnosis. There are relatively few therapists familiar with AvPD, and I have gotten many letters from patients complaining that their therapists called them depressed or paranoid, when they were in fact avoidant. Because avoidants need to face their fears gradually, but inexorably through graded exposure, before they can obtain full, useful self-understanding, the most effective therapists are action oriented, rather than purely intellectual healers; that is, they do not rely exclusively on imparting insight then expect avoidants to attempt, and be able to take, nonavoidant action simply because they understand themselves. Effective therapists also do not rely solely on cognitive-behavioral therapy alone, without simultaneously employing insight-oriented, interpersonal, and supportive methods. The latter methods are often criticized in the cognitive-behavioral literature as inadequate—for example, Anthony and Swinson say, "As for other psychological therapies, although they certainly have a place for treating certain types of problems, they are not proven when it comes to treating social phobia and other anxiety-related conditions."[5] But this so-called inadequacy is often not the product of the methods themselves, but due to the therapist relying on them exclusively.

Avoidants often need to do their own research and ask their therapists specific questions about indications and contraindications, adverse effects, and the risks and rewards of being medicated for anxiety and depression. Many individuals with AvPD benefit from pharmacotherapy to reduce anxiety and depression. On the positive side, prescribed benzodiazepines and antidepressants can help avoidants become less anxious and fearful, while antidepressants can help relieve an avoidant's depression. But on the negative side, both can interfere with relationship formation and maintenance. Both can create a chemical nirvana that removes motivating anxiety and depression, which warn avoidants to do something with their lives before it's too late; take a needed edge off the socially useful protective paranoia that allows avoidants to determine if there is anything wrong with, or even dangerous about, certain others; soften the "craggy neurotic profile" an avoidant needs to be interesting, not bland/pedestrian/ordinary; and lyse the pro-social interpersonal (hyper-) sensitivity and capacity for empathy that so often originates with, and depends for its continuance on, being anxious, depressed, and paranoid.

SUMMING IT ALL UP AND PUTTING IT ALL TOGETHER

Avoidants should apply the lessons learned as often as they can, and preferably on a daily basis, ultimately bringing all helpful therapeutic methods to bear on each and every troublesome interpersonal encounter, effectively using multiple approaches to chip away at the avoidant problem and reduce relational anxiety to the point that it becomes sufficiently tolerable to allow them to feel comfortable and fearless enough to be transactionally active and interpersonally venturesome.

Throughout, avoidants should continue to expose themselves to one feared situation after another, until they prove to themselves that relationships are in fact, if not entirely safe, then at least less dangerous than they fear. To keep moving forward and keep their avoidance from coming back, taking hold, and escalating once again, they should constantly review, rethink, and rework what they learned and practice the remedies over and over again, until practice makes perfect. As their fear and anxiety subside, they can begin to think more clearly and take on more and more challenges, until they have attained the level of nonavoidance that is both possible and right for them.

Getting over avoidance is a lifetime job. Avoidance can be more easily reduced than entirely eliminated. Therefore, every day of their lives, avoidants have to be on the alert for distancing, and every time they detect that the distance between themselves and others is resurfacing and increasing, they should repeat the step-by-step remedies outlined in this chapter and in the rest of this book, until they can cope with and master their anxiety and avoidance and so change themselves and their lives in the direction that they, not their psychopathologies, want things to go.

Notes

PREFACE

1. Oldham, J.M., & Morris, L.B. (1995). *New personality self-portrait: Why you think, work, love, and act the way you do.* New York: Bantam Books, p. 200.

2. Dalrymple, K., & Zimmerman, M. (2007, October). Social anxiety disorder and comorbid depression; challenges in diagnosis and treatment. *Psychiatric Times*, p. 27.

3. PDM Task Force. (2006). *Psychodynamic diagnostic manual.* Silver Spring, MD: Alliance of Psychoanalytic Organizations, p. 54.

CHAPTER 1

1. Fenichel, O. (1945). *The psychoanalytic theory of neurosis.* New York: W. W. Norton, p. 180.

2. American Psychiatric Association. (1987). *Diagnostic and statistical manual of mental disorders* (4th ed.). Washington, DC: Author, pp. 662–665.

3. Quality Assurance Project. (1991). Treatment outlines for avoidant, dependent and passive-aggressive personality disorders. *Australian and New Zealand Journal of Psychiatry, 25*, p. 410.

4. Francis, A., & Widiger, T.A. (1987). A critical review of four DSM-III personality disorders. In G.L. Tischler (Ed.), *Diagnosis and classification in psychiatry.* New York: Cambridge University Press, p. 280.

5. Millon, T. (1981). *Disorders of personality: DSM-III: Axis II.* New York: John Wiley, p. 313.

6. Benjamin, L.S. (1996). *Interpersonal diagnosis and treatment of personality disorders.* New York: Guilford Press, p. 293.

7. Portnoy, I. (1959). The anxiety states. In S. Arieti (Ed.), *American handbook of psychiatry*. New York: Basic Books, p. 316.

8. PDM Task Force. (2006). *Psychodynamic diagnostic manual*. Silver Spring, MD: Alliance of Psychoanalytic Organizations, p. 55.

9. Gabbard, G. O. (1992, Spring). Psychodynamics of panic disorder and social phobia. *Bulletin of the Menninger Clinic, 56*(Suppl. A), p. A8.

10. APA Help Center. (n.d.). *Painful shyness in children and adults*. Retrieved June 7, 2009, from http://www. apahelpcenter.org/featuredtopics/feature. php?id=5&ch=1, p. 1.

11. American Psychiatric Association. (1987). *Diagnostic and statistical manual of mental disorders* (4th ed.). Washington, DC: Author, pp. 662–665.

12. Sullivan, H. S. (1953). *The interpersonal theory of psychiatry*. New York: W. W. Norton, p. 267.

13. Quality Assurance Project. (1991). Treatment outlines for avoidant, dependent and passive-aggressive personality disorders. *Australian and New Zealand Journal of Psychiatry, 25*, p. 410.

14. Millon, T., & Davis, R. D. (1996). *Disorders of personality DSM-IV and beyond*. New York: John Wiley, p. 154.

15. Freud, S. (1924). The economic problem in masochism. In J. D. Sutherland (Ed.) & J. Riviere (Trans.), *Collected papers* (Vol. 2). London: Hogarth Press, pp. 266–267.

16. Freud, S. (1957). Some character-types met with in psycho-analytic work. In J. D. Sutherland (Ed.) & J. Riviere (Trans.), *Collected papers* (Vol. 4). London: Hogarth Press, pp. 324–325.

17. Benjamin, L. S. (1996). *Interpersonal diagnosis and treatment of personality disorders*. New York: Guilford Press, p. 293.

18. Hagey, L. M. (2009, January 21). *Review of Distancing*. Amazon.com. Retrieved October 23, 2009, from http://www.Amazon.com/Distancing-Avoidant-Personality-Disorder-Expanded/product-reviews/027597829X/ref=cm_cr_dp_hist_2?ie=UTF8showViewpoints0&filterBy=addTwoStar.

19. Hagey, L. M. (2007, September 10). *Review of Forever Flashlight—9" Shake Electromagnetic Induction*. Amazon.com. Retrieved October 23. 2009, from http://www.amazon.com/Forever-Flashlight-Shake-Electromagnetic-Induction/dp/B00027U880/ref=cm=cr-mr-title

20. Sullivan, H. S. (1953). *The interpersonal theory of psychiatry*. New York: W. W. Norton, p. 216.

21. Fenichel, O. (1945). *The psychoanalytic theory of neurosis*. New York: W. W. Norton, p. 169.

22. Millon, T. (1981). *Disorders of personality: DSM-III: Axis II*. New York: John Wiley, p. 313.

23. Francis, A., & Widiger, T. A. (1987). A critical review of four DSM-III personality disorders. In G. L. Tischler (Ed.), *Diagnosis and classification in psychiatry*. New York: Cambridge University Press, p. 278.

24. Beck, A. T. (1999). *Prisoners of hate: The cognitive basis of anger, hostility, and violence*. New York: HarperCollins, p. 273.

25. Millon, T., & Davis, R. D. (1996). *Disorders of personality DSM-IV and beyond.* New York: John Wiley, p. 253.

26. Sullivan, H. S. (1953). *The interpersonal theory of psychiatry.* New York: W. W. Norton, p. 57.

27. Fenichel, O. (1945). *The psychoanalytic theory of neurosis.* New York: W. W. Norton, p. 169.

28. Freud, S. (1957). The most prevalent form of degradation in erotic life (from *Contributions to the psychology of love*). In J. D. Sutherland (Ed.) & J. Riviere (Trans.), *Collected papers* (Vol. 4). London: Hogarth Press, p. 215.

29. Francis, A., & Widiger, T. A. (1987). A critical review of four DSM-III personality disorders. In G. L. Tischler (Ed.), *Diagnosis and classification in psychiatry.* New York: Cambridge University Press, p. 280.

CHAPTER 2

1. PDM Task Force. (2006). *Psychodynamic diagnostic manual.* Silver Spring, MD: Alliance of Psychoanalytic Organizations, pp. 55–56.

2. Sullivan, H. S. (1953). *The interpersonal theory of psychiatry.* New York: W. W. Norton, p. 306.

3. Coleman, E. (1992). Is your patient suffering from compulsive sexual behavior? *Psychiatric Annals, 22,* 320–325.

4. Thompson, C. (1959). An introduction to minor maladjustments. In S. Arieti (Ed.), *American handbook of psychiatry.* New York: Basic Books, pp. 239–240.

5. Berne, E. (1964). *Games people play.* New York: Grove Press, p. 126.

6. Beatty, M. (1987). *Codependent no more: How to stop controlling others and start caring for yourself.* Center City, MN: Hazelden.

CHAPTER 3

1. Sullivan, H. S. (1953). *The interpersonal theory of psychiatry.* New York: W. W. Norton, p. 351.

CHAPTER 4

1. Fenichel, O. (1945). *The psychoanalytic theory of neurosis.* New York: W. W. Norton, p. 169.

2. Freud, S. (1957). The most prevalent form of degradation in erotic life (from Contributions to the psychology of love). In J. D. Sutherland (Ed.) and J. Riviere (Trans.), *Collected papers* (Vol. 4). London: Hogarth Press, p. 212.

3. Ibid., p. 203.

4. Jones, E. (1953–1957). *The life and works of Sigmund Freud* (Vols. 1–3). New York: Basic Books, p. 2.299.

CHAPTER 5

1. Berne, E. (1964). *Games people play.* New York: Grove Press, p. 14.
2. Millon, T. (1981). *Disorders of personality: DSM-III: Axis II.* New York: John Wiley, p. 313.

CHAPTER 6

1. American Psychiatric Association. (1987). *Diagnostic and statistical manual of mental disorders* (4th ed.). Washington, DC: Author, p. 396.
2. Ballenger, J. (1991). *Masters in psychiatry.* Kalamazoo, MI: Upjohn, pp. 4–5.
3. American Psychiatric Association. (1987). *Diagnostic and statistical manual of mental disorders* (4th ed.). Washington, DC: Author, p. 410.
4. PDM Task Force. (2006). *Psychodynamic diagnostic manual.* Silver Spring, MD: Alliance of Psychoanalytic Organizations, p. 54.
5. Anthony, M. M., & Swinson, R. P. (2000). *Shyness & social anxiety workbook: Proven techniques for overcoming your fears.* Oakland, CA: New Harbinger, p. 16.
6. Rettew, D. C. (2000). Avoidant personality disorder, generalized social phobia, and shyness: Putting the personality back into personality disorders. *Harvard Review of Psychiatry, 8,* 283–297.
7. PDM Task Force. (2006). *Psychodynamic diagnostic manual.* Silver Spring, MD: Alliance of Psychoanalytic Organizations, p. 55.
8. Millon, T., & Davis, R. D. (1996). *Disorders of personality: DSM-IV and beyond.* New York: John Wiley, p. 274.
9. Reich, W. (1949). *Character analysis.* New York: Orgone Institute Press, p. 44.
10. Millon, T., & Davis, R. D. (1996). *Disorders of personality: DSM-IV and beyond.* New York: John Wiley, p. 274.
11. Benjamin, L. S. (1996). *Interpersonal diagnosis and treatment of personality disorders.* New York: Guilford Press, p. 291.
12. Ibid., p. 298.
13. Ibid., p. 290.
14. American Psychiatric Association. (1987). *Diagnostic and statistical manual of mental disorders* (4th ed.). Washington, DC: Author, p. 654.

CHAPTER 7

1. Millon, T. (1981). *Disorders of personality: DSM-III: Axis II.* New York: John Wiley, pp. 313–314.
2. Beck, A. T. (1990). *Psychotherapy of an avoidant personality* [Audiotape]. New York: Guilford Press.
3. Berne, E. (1964). *Games people play.* New York: Grove Press, p. 126.

CHAPTER 8

1. Burns, D. D., & Epstein, N. (1983). Passive-aggressiveness: A cognitive-behavioral approach. In R. D. Parsons & R. M. Wicks (Eds.), *Passive-aggressiveness: Theory and practice*. New York: Brunner/Mazel, p. 75.

2. Ibid.

CHAPTER 9

1. American Psychiatric Association. (1987). *Diagnostic and statistical manual of mental disorders* (3rd rev. ed.). Washington, DC: Author, p. 61.

2. Millon, T. (1981). *Disorders of personality: DSM-III: Axis II*. New York: John Wiley, p. 318.

3. Benjamin, L. S. (1996). *Interpersonal diagnosis and treatment of personality disorders*. New York: Guilford Press, pp. 292–293.

4. Rosenthal, E. (1992, August 18). Troubled marriage? Sibling relations may be at fault. *New York Times*, pp. C1, C9.

5. Millon, T. (1981). *Disorders of personality: DSM-III: Axis II*. New York: John Wiley, p. 320.

6. Ballenger, J. (1991). *Masters in psychiatry*. Kalamazoo, MI: Upjohn, p. 4.

7. Millon, T. (1981). *Disorders of personality: DSM-III: Axis II*. New York: John Wiley, pp. 316–317.

8. Galvin, R. (1992, March–April). The nature of shyness. *Harvard Magazine*, *94*, pp. 41, 43.

CHAPTER 10

1. Oldham, J. M., & Morris, L. B. (1995). *New personality self-portrait: Why you think, work, love, and act the way you do*. New York: Bantam Books, 2001.

2. Millon, T., & Davis, R. D. (1996). *Disorders of personality: DSM-IV and beyond*. New York: John Wiley, pp. 321–324.

3. Ibid., pp. 282–284.

4. Anthony, M. M., & Swinson, R. P. (2000). *Shyness & social anxiety workbook: Proven techniques for overcoming your fears*. Oakland, CA: New Harbinger, pp. 100–101.

5. Benjamin, L. S. (1996). *Interpersonal diagnosis and treatment of personality disorders*. New York: Guilford Press, p. 302.

CHAPTER 11

1. Quality Assurance Project. (1991). Treatment outlines for avoidant, dependent and passive-aggressive personality disorders. *Australian and New Zealand Journal of Psychiatry*, *25*, p. 405.

2. Millon, T. (1981). *Disorders of personality: DSM-III: Axis II*. New York: John Wiley, p. 324.

CHAPTER 12

1. Beck, A. T. (1999). *Prisoners of hate: The cognitive basis of anger, hostility, and violence.* New York: HarperCollins, p. 54.
2. Ibid., pp. 252–254.
3. Rapee, R. M. (1998). *Overcoming shyness and social phobia: A step-by-step guide.* Northvale, NJ: Jason Aronson.
4. Quality Assurance Project. (1991). Treatment outlines for avoidant, dependent and passive-aggressive personality disorders. *Australian and New Zealand Journal of Psychiatry, 25,* pp. 404–405.
5. Anthony, M. M., & Swinson, R. P. (2000). *Shyness & social anxiety workbook: Proven techniques for overcoming your fears.* Oakland, CA: New Harbinger, pp. 193–219.
6. Benjamin, L. S. (1996). *Interpersonal diagnosis and treatment of personality disorders.* New York: Guilford Press, pp. 304–305.
7. Rapee, R. M. (1998). *Overcoming shyness and social phobia: A step-by-step guide.* Northvale, NJ: Jason Aronson, p. 76.
8. Auden, W. H. (n.d.). *The more loving one.* Retrieved July 9, 2009, from http://www.poets.org/viewmedia.php/prmMID/15550
9. Haley, personal communication, 1961.

CHAPTER 13

1. Sullivan, H. S. (1953). *The interpersonal theory of psychiatry.* New York: W. W. Norton, p. 302.
2. Fromm-Reichmann, F. (1960). *Principles of intensive psychotherapy.* Chicago: University of Chicago Press, p. 34.
3. Millon, T., & Davis, R. D. (1996). *Disorders of personality: DSM-IV and beyond.* New York: John Wiley, p. 283.
4. Mitchell, J. (2008, November 4). A 65th birthday tribute to Joni Mitchell. *Wall Street Journal,* p. D7.

CHAPTER 14

1. Benjamin, L. S. (1996). *Interpersonal diagnosis and treatment of personality disorders.* New York: Guilford Press, p. 302.
2. Pinsker, H. (1997). *A primer of supportive therapy.* Hillsdale, NJ: Analytic Press, p. 162.

CHAPTER 15

1. Bandura, A. (n.d.). *Observational learning.* Retrieved July 22, 2009, from http://en.wikipedia.org/wiki/Observational_Learning

2. Buggey, T. (n.d.). *A picture is worth . . . Video self-modeling applications at school and home.* Retrieved July 9, 2009, from http://education.ucsb.edu/autism/JPBI-abstracts/JPBIv9n3su07.htm

3. Beavers, W.R. (1982). Indications and contraindications for couples therapy. *Psychiatric Clinics of North America: Marital Therapy, 5,* p. 474.

4. Benjamin, L.S. (1996). *Interpersonal diagnosis and treatment of personality disorders.* New York: Guilford Press, p. 305.

5. Gabbard, G.O. (1992). Psychodynamics of panic disorder and social phobia. *Bulletin of the Menninger Clinic, 56*(Suppl. A), p. A8.

6. Marshall, J.R. (1992). The psychopharmacology of social phobia. *Bulletin of the Menninger Clinic, 56*(Suppl. A), pp. 42–49.

7. Rapee, R.M. (1998). *Overcoming shyness and social phobia: A step-by-step guide.* Northvale, NJ: Jason Aronson, p. 116.

CHAPTER 17

1. American Psychiatric Association. (1987). *Diagnostic and statistical manual of mental disorders* (4th ed.). Washington, DC: Author, p. 662.

2. Keating, C.J. (1984). *Dealing with difficult people.* Ramsey, NJ: Paulist Press, p. 150.

3. Freud, S. (1957). Certain neurotic mechanisms in jealousy, paranoia and homosexuality. In J.D. Sutherland (Ed.) & J. Riviere (Trans.), *Collected papers* (Vol. 2). London: Hogarth Press, pp. 232–243.

4. Franklin, B. (n.d.). BrainyQuote. Retrieved October 26, 2009, from http://www.brainyquote.com/quotes/quotes/b/benjaminfr151684.html

CHAPTER 18

1. Beck, A.T. (1999). *Prisoners of hate: The cognitive basis of anger, hostility, and violence.* New York: HarperCollins, p. 251.

2. Ibid., p. 53.

CHAPTER 19

1. PDM Task Force. (2006). *Psychodynamic diagnostic manual.* Silver Spring, MD: Alliance of Psychoanalytic Organizations, p. 128.

CHAPTER 20

1. Oldham, J.M., & Morris, L.B. (1995). *New personality self-portrait: Why you think, work, love, and act the way you do.* New York: Bantam Books and Morris, p. 201.

2. Winter, D.A. (n.d.). *The internet encyclopaedia of personal construct psychology: Fixed-role therapy*. Retrieved July 22, 2009, from http://www.pcp-net.org/encyclopaedia/fixed-role-ther.html

3. New introductory lectures on psycho-analysis. (n.d.). Answers.com. Retrieved October 22, 2009, from http://www.answers.com/topic/new-introductory-lectures-on-psycho-analysis

4. Mitchell, J. (2008, November 4). A 65th birthday tribute to Joni Mitchell. *Wall Street Journal*, p. D7.

5. Anthony, M.M., & Swinson, R.P. (2000). *Shyness & social anxiety workbook: Proven techniques for overcoming your fears*. Oakland, CA: New Harbinger, p. 78.

Index

therapeutic errors, 192; treatment, 185–92
Shyness, timidity, and withdrawal, 3, 6–7, 106–7. *See also* Self-help
Siblings, 103, 105
Social anxiety, 148
Social awkwardness, 10–11
Social phobia, 61–66, 166
Social skills training, 137
Society, identification with, 19–28
Somatic complaints, 74
"Some Character-Types Met with in Psychoanalytic Work" (Freud), 12
Sons, sexual avoidance development in, 51–52
Sour grapes, 59
Specific phobia, 61
Stimulation enhancement, in sexual avoidance reduction, 186
Successophobia, 86–88
Supplemental approaches, 127–31, 155–57, 165–66
Supportive therapy, 147–57; advice, bad, 155; advice, good, 150–55; liking and respecting patients, 147; overview, 112, 116–17; reassurance, 148–50; supplemental approaches, 155–57
Sympathy, 170

Temperament, inherited, 106–7
Therapy: avoidance creation in, 167–68; cognitive, 112, 133–37; dimensions, 112; evaluating need for, 213–14; family, 117–18, 168–69; fixed role, 202; group, 160; ideal techniques, 163–70; interpersonal, 112, 116, 143–45, 159–60; marital/couple, 159–60; normal avoidance as part of, 41; paradoxical, 140–41; pharmacotherapy, 112, 160–61; technique of last resort, 161–62; video self-modeling, 159, 165–66.

See also Behavioral therapy; Cognitive-behavioral therapy; Psychodynamically oriented psychotherapy; Supportive therapy
Thinking: catastrophic, 96–97, 136; errors in, 144, 209; negative, 95; projective/paranoid, 93–94
Third parties, putting between avoidants and critics, 176
Thompson, Clara, 31
Time to meet people, lack of, as rationalization, 58
Timidity, 3, 6–7, 106–7. *See also* Self-help
Total push techniques, 163–65
Transference resistances, 120–21, 127, 169–70
Trauma, early, 102, 204–5
Type I avoidant personality disorder, 3–28; *DSM-IV* criteria, 3–4, 6–11; non-*DSM-IV* criteria, 4–6, 11–28; push techniques, 165; Type II *versus*, 29
Type II avoidant personality disorder, 29–36; Type IIa, 30–34, 165; Type IIb, 34–36, 165; Type IIc, 36
Type IIa avoidant personality disorder, 30–34, 165
Type IIb avoidant personality disorder, 34–36, 165
Type IIc avoidant personality disorder, 36

Unhealthy defenses, 126
Unhealthy projection, 204
Unworthiness, projection of, 94

Validation, consensual, 151
Vicious cycles, interrupting, 180–81, 208–9
Video self-modeling, 159, 165–66

Withdrawal, 3, 6–7, 106–7. *See also* Self-help
Women, sexual avoidance in, 52, 53

About the Author

MARTIN KANTOR, MD, is a Harvard psychiatrist who has been in full private practice in Boston and New York City and active in residency training programs at several hospitals, including Massachusetts General and Beth Israel in New York. He also served as assistant clinical professor of psychiatry at Mount Sinai Medical School and as clinical assistant professor of psychiatry at the University of Medicine and Dentistry of New Jersey–New Jersey Medical School. He is author of 18 other books, including *Homophobia: The State of Sexual Bigotry Today* (Praeger, 2009); *Uncle Sam's Shame: Inside the Veteran's Administration* (Praeger, 2008); *Lifting the Weight: Understanding Depression in Men: Its Causes and Solutions* (Praeger, 2007); *The Psychopathy of Everyday Life: How Antisocial Personality Disorder Affects All of Us* (Praeger, 2006); *Understanding Paranoia: A Guide for Professionals, Families, and Sufferers* (Praeger, 2004); *Distancing: Avoidant Personality Disorder, Revised and Expanded* (Praeger, 2003); *Passive-Aggression: A Guide for the Therapist, the Patient, and the Victim* (Praeger, 2002); and *Treating Emotional Disorder in Gay Men* (Praeger, 1999).